The Right Thing to Do

Basic Readings in Moral Philosophy

FOURTH EDITION

Edited by

JAMES RACHELS

and

STUART RACHELS

Boston Burr Ridge, IL Dubuque, IA Madison, WI New York
San Francisco St. Louis Bangkok Bogotá Caracas Kuala Lumpur
Lisbon London Madrid Mexico City Milan Montreal New Delhi
Santiago Seoul Singapore Sydney Taipei Toronto

Mc Graw Hill **Higher Education**

Published by McGraw-Hill, a business unit of The McGraw-Hill Companies, Inc., 1221 Avenue of the Americas, New York, NY, 10020. Copyright © 2007 by The McGraw-Hill Companies, Inc. All rights reserved. No part of this publication may be reproduced or distributed in any form or by any means, or stored in a database or retrieval system, without the prior written consent of The McGraw-Hill Companies, Inc., including, but not limited to, in any network or other electronic storage or transmission, or broadcast for distance learning. Some ancillaries, including electronic and print components, may not be available to customers outside the United States.

This book is printed on acid-free paper.

1 2 3 4 5 6 7 8 9 0 DOC/DOC 0 9 8 7 6

ISBN-13: 978-0-07-312546-6
ISBN-10: 0-07-312546-6

Publisher: *Lyn Uhl*
Sponsoring Editor: *Jon-David Hague*
Production Editor: *David Blatty*
Production Supervisor: *Tandra Jorgensen*
Design Manager: *Kim Menning*
Typeface: *11/12 Baskerville*
Compositor: *International Typesetting & Composition*
Printer: *R.R. Donnelley & Sons*

Cover art: Aleksandr Rodchenko. (Russian, 1891–1956). Non-Objective Painting no. 80 (Black on Black). 1918. Oil on canvas, 32 1/4 × 31 1/4" (81.9 × 79.4 cm). Gift of the artist, through Jay Leyda. The Museum of Modern Art, New York. Digital Image © 2006 The Museum of Modern Art/Licensed by Scala/Art Resource, NY. © Alexander Rodchenko/RAO, Moscow/VAGA, New York.

Library of Congress Cataloging-in-Publication Data

The right thing to do : basic readings in moral philosophy/edited by James Rachels and
   Stuart Rachels.—4th ed.
      p. cm.
   Includes bibliographical references.
   ISBN-13: 978-0-07-312546-6 (alk. paper)
      1. Ethics—Textbooks. I. Rachels, James, 1941–2003. II. Rachels, Stuart, 1969–
BJ1012.R5 2006
170—dc22   2006041045

www.mhhe.com

Contents

Preface

Moral philosophy is the attempt to achieve a systematic understanding of what morality is and what it requires of us—of how we ought to live, and why. This anthology is an introduction to moral philosophy, conceived in this broad sense. The readings spotlight some of the main moral theories from the Western tradition and showcase some of the best arguments that philosophers have offered on practical moral issues.

This anthology is a companion to *The Elements of Moral Philosophy*, also published by McGraw-Hill. Both books were written by James Rachels and revised most recently by Stuart Rachels. These two books complement one another and may be profitably read together. However, nothing in either book presupposes acquaintance with the other.

About the Authors

JAMES RACHELS (1941–2003) was University Professor of Philosophy at the University of Alabama at Birmingham. He wrote *The End of Life: Euthanasia and Morality* (1986), *Created from Animals: The Moral Implications of Darwinism* (1990), *Can Ethics Provide Answers?* (1997), *Problems from Philosophy* (2005), *The Elements of Moral Philosophy*, and *The Legacy of Socrates* (forthcoming).

STUART RACHELS is Associate Professor of Philosophy at the University of Alabama. A former United States Chess Champion and a Life Master at bridge, he wrote the fifth edition of *The Elements of Moral Philosophy* (2006; previous editions were by James Rachels). His scholarly articles have appeared in numerous journals.

CHAPTER 1

A Short Introduction to Moral Philosophy

James Rachels

An ancient legend tells the story of Gyges, a poor shepherd who found a magic ring in a fissure opened by an earthquake. The ring would make its wearer invisible, so he could go anywhere and do anything undetected. Gyges was an unscrupulous fellow, and he quickly realized that the ring could be put to good advantage. We are told that he used its power to gain entry to the royal palace where he seduced the queen, murdered the king, and seized the throne. (It is not explained how invisibility helped him to seduce the queen—but let that pass.) In no time at all, he went from being a poor shepherd to being king of all the land.

This story is recounted in Book II of Plato's *Republic*. Like all of Plato's works, the *Republic* is written in the form of a dialogue between Socrates and his companions. Glaucon, who is having an argument with Socrates, uses the story of Gyges's ring to make a point.

Glaucon asks us to imagine that there are two such rings, one given to a man of virtue and the other given to a rogue. How might we expect them to behave? The rogue, of course, will do anything necessary to increase his own wealth and power. Since the cloak of invisibility will protect him from discovery, he can do anything he pleases without fear of being caught. Therefore, he will recognize no moral constraints on his conduct, and there will be no end to the mischief he will do.

But how will the so-called virtuous man behave? Glaucon suggests that he will do no better than the rogue:

> No one, it is commonly believed, would have such iron strength of mind as to stand fast in doing right or keep his hands off other men's goods, when he could go to the market-place and fearlessly help himself to anything he wanted, enter houses and sleep with any

woman he chose, set prisoners free and kill men at his pleasure, and in a word go about among men with the powers of a god. He would behave no better than the other; both would take the same course.

Moreover, Glaucon asks, why shouldn't he? Once he is freed from the fear of reprisal, why shouldn't a person simply do what he pleases, or what he thinks is best for himself? Why should he care at all about "morality"?

The *Republic,* written over 2300 years ago, was one of the first great works of moral philosophy in Western history. Since then, philosophers have formulated theories to explain what morality is, why it is important, and why it has the peculiar hold on us that it does. What, if anything, justifies us in believing that we *morally ought* to act in one way rather than another?

Relativism

Perhaps the oldest philosophical theory about morality is that right and wrong are relative to the customs of one's society—on this view, there is nothing behind the demands of morality except social convention. Herodotus, the first of the great Greek historians, lived at about the time of Socrates. His *History* is full of wonderful anecdotes that illustrate his belief that "right" and "wrong" are little more than names for social conventions. Of the Massagetae, a tribe in Central Asia, he writes:

> The following are some of their customs—Each man has but one wife, yet all the wives are held in common . . . Human life does not come to its natural close with these people; but when a man grows very old, all his kinsfolk collect together and offer him up in sacrifice; offering at the same time some cattle also. After the sacrifice they boil the flesh and feast on it; and those who thus end their days are reckoned the happiest. If a man dies of disease they do not eat him, but bury him in the ground, bewailing his ill-fortune that he did not come to be sacrificed. They sow no grain, but live on their herds, and on fish, of which there is great plenty in the Araxes. Milk is what they chiefly drink. The only god they worship is the sun, and to him they offer the horse in sacrifice; under the notion of giving the swiftest of the gods the swiftest of all mortal creatures.

Herodotus did not think the Massagetae were to be criticized for such practices. Their customs were neither better nor worse than those of other peoples; they were merely different. The Greeks, who considered themselves more "civilized," may have thought that their customs were superior, but, Herodotus says, that is only because everyone believes the customs of his own society to be the best. The "truth" depends on one's point of view—that is, on the society in which one happens to have been raised.

Relativists think that Herodotus was obviously on to something and that those who believe in "objective" right and wrong are merely naive. Critics, however, object to the theory on a number of grounds. First, it is exceedingly conservative, in that the theory endorses whatever moral views happen to be current in a society. Consider our own society. Many people believe that our society's moral code is mistaken, at least on some points—for example, they may disagree with the dominant social view regarding capital punishment, or homosexuality, or the treatment of nonhuman animals. Must we conclude that these would-be reformers are wrong, merely because they oppose the majority view? Why must the majority always be right?

But there is a deeper problem with Relativism, emphasized by Socrates. Some social customs are, indeed, merely arbitrary, and when these customs are at issue it is fruitless to insist that one society's practices are better than another's. Funerary practices are a good example. The Greeks burned their dead, while the Callatians ate their dead, but neither practice is better than the other. However, it does not follow from this that *all* social practices are arbitrary in the same way. Some are, and some are not. The Greeks and the Callatians were free to accept whatever funerary practices they liked because no objective reason could be given why one practice was superior to the other. In the case of other practices, however, there may be good reasons why some are superior. It is not hard, for example, to explain why honesty and respect for human life are socially desirable, and similarly it is not hard to explain why slavery and racism are undesirable. Because we can support our judgments about these matters with rational arguments, we do not have to regard those judgments as "merely" the expression of our particular society's moral code.

Divine Commands

A second ancient idea, also familiar to Socrates, was that moral living consists in obedience to divine commands. If this were true, then we could easily answer the challenge of Gyges's ring—even if we had the power of invisibility, we would still be subject to divine retribution, so ultimately we could not "get away with" doing whatever we wanted.

But Socrates did not believe that right living could consist merely in trying to please the gods. In the *Euthyphro,* another of Plato's dialogues, Socrates is shown considering at some length whether "right" can be the same as "what the gods command." Now we may notice, to begin with, that there are considerable practical difficulties with this as a general theory of ethics. How, for example, are we supposed to *know* what the gods command? There are, of course, those who claim to have spoken with God about the matter and who therefore claim to be in a position to pass on his instructions to the rest of us. But people who claim to speak for God are not the most trustworthy folks—hearing voices can be a sign of schizophrenia or a megalomania just as easily as an instance of divine communication. Others, more modestly, rely on scripture or church tradition for guidance. But those sources are notoriously ambiguous— they give vague and often contradictory instructions—so, when people consult these authorities, they typically rely on whatever elements of scripture or church tradition support the moral views they are already inclined to agree with. Moreover, because scripture and church tradition have been handed down from earlier times, they provide little direct help in addressing distinctively contemporary problems: the problem of environmental preservation, for example, or the problem of how much of our resources should be allocated to AIDS research as opposed to other worthy endeavors.

Still, it may be thought that God's commands provide the ultimate *authority* for ethics, and that is the issue Socrates addressed. Socrates accepted that the gods exist and that they may issue instructions. But he showed that this cannot be the ultimate basis of ethics. He points out that we have to distinguish two possibilities: Either the gods have some reason for the instructions they issue, or they do not. If they do not, then their commands are merely arbitrary—the gods are like petty tyrants who demand that we act in this way and that, even though there is no good reason for it. But this is an impious view that religious people will not want to accept. On the other hand, if we say that the gods do have good reasons for their instructions, then we have admitted that there is a standard of rightness independent of their commands—namely, the standard to which the gods themselves refer in deciding what to require of us.

It follows, then, that even if one accepts a religious picture of the world, the rightness or wrongness of actions cannot be understood merely in terms of their conformity to divine prescriptions. We may always ask why the gods command what they do, and the answer to *that* question will reveal why right actions are right and why wrong actions are wrong.

Aristotle

Although Relativism and the Divine Command Theory have always had supporters, they have never been popular among serious students of moral philosophy. The first extended, systematic treatise on moral philosophy, produced two generations after Socrates, was Aristotle's *Nicomachean Ethics* (ca. 330 B.C.), and Aristotle wasted no time on such notions. Instead, Aristotle offered a detailed account of the virtues—the qualities of character that people need to do well in life. The virtues include courage, prudence, generosity, honesty, and many more; Aristotle sought to explain what each one is and why it is important. His answer to the question of Gyges's ring was that virtue is necessary for human beings to achieve happiness; therefore, the man of virtue is ultimately better off *because* he is virtuous.

Aristotle's view of the virtuous life was connected with his overall way of understanding the world and our place in it. Aristotle's conception of what the world is like was enormously influential; it dominated Western thinking for over 1700 years. A central feature of this conception was that *everything in nature exists for a purpose.* "Nature," Aristotle said, "belongs to the class of causes which act for the sake of something."

It seems obvious that artifacts such as knives and chariots have purposes, because we have their purposes in mind when we make them. But what about natural objects that we do not make? Do they have purposes too? Aristotle thought so. One of his examples was that we have teeth so that we can chew. Such biological examples are quite persuasive; the parts of our bodies do seem, intuitively, to have particular purposes— eyes are for seeing, the heart is for pumping blood, and so on. But Aristotle's thesis was not limited to organic beings. According to him, *everything* in nature has a purpose. He also thought, to take a different sort of example, that rain falls so that plants can grow. As odd as it may seem to a modern reader, Aristotle was perfectly serious about this. He considered other alternatives, such as that the rain falls "of necessity" and that this helps the plants only "by coincidence," and rejected them. His considered view was that plants and animals are what they are, and that the rain falls as it does, "because it is better so."

The world, therefore, is an orderly, rational system, with each thing having its own proper place and serving its own special purpose.

There is a neat hierarchy: The rain exists for the sake of the plants, the plants exist for the sake of the animals, and the animals exist—of course—for the sake of people, whose well-being is the point of the whole arrangement. In the *Politics* he wrote:

> [W]e must believe, first that plants exist for the sake of animals, second that all other animals exist for the sake of man, tame animals for the use he can make of them as well as for the food they provide; and as for wild animals, most though not all of these can be used for food or are useful in other ways; clothing and instruments can be made out of them. If then we are right in believing that nature makes nothing without some end in view, nothing to no purpose, it must be that nature has made all things specifically for the sake of man.

It was a stunningly anthropocentric view. Aristotle may be forgiven, however, when we consider that virtually every important thinker in our history has entertained some such thought. Humans are a remarkably vain species.

Natural Law

The Christian thinkers who came later found Aristotle's view of the world to be congenial. There was only one thing missing: The addition of God was required to make the picture complete. (Aristotle had denied that God was a necessary part of the picture. For him, the worldview we have outlined was not religious; it was simply a description of how things are.) Thus, the Christian thinkers said that the rain falls to help the plants because *that is what the Creator intended,* and the animals are for human use because *that is what God made them for.* Values and purposes were, therefore, conceived to be a fundamental part of the nature of things, because the world was believed to have been created according to a divine plan.

This view of the world had a number of consequences for ethics. On the most general level, it affirmed the supreme value of human life, and it explained why humans are entitled to do whatever they please with the rest of nature. The basic moral arrangement—human beings, whose lives are sacred, dominating a world made for their benefit—was enshrined as the Natural Order of Things.

At a more detailed level, a corollary of this outlook was that the "laws of nature" specify how things *ought to be,* as well as describing how things *are.* In turn, knowing how things ought to be enables us to evaluate states of affairs as objectively good or bad. Things are as they ought to be when they are serving their natural purposes; when they do not or cannot serve those purposes, things have gone wrong. Thus, teeth that have decayed and cannot be used for chewing are defective; and drought, which deprives plants of the rain they need, is a natural, objective evil.

There are also implications for human action: On this view, moral rules are one type of law of nature. The key idea here is that some forms of human behavior are "natural" while others are not; and "unnatural" acts are said to be wrong. Beneficence, for example, is natural for us because God has made us as social creatures. We want and need the friendship of other people, and we have natural affections for them; hence, behaving brutishly toward them is unnatural. Or to take a different sort of example, the purpose of the sex organs is procreation. Thus, any use of them for other purposes is "contrary to nature"— which is why the Christian church has traditionally regarded any form of sexual activity that does not result in procreation, such as masturbation, gay sex, or the use of contraceptives, as impermissible.

This combination of ideas, together with others like them, formed the core of an outlook known as natural-law ethics. The Theory of Natural Law was developed most fully by Saint Thomas Aquinas (1225–1274), who lived at a time when the Aristotelian worldview was unchallenged. Aquinas was the foremost thinker among traditional Catholic theologians. Today natural-law theory still has adherents inside the Catholic Church, but few outside. The reason is that the Aristotelian worldview, on which natural-law ethics depended, has been replaced by the outlook of modern science.

Galileo, Newton, Darwin, and others developed ways of understanding natural phenomena that made no use of evaluative notions. In their way of thinking, the rain has no purpose. It does not fall in order to help the plants grow. Plants typically get the amount of water they need because each species has evolved, by natural selection, in the environment in which that amount of water is available. Natural selection produces an orderly arrangement that *appears* to have been designed, but that is only an illusion. To explain nature there is no need to assume teleological principles, neither Aristotle's "final causes" nor the Christians' God. This changed outlook was by far the most insidious feature of the new science; it is little wonder that the church's first response was to condemn it.

Modern science transformed people's view of what the world is like. But part of the transformation, inseparable from the rest, was an altered view of the nature of ethics. Right and wrong could no longer be deduced from the nature of things, for on the new view the natural world does not, in and of itself, manifest value and purpose. The *inhabitants* of the world may have needs and desires that generate values special to them, but that is all. The world apart from those inhabitants knows and cares nothing for their values, and it has no values of its own. A hundred and fifty years before Nietzsche declared, "There are no moral facts," the Scottish philosopher David Hume had come to the same conclusion. Hume summed up the moral implications of the new worldview in his *Treatise of Human Nature* (1739) when he wrote:

> Take any action allow'd to be vicious: Willful murder, for instance. Examine it in all lights, and see if you can find that matter of fact, or real existence, which you call *vice*. In whichever way you take it, you find only certain passions, motives, volitions and thoughts. There is no other matter of fact in the case.

To Aristotle's idea that "nature has made all things for the sake of man," Hume replied: "The life of a man is of no greater importance to the universe than that of an oyster."

The Social Contract

If there are no moral facts and no God, what becomes of morality? Ethics must somehow be understood as a purely human phenomenon—as the product of human needs, interests, and desires—and nothing else. Figuring out how to do this has been the basic project of moral philosophy from the 17th century on.

Thomas Hobbes, the foremost English philosopher of the 17th century, suggested one way in which ethics might be understood in purely human terms. Hobbes assumed that "good" and "bad" are just names we give to things we like and dislike. Thus, because we may like different things, we may disagree about what is good or bad. However, Hobbes said, in our fundamental psychological makeup we are all very much alike. We are all basically self-interested creatures who want to live and to live as well as possible. This is the key to understanding ethics. Ethics arises when people realize *what they must do* to live well.

Hobbes was the first important modern thinker to provide a secular, naturalistic basis for ethics. He pointed out that each of us is enormously better off living in a mutually cooperative society than we would be if we tried to make it on our own. The benefits of social living go far beyond companionship: Social cooperation makes possible schools, hospitals, and highways; houses with electricity and central heating; airplanes and telephones; newspapers and books; movies, opera, and bingo; science and agriculture. Without social cooperation we would lose these benefits and more. Therefore, it is to the advantage of each of us to do whatever is necessary to establish and maintain a cooperative society.

But it turns out that a mutually cooperative society can exist only if we adopt certain rules of behavior—rules that require telling the truth, keeping our promises, respecting one another's lives and property, and so on:

- Without the presumption that people will tell the truth, there would be no reason for people to pay any attention to what other people say. Communication would be impossible. And without communication among its members, society would collapse.
- Without the requirement that people keep their promises, there could be no division of labor—workers could not count on getting paid, retailers could not rely on their agreements with suppliers, and so on—and the economy would collapse. There could be no business, no building, no agriculture, no medicine.
- Without assurances against assault, murder, and theft, no one could feel secure; everyone would have to be constantly on guard against everyone else, and social cooperation would be impossible.

Thus, to obtain the benefits of social living, we must strike a bargain with one another, with each of us agreeing to obey these rules, provided others do likewise. (We must also establish mechanisms for enforcing these rules—such as legal sanctions and other, less formal methods of enforcement—so that we can *count on* one another to obey them.) This "social contract" is the basis of morality. Indeed, morality can be defined as nothing more or less than *the set of rules that rational people will agree to obey, for their mutual benefit, provided that other people will obey them as well.*

This way of understanding morality has a number of appealing features. First, it takes the mystery out of ethics and makes it a practical, down-to-earth business. Living morally is not a matter of blind obedience to the mysterious dictates of a supernatural being; nor is it a matter of fidelity to lofty but pointless abstract rules. Instead, it is a matter of doing what it takes to make social living possible.

Second, this theory makes it clear how morality can be rational and objective even if there are no moral facts. It is not merely a matter of opinion that the rule against murder must be a part of any workable social scheme or that rational people, to secure their own welfare, must agree to adopt such a rule. Nor is it merely a matter of opinion that rules requiring truthfulness and promise keeping are needed for people to flourish in a social setting. Even if there are no moral facts, the reasoning that leads to such conclusions is perfectly objective.

Third, the Social Contract Theory explains why we should *care* about ethics—it offers at least a partial response to the problem of Gyges's ring. If there is no God to punish us, why should we bother to do what is "right," especially when it is not to our advantage? The answer is that it *is* to our advantage to live in a society where people behave morally—thus, it is rational for us to accept moral restrictions on our conduct as part of a bargain we make with other people. We benefit directly from the ethical conduct of others, and our own compliance with the moral rules is the price we pay to secure their compliance.

Fourth, the Social Contract approach gives us a sensible and mature way of determining what our ethical duties really are. When "morality" is mentioned, the first thing that pops into many people's minds is an attempt to restrict their sex lives. It is unfortunate that the word *morals* has come to have such a connotation. The whole purpose of having a system of morality, according to Social Contract Theory, is to make it possible for people to live their individual lives in a setting of social cooperation—its purpose is not to tell people what kinds of lives they should live (except insofar as it is necessary to restrict conduct in the interests of maintaining social cooperation). Therefore, an ethic based on the Social Contract would have little interest in what people do in their bedrooms.

Finally, we may note again that Social Contract Theory assumes relatively little about human nature. It treats human beings as self-interested creatures and does not assume that they are naturally altruistic, even to the slightest degree. One of the theory's charms is that it can reach the conclusion that we ought, often, to *behave* altruistically, without assuming that we *are* naturally altruistic. We want to live as well as possible, and moral obligations are created as we band together with other people to form the cooperative societies that are necessary for us to achieve this fundamentally self-interested goal.

Altruism and Self-Interest

Are people essentially self-interested? Although the Social Contract Theory continues to attract supporters, not many philosophers and psychologists today would accept Hobbes's egoistic view of human nature. It seems evident that humans have at least *some* altruistic feelings, if only for their family and friends. We have evolved as so-cial creatures just as surely as we have evolved as creatures with legs—thus, caring for our kin and members of our local group is as natural for us as walking.

If humans do have some degree of natural altruism, does this have any significance for morals? Hume thought so. Hume agreed with Hobbes that our moral opinions are expressions of our feel-ings. In 1739, when he invited his readers to consider "willful mur-der" and see if they could find that "matter of fact" called "vice," Hume concluded:

> You can never find it, till you turn your reflexion into your own breast, and find a sentiment of disapprobation, which arises in you, towards this action. Here is a matter of fact; but 'tis the ob-ject of feeling . . . It lies in yourself, not in the object. So that when you pronounce any action or character to be vicious, you mean nothing, but that from the constitution of your nature you have a feeling or sentiment of blame from the contemplation of it.

And what, exactly, is "the constitution of our nature"? Of course, it is part of our nature to care about ourselves and our own welfare. But Hume added that we also have "*social* sentiments"—feelings that con-nect us with other people and make us concerned about their welfare. That is why, Hume said, we measure right and wrong by "the true in-terests of mankind":

> In all determinations of morality, this circumstance of public util-ity is ever principally in view; and wherever disputes arise, either in philosophy or common life, concerning the bounds of duty, the question cannot, by any means, be decided with greater cer-tainty than by ascertaining, on any side, the true interests of mankind.

This view came to be known as Utilitarianism. In modern moral phi-losophy, it is the chief alternative to the Theory of the Social Contract.

Utilitarianism

Utilitarians hold that there is one principle that sums up all our moral duties. The ultimate moral principle is that *we should always do whatever will produce the greatest possible balance of happiness over unhap-piness for everyone who will be affected by our action*. This "principle of util-ity" is deceptively simple. It is actually a combination of three ideas: First, in determining what to do, we should be guided by the expected consequences of our actions—we should do whatever will have the best consequences. Second, in determining which consequences are best, we should give the greatest possible weight to the happiness or unhappiness that would be caused—we should do whatever will cause the most happiness or the least unhappiness. And finally, the principle of utility assumes that each individual's happiness is equally as important as anyone else's.

Although Hume expressed the basic idea of Utilitarianism, two other philosophers elaborated it in greater detail. Jeremy Bentham, an Englishman who lived in the late 18th and early 19th centuries, was the leader of a group of philosophical radicals who aimed to reform the laws of Britain along utilitarian lines. They were remarkably successful in advancing such causes as prison reform and restrictions on the use of child labor. John Stuart Mill, the son of one of Bentham's original followers, gave the theory its most popular and influential defense in his book *Utilitarianism,* published in 1861.

The utilitarian movement attracted critics from the outset. It was an easy target because it ignored conventional religious notions. The point of morality, according to the Utilitarians, had nothing to do with obeying God or gaining credit in Heaven. Rather, the point was just to make life in this world as comfortable and happy as possible. So some critics condemned Utilitarianism as a godless doctrine. To this Mill replied:

> [T]he question depends upon what idea we have formed of the moral character of the Deity. If it be a true belief that God desires, above all things, the happiness of his creatures, and that this was his purpose in their creation, utility is not only not a godless doctrine, but more profoundly religious than any other.

Utilitarianism was also an easy target because it was (and still is) a *subversive* theory, in that it turned many traditional moral ideas upside down. Bentham argued, for example, that the purpose of the criminal justice system cannot be understood in the traditional way as "paying back" miscreants for their wicked deeds—that only piles misery upon misery. Instead, the social response to crime should be threefold: to identify and deal with the causes of criminal behavior; where possible, to reform individual lawbreakers and make them into productive citizens; and to "punish" people only insofar as it is necessary to deter others from committing similar crimes. (Today, of course, these are familiar ideas, but only because the Utilitarians' victory was so sweeping.) Or, to take a different example, by insisting that everyone's happiness is equally important, the Utilitarians offended various elitist notions of group superiority. According to the Utilitarian standard, neither race, sex, nor social class makes a difference to one's moral status. Mill himself wrote a book on *The Subjection of Women* that became a classic of the 19th-century suffragist movement.

Finally, Utilitarianism was controversial because it had no use for "absolute" moral rules. The Utilitarians regarded the traditional rules—against killing, lying, breaking one's promises, and so on—as "rules of thumb," useful because following them will generally be for the best. But they are not absolute—whenever breaking such a rule will have better results for everyone concerned, the rule should be broken. The rule against killing, for example, might be suspended in the case of voluntary euthanasia for someone dying of a painful illness. Moreover, the Utilitarians regarded some traditional rules as dubious, even as rules of thumb. For example, Christian moralists had traditionally said that masturbation is evil because it violates the Natural Law; but from the point of view of the Principle of Utility, it appears to be harmless. A more serious matter is the traditional religious condemnation of homosexuality, which has resulted in misery for countless people. Utilitarianism implies that if an activity makes people happy, without anyone being harmed, it cannot be wrong.

But it is one thing to describe a moral view; it is another thing to justify it. Utilitarianism says that our moral duty is to "promote the general happiness." Why should we do that? How can the challenge of Gyges's ring be answered? As Mill puts it:

> I feel that I am bound not to rob or murder, betray or deceive; but why am I bound to promote the general happiness? If my own happiness lies in something else, why may I not give that the preference?

Aside from the "external sanctions" of law and public opinion, Mill thinks there is only one possible reason for accepting this or any other moral standard. The "internal sanction" of morality must always be "a feeling in our minds," regardless of what sort of ethic this feeling endorses:

> The ultimate sanction, therefore, of all morality (external motives apart) being a subjective feeling in our own minds, I see nothing embarrassing to those whose standard is utility in the question, What is the sanction of that particular standard? We may answer, the same as all other moral standards—the conscientious feelings of mankind. Undoubtedly this sanction has no binding efficacy on those who do not possess the feelings it appeals to; but neither will these persons be more obedient to any other moral principle than the utilitarian one.

The kind of morality we accept will, therefore, depend on the nature of our feelings: If human beings have "social feelings," then Mill says that utilitarian morality will be the natural standard for them:

> The firm foundation [of utilitarian morality] is that of the social feelings of mankind—the desire to be in unity with our fellow creatures, which is already a powerful principle in human nature, and happily one of those which tend to become stronger, even without express inculcation, from the influences of advancing civilization.

Impartiality

Utilitarianism, as we have seen, has implications that are at odds with traditional morality. Much the same could be said about the Social Contract Theory. In most of the practical matters that have been mentioned—punishment, racial discrimination, women's rights, euthanasia, homosexuality—the two theories have similar implications. But there is one matter on which they differ dramatically. Utilitarians believe that we have a very extensive moral duty to help other people. Social Contract theorists deny this.

Suppose, for example, you are thinking of spending $1000 for a new living room carpet. Should you do this? What are the alternatives? One alternative is to give the money to an agency such as the United Nations Children's Fund. Each year between 10 and 20 million third-world children die of easily preventable diseases, because there isn't enough money to provide the vitamin-A capsules, antibiotics, and oral rehydration treatments they need. By giving the money to UNICEF, and making do a while longer with your old carpet, you could provide much-needed medical care for dozens of children. From the point of view of utility—seeking the best overall outcome for everyone concerned—there is no doubt you should give the money to UNICEF. Obviously, the medicine will help the kids a lot more than the new rug will help you.

But from the point of view of the Social Contract, things look very different. If morality rests on an agreement between people— remember, an agreement they enter into *to promote their own interests*— what would the agreement say about helping other people? Certainly, we would want the contract to impose a duty not to harm other people, even strangers. Each of us would obviously benefit from that. And it might be in our best interests to accept a mutual obligation to provide aid to others when it is easy and convenient to do so. But would rational people accept a general duty to provide virtually unlimited aid to strangers, even at great cost to themselves? From the standpoint of self-interest, that sounds crazy. Jan Narveson, a contract theorist who teaches philosophy at the University of Waterloo in Canada, writes in his book *Moral Matters* (1993):

> [M]orals, if they are to be rational, must amount to agreements among people—people of all kinds, each pursuing his or her own interests, which are various and do not necessarily include much concern for others and their interests. But people have minds, and apply information gleaned from observing the world around them to the task of promoting their interests, and they have a broad repertoire of powers including some that can make them exceedingly dangerous, as well as others that can make them very helpful. This gives us reason to agree with each other that we will refrain from harming others in the pursuit of our interests, to respect each other's property and grant extensive civil rights, but not necessarily to go very far out of our way to be very helpful to those we don't know and may not particularly care for. . . .
>
> It is reasonable, then, to arrive at a general understanding that we shall be ready to help when help is urgent and when giving it is not very onerous to us. But a general understanding that we shall help everyone as if they were our spouses or dearest friends is quite another matter.

Unlike many philosophers who prefer to keep things abstract, Narveson is good about spelling out the implications of his view in a way that leaves no room for misunderstanding:

> What about parting with the means for making your sweet little daughter's birthday party a memorable one, in order to keep a dozen strangers alive on the other side of the world? Is this something you are morally required to do? Indeed not. She may well *matter* to you more than they. This illustrates again the fact that people do *not* "count equally" for most of us. Normal people care more about some people than others, and build their very lives around those carings.

Which view is correct? Do we have a moral duty to provide extensive aid to strangers, or not? Both views appeal ultimately to our emotions. A striking feature of Narveson's contractarian argument is its appeal to the fact that we *care more* for some people than others. This is certainly true: As he says, we care more for our own children than for "strangers on the other side of the world." But does this really mean that I may choose some trivial benefit for my children over the very lives of the strangers? Suppose there are two buttons on my desk at this moment, and by pressing button A, I can provide my son with a nice party; by pressing B, I can save the lives of a dozen strangers. Is it really all right for me to press A, just because I "care more" for my son? Mill agrees that the issue must be decided on the basis of feelings (how else could it be?), but for him it is not these small-scale personal feelings that have the final say. Instead, it is one's "conscientious feelings"—the feelings that prevail after everything has been thought through—that finally determine one's obligations. Mill assumes that we cannot, when we are thoughtful and reflective, approve of ourselves pushing button A.

However, some contemporary Utilitarians have argued that the matter need not be left to the vicissitudes of individual feeling. It may be true, they say, that we all care more for ourselves, our family, and our friends than we care for strangers. But we have rational capacities as well as feelings, and if we think objectively about the matter, we will realize that other people are no different. Others, even strangers, also care about themselves, their families, and their friends, in the same way that we do. Their needs and interests are comparable to our own. In fact, *there is nothing of this general sort that makes anyone different from anyone else*—and if we are in all relevant respects similar to one another, then there is no justification for anyone taking his or her own interests to be more important. Peter Singer, a utilitarian philosopher at Princeton University, writes in his book *How Are We to Live?* (1995):

> Reason makes it possible for us to see ourselves in this way . . . I am able to see that I am just one being among others, with interests and desires like others. I have a personal perspective on the world, from which my interests are at the front and centre of the stage, the interests of my family and friends are close behind, and the interests of strangers are pushed to the back and sides. But reason enables me to see that others have similarly subjective perspectives, and that from "the point of view of the universe" my perspective is no more privileged than theirs. Thus my ability to reason shows me the possibility of detaching myself from my own perspective, and shows me what the universe might look like if I had no personal perspective.

So, from an objective viewpoint, each of us must acknowledge that our own perspective—our own particular set of needs, interests, likes, and dislikes—is only one among many and has no special status.

Kant

The idea of impartiality is also central to the third major alternative in modern moral philosophy, the system of ethical ideas devised by the great German philosopher Immanuel Kant (1724–1804). Like the Social Contract theorists and the Utilitarians, Kant sought to explain ethics without appealing to divine commands or "moral facts." Kant's solution was to see morality as a product of "pure reason." Just as we must do some things because of our *desires*—for example, because I desire to attend a concert, I must reserve a ticket—the moral law is binding on us because of our *reason*.

Like the Utilitarians, Kant believed that morality can be summed up in one ultimate principle, from which all our duties and obligations are derived. But his version of the "ultimate moral principle" was very different from the Principle of Utility, because Kant did not emphasize the outcomes of actions. What was important for him was "doing one's duty," and he held that a person's duty is not determined by calculating consequences.

Kant called his ultimate moral principle the "Categorical Imperative." But he gave this principle two very different formulations. The first version of the Categorical Imperative, as expressed in his *Fundamental Principles of the Metaphysics of Morals* (1785), goes like this:

> Act only according to that maxim by which you can at the same time will that it should become a universal law.

Stated in this way, Kant's principle summarizes a procedure for deciding whether an act is morally permissible. When you are contemplating a particular action, you are to ask what rule you would be following if you were to do it. (This will be the "maxim" of the act.) Then you are to ask whether you would be willing for that rule to be followed by everyone all the time. (That would make it a "universal law" in the relevant sense.) If so, the rule may be followed, and the act is permissible. However, if you would not be willing for everyone to follow the rule, then you may not follow it, and the act is morally impermissible.

This explains why the Moral Law is binding on us simply by virtue of our rationality. The first requirement of rationality is that we be consistent, and it would not be consistent to act on a maxim that we could not want others to adopt as well. Kant believed, in addition, that consistency requires us to interpret moral rules as having no exceptions. For this reason, he endorsed a whole range of absolute prohibitions, covering everything from lying to suicide.

However, Kant also gave another formulation of the Categorical Imperative. Later in the same book, he said that the ultimate moral principle may be understood as saying:

> So act that you treat humanity, whether in your own person or in that of another, always as an end and never as means only.

What does it mean to say that persons are to be treated as "ends" and never as "means"? Kant gives this example: Suppose you need money, and so you want a "loan," but you know you could not repay it. In desperation, you consider making a false promise (to repay) in order to trick a friend into giving you the money. May you do this? Perhaps you need the money for a good purpose—so good, in fact, that you might convince yourself the lie would be justified. Nevertheless, if you lied to your friend, you would merely be manipulating him and using him "as a means."

On the other hand, what would it be like to treat your friend "as an end"? Suppose you told the truth—that you need the money for a certain purpose but could not repay it. Then your friend could make up his own mind about whether to let you have it. He could exercise his own powers of reason, consulting his own values and wishes, and make a free, autonomous choice. If he did decide to give the money for this purpose, he would be choosing to make that purpose his own. Thus, you would not merely be using him as a means to achieving your goal. This is what Kant meant when he said that "rational beings . . . ought always be esteemed also as ends, that is, as beings who must be capable of containing in themselves the end of the very same action."

Conclusion

Our purpose here is not to reach any firm conclusion about which of these approaches, if any, is correct. But we may end with an observation about how that project might be undertaken.

Philosophical ideas are often very abstract, and it is difficult to see what sort of evidence counts for or against them. It is easy enough to appreciate, intuitively, the ideas behind each of these theories, but how do we determine which, if any, is correct? It is a daunting question. Faced with this problem, people are tempted to accept or reject philosophical ideas on the basis of their intuitive appeal—if an idea sounds good, one may embrace it; or if it rubs one the wrong way, it may be discarded. But this is hardly a satisfactory way to proceed if we want to discover the truth. How an idea strikes us is not a reliable guide, for our "intuitions" may be mistaken.

Happily, there is an alternative. An idea is no better than the arguments that support it. So, to evaluate a philosophical idea, we may examine the reasoning behind it. The great philosophers knew this very well: They did not simply announce their philosophical opinions; instead, they presented arguments in support of their views. The leading idea, from the time of Socrates to the present, has been that truth is discovered by considering the reasons for and against the various alternatives—the "correct" theory is the one that has the best arguments on its side. Thus, philosophical thinking consists, to a large extent, in formulating and assessing arguments. This is not the whole of philosophy, but it is a big part of it. It is what makes philosophy a rational enterprise, rather than an empty exercise in theory mongering.

CHAPTER 2

Some Basic Points about Arguments

James Rachels

Philosophy without argument would be a lifeless exercise. What good would it be to produce a theory, if there were no reasons for thinking it correct? And of what interest is the rejection of a theory, if there are no good reasons for thinking it incorrect? A philosophical idea is exactly as good as the arguments in its support.

Therefore, if we want to think clearly about philosophical matters, we have to learn something about the evaluation of arguments. We have to learn to distinguish the sound ones from the unsound ones. This can be a tedious business, but it is indispensable if we want to come within shouting distance of the truth.

Arguments

In ordinary English, the word *argument* often means a quarrel, and there is a hint of acrimony in the word. That is not the way the word is used here. In the logician's sense, an argument is a chain of reasoning designed to prove something. It consists of one or more *premises* and a *conclusion,* together with the claim that the conclusion *follows from* the premises. Here is a simple argument. This example is not particularly interesting in itself, but it is short and clear, and it will help us grasp the main points we need to understand about the nature of arguments.

(1) All men are mortal.

Socrates is a man.

Therefore, Socrates is mortal.

The first two statements are the premises; the third statement is the conclusion; and it is claimed that the conclusion follows from the premises.

What does it mean to say that the conclusion "follows from" the premises? It means that a certain logical relation exists between the premises and the conclusion, namely, that *if* the premises are true, then the conclusion must be true also. (Another way to put the same point is: The conclusion follows from the premises if and only if it is impossible for the premises to be true, and the conclusion false, at the same time.) In example (1), we can see that the conclusion does follow from the premises. If it is true that all men are mortal, and Socrates is a man, then it must be true that Socrates is mortal. (Or, it is impossible for it to be true that all men are mortal, and for Socrates to be a man, and yet be false that Socrates is mortal.)

In example (1), the conclusion follows from the premises, *and* the premises are in fact true. However, the conclusion of an argument may follow from the premises even if the premises are not actually true. Consider this argument:

(2) All people from Georgia are famous.

Jimmy Carter is from Georgia.

Therefore, Jimmy Carter is famous.

Clearly, the conclusion of this argument does follow from the premises: *If* it were true that all Georgians were famous, and Jimmy Carter was from Georgia, then it follows that Jimmy Carter would be famous. This logical relation holds between the premises and conclusion even though one of the premises is in fact false.

At this point, logicians customarily introduce a bit of terminology. They say that an argument is *valid* just in case its conclusion follows from its premises. Both the examples given above are valid arguments, in this technical sense.

In order to be a *sound* argument, however, two things are necessary: The argument must be valid, *and* its premises must be true. Thus, the argument about Socrates is a sound argument, but the argument about Jimmy Carter is not sound, because even though it is valid, its premises are not all true.

It is important to notice that an argument may be unsound even though its premises and conclusion are both true. Consider the following silly example:

(3) The earth has one moon.

John F. Kennedy was assassinated.

Therefore, snow is white.

The premises of this "argument" are both true, and the conclusion is true as well. Yet it is obviously a bad argument, because it is not valid—the conclusion does not follow from the premises. The point is that *when we ask whether an argument is valid, we are not asking whether the premises actually are true, or whether the conclusion actually is true. We are only asking whether,* if *the premises were true, the conclusion would really follow from them.*

So far, our examples have all been trivial. I have used these trivial examples because they permit us to make the essential logical points clearly and uncontroversially. But these points are applicable to the analysis of any argument, trivial or not. To illustrate, let us consider how these points can be used in analyzing a more important and controversial issue. We will look at the arguments for Moral Skepticism in some detail.

Moral Skepticism

Moral Skepticism is the idea that *there is no such thing as objective moral truth.* It is not merely the idea that we cannot *know* the truth about right and wrong. It is the more radical idea that, where ethics is concerned, "truth" does not exist. The essential point may be put in several different ways. It may be said that:

- Morality is subjective; it is a matter of how we feel about things, not a matter of how things *are.*
- Morality is only a matter of opinion, and one person's opinion is just as good as another's.
- Values exist only in our minds, not in the world outside us.

However the point is put, the underlying thought is the same: The idea of "objective moral truth" is only a fiction; in reality, there is no such thing.

We want to know whether Moral Skepticism is correct. Is the idea of moral "truth" only an illusion? What arguments can be given in favor of this idea? In order to determine whether it is correct, we need to ask what arguments can be given for it and whether those arguments are sound.

The Cultural Differences Argument. One argument for Moral Skepticism might be based on the observation that in different cultures people have different ideas concerning right and wrong. For example, in traditional Eskimo society, infanticide was thought to be morally acceptable—if a family already had too many children, a new baby might have been left to die in the snow. (This was more likely to happen to girl babies than to boys.) In our own society, however, this would be considered wrong. There are many other examples of the same kind. Different cultures have different moral codes.

Reflecting on such facts, many people have concluded that there is no such thing as objective right and wrong. Thus, they advance the following argument:

> **(4)** In some societies, such as among the Eskimos, infanticide is thought to be morally acceptable.
>
> In other societies, such as our own, infanticide is thought to be morally odious.
>
> Therefore, infanticide is neither objectively right nor objectively wrong; it is merely a matter of opinion that varies from culture to culture.

We may call this the "Cultural Differences Argument." This kind of argument has been tremendously influential; it has persuaded many people to be skeptical of the whole idea of moral "truth." But is it a *sound* argument? We may ask two questions about it: First, are the premises true, and second, does the conclusion really follow from them? If the answer to either question is no, then the argument must be rejected. In this case, the premises seem to be correct—there have been many cultures in which infanticide was accepted. Therefore, our attention must focus on the second matter: Is the argument *valid?*

To figure this out, we may begin by noting that the premises concern *what people believe.* In some societies, people think infanticide is all right. In others, people believe it is immoral. The conclusion, however, concerns not what people believe, but whether infanticide *really is* immoral. The problem is that this sort of conclusion does not follow from those sorts of premises. It does not follow, from the mere fact that people have different beliefs about something, that there is no "truth" in the matter. Therefore, the Cultural Differences Argument is not valid.

To make the point clearer, consider this analogous argument:

> **(5)** In some societies, the world is thought to be flat.
>
> In other societies, the world is thought to be round.
>
> Therefore, objectively speaking, the world is neither flat nor round. It is merely a matter of opinion that varies from culture to culture.

Clearly, *this* argument is not valid. We cannot conclude that the world is shapeless simply because not everyone agrees what shape it has. But exactly the same can be said about the Cultural Differences Argument: We cannot validly move from premises about what people *believe* to a conclusion about what is so, because people—even whole societies—may be wrong. The world has a definite shape, and those who think it is flat are mistaken. Similarly, infanticide might be objectively wrong (or not wrong), and those who think differently might be mistaken. Therefore, the Cultural Differences Argument is not valid, and so it provides no legitimate support for the idea that moral "truth" is only an illusion.

There are two common reactions to this analysis. These reactions illustrate traps that people often fall into.

1. The first reaction goes like this: Many people find the conclusion of the Cultural Differences Argument very appealing. This makes it hard for them to believe that the argument is invalid—when it is pointed out that the argument is fallacious, they tend to respond: "But right and wrong really *are* only matters of opinion!" They make the mistake of thinking that, if we reject an argument, we are somehow impugning the truth of its conclusion. But that is not so. Remember example (3) above; it illustrates how an argument may have a true conclusion and still be a bad argument. If an argument is unsound, then it fails to provide any reason for thinking the conclusion is true. The conclusion may still be true—that remains an open question—but the point is just that the unsound argument gives it no support.

2. It may be objected that it is unfair to compare morality with an obviously objective matter like the shape of the earth, because we can prove what shape the earth has by scientific methods. Therefore, we know that the flat-earthers are simply wrong. But morality is different. There is no way to prove a moral opinion is true or false.

This objection misses the point. The Cultural Differences Argument tries to derive the skeptical conclusion about morality *from a certain set of facts,* namely, the facts about cultural disagreements. This objection suggests that the conclusion might be derived from a *different* set of facts, namely, facts about what is and what is not provable. It suggests, in effect, a different argument, which might be formulated like this:

> **(6)** If infanticide (or anything else, for that matter) is objectively right or wrong, then it should be possible to *prove* it right or wrong.
>
> But it is not possible to prove infanticide right or wrong.

Therefore, infanticide is neither objectively right nor objectively wrong. It is merely a matter of opinion that varies from culture to culture.

This argument is fundamentally different from the Cultural Differences Argument, even though the two arguments have the same conclusion. They are different because they appeal to different considerations in trying to prove that conclusion—in other words, they have different premises. Therefore, the question of whether argument (6) is sound is separate from the question of whether the Cultural Differences Argument is sound. The Cultural Differences Argument is not valid, for the reason given above.

We should emphasize the importance of *keeping arguments separate*. It is easy to slide from one argument to another without realizing what one is doing. It is easy to think that, if moral judgments are "unprovable," then the Cultural Differences Argument is strengthened. But it is not. Argument (6) merely introduces a different set of issues. It is important to pin down an argument and evaluate *it* as carefully as possible, before moving on to different considerations.

The Provability Argument. Now let us consider in more detail the question of whether it is possible to prove a moral judgment true or false. The following argument, which we might call the "Provability Argument," is a more general form of argument (6):

(7) If there were any such thing as objective truth in ethics, we should be able to prove that some moral opinions are true and others false.

But in fact we cannot prove which moral opinions are true and which are false.

Therefore, there is no such thing as objective truth in ethics.

Once again, we have an argument with a certain superficial appeal. But are the premises true? And does the conclusion really follow from them? It seems that the conclusion does follow. Therefore, the crucial question will be whether the premises are in fact true.

The general claim that moral judgments can't be proven *sounds* right: Anyone who has ever argued about a matter like abortion knows how frustrating it can be to try to "prove" that one's point of view is correct. However, if we inspect this claim more closely, it turns out to be dubious.

Suppose we consider a matter that is simpler than abortion. A student says that a test given by a teacher was unfair. This is clearly a moral judgment—fairness is a basic moral value. Can the student prove the test was unfair? She might point out that the test was so long that not even the best students could complete it in the time allowed (and the test was to be graded on the assumption that it should be completed). Moreover, the test covered trivial matters in detail while ignoring matters the teacher had stressed as very important. And finally, the test included questions about some matters that were not covered in either the assigned readings or the class discussions.

Suppose all this is true. And further suppose that the teacher, when asked to explain, has no defense to offer. (In fact, the teacher, who is rather inexperienced, seems muddled about the whole thing and doesn't seem to have had any very clear idea of what he was doing.) Now, hasn't the student proved the test was unfair? What more in the way of proof could we possibly want?

It is easy to think of other examples that make the same point:

- *Jones is a bad man.* To prove this, one might point out that Jones is a habitual liar; he manipulates people; he cheats when he thinks he can get away with it; he is cruel to other people; and so on.
- *Dr. Smith is irresponsible.* She bases her diagnoses on superficial considerations; she drinks before performing delicate surgery; she refuses to listen to other doctors' advice; and so on.
- A *certain used-car salesman is unethical.* He conceals defects in his cars; he takes advantage of poor people by pressuring them into paying exorbitant prices for cars he knows to be defective; he runs false advertisements in any newspaper that will carry them; and so on.

The point is that we can, and often do, back up our ethical judgments with good reasons. Thus, it does not seem right to say that they are all unprovable, as though they were nothing more than "mere opinions." If a person has good reasons for his judgments, then he is not *merely* giving "his opinion." On the contrary, he may be making a judgment with which any reasonable person would have to agree.

If we can sometimes give good reasons for our moral judgments, what accounts for the persistent impression that they are "unprovable"? There are two reasons why the Provability Argument appears to be more potent than it actually is.

First, there is a tendency to focus attention only on the most difficult moral issues. The question of abortion, for example, is an enormously difficult and complicated matter. If we think only of questions like *this*, it is easy to believe that "proof" in ethics is impossible. The same could be said of the sciences. There are many complicated matters that physicists cannot agree on; if we focused our attention entirely on *them*, we might conclude that there is no "proof" in physics. But, of course, there are many simpler matters in physics that can be proven and about which all competent physicists agree. Similarly, in ethics, there are many matters far simpler than abortion, about which all reasonable people must agree.

Second, it is easy to confuse two matters that are really very different:

1. Proving an opinion to be correct
2. Persuading someone to accept your proof

Suppose you are having an argument with someone about some moral issue, and you have perfectly cogent reasons in support of your position, while they have no good reasons on their side. Still, they refuse to accept your logic and continue to insist they are right. This is a common, if frustrating, experience. You may be tempted to conclude that it is impossible to prove you are right. But this would be a mistake. Your proof may be impeccable; the trouble may be that the other person is being pig-headed. (Of course, that is not the *only* possible explanation of what is going on, but it is one possible explanation.) The same thing can happen in any sort of discussion. You may be arguing about intelligent design versus evolution, and the other person may be unreasonable. But that does not necessarily mean there is something wrong with your arguments. There may be something wrong with him.

Conclusion

We have examined two of the most important arguments in support of Moral Skepticism and seen that these arguments are no good. Moral Skepticism might still turn out to be true, but if so, then other, better arguments will have to be found. Provisionally, at least, we have to conclude that Moral Skepticism is not nearly as plausible as we might have thought.

The purpose of this exercise, however, was to illustrate the process of evaluating philosophical arguments. We may summarize what we have learned about evaluating arguments like this:

1. Arguments are offered to provide support for a theory or idea; a philosophical theory may be regarded as acceptable only if there are sound arguments in its favor.

2. An argument is sound only if its premises are true and the conclusion follows logically from them.

   (a) A conclusion "follows from" the premises just in case the following is so: *If* the premises were true, then the conclusion would have to be true also. (An alternative way of saying the same thing: A conclusion follows from the premises just in case it is impossible for the premises to be true and the conclusion false at the same time.)

   (b) A conclusion can follow from premises even if those premises are in fact false.

   (c) A conclusion can be true and yet not follow from a given set of premises.

3. Therefore, in evaluating an argument, we ask two *separate* questions: Are the premises true? And, does the conclusion follow from them?

4. It is important to avoid two common mistakes. We should be careful to keep arguments separate, and not slide from one to the other, confusing different issues. And, we should not think an argument stronger than it is simply because we happen to agree with its conclusion. Moreover, we should remember that, if an argument is unsound, that does not mean the conclusion must be false—it only means that *this* argument does nothing to show it is true.

*T*heories about the Nature of Morality

CHAPTER 3

The Subjectivity of Values

J. L. Mackie

Everyone agrees that ethics is subjective in the sense that people have their own personal moral beliefs, and yours may be different from mine. In this selection, John L. Mackie contends that ethics is subjective in a much more radical sense—that really there is no right or wrong.

Consider this analogy: The earth is spherical, and not flat, because there is this thing—the earth—that has the property of being spherical. But when someone says abortion is wrong, according to Mackie, there is no property of wrongness corresponding to the property of being spherical; there is just the feeling, or belief, that abortion is wrong.

In Mackie's view, the belief that Abraham Lincoln is morally better than John Wilkes Booth is similar to Homer Simpson's belief that syrup is better than jelly. Homer might like syrup more than jelly, but he's not "right" in feeling that way. Similarly, Mackie thinks, you might approve of the man who emancipated the slaves more than the man who shot him, but you're not "right" in feeling that way. It's just how you feel.

John L. Mackie (1917–1981) was born in Australia and taught at the University of Oxford for the last 14 years of his life. This selection is from his book *Ethics: Inventing Right and Wrong*.

Moral Scepticism

There are no objective values. This is a bald statement of the thesis of this chapter, but before arguing for it I shall try to clarify and restrict it in ways that may meet some objections and prevent some misunderstanding.

J. L., Mackie, *Ethics: Inventing Right and Wrong*, Penguin, 1977, pp. 15–17, 25–28, 29–31, 34–35, 35–39, 40, 41. Reproduced by permission of Penguin Books, Ltd.

The statement of this thesis is liable to provoke one of three very different reactions. Some will think it not merely false but pernicious; they will see it as a threat to morality and to everything else that is worthwhile, and they will find the presenting of such a thesis in what purports to be a book on ethics paradoxical or even outrageous. Others will regard it as a trivial truth, almost too obvious to be worth mentioning, and certainly too plain to be worth much argument. Others again will say that it is meaningless or empty, that no real issue is raised by the question whether values are or are not part of the fabric of the world. But, precisely because there can be these three different reactions, much more needs to be said.

The claim that values are not objective, are not part of the fabric of the world, is meant to include not only moral goodness, which might be most naturally equated with moral value, but also other things that could be more loosely called moral values or disvalues—rightness and wrongness, duty, obligation, an action's being rotten and contemptible, and so on. It also includes non-moral values, notably aesthetic ones, beauty and various kinds of artistic merit. I shall not discuss these explicitly, but clearly much the same considerations apply to aesthetic and to moral values, and there would be at least some initial implausibility in a view that gave the one a different status from the other.

Since it is with moral values that I am primarily concerned, the view I am adopting may be called moral scepticism. But this name is likely to be misunderstood: "moral scepticism" might also be used as a name for either of two first order views, or perhaps for an incoherent mixture of the two. A moral sceptic might be the sort of person who says "All this talk of morality is tripe," who rejects morality and will take no notice of it. Such a person may be literally rejecting all moral judgements; he is more likely to be making moral judgements of his own, expressing a positive moral condemnation of all that conventionally passes for morality; or he may be confusing these two logically incompatible views, and saying that he rejects all morality, while he is in fact rejecting only a particular morality that is current in the society in which he has grown up. But I am not at present concerned with the merits or faults of such a position. These are first order moral views, positive or negative: the person who adopts either of them is taking a certain practical, normative, stand. By contrast, what I am discussing is a second order view, a view about the status of moral values and the nature of moral valuing, about where and how they fit into the world. These first and second order views are not merely distinct but completely independent: one could be a second order moral sceptic without being a first order one, or again the other way round. A man could hold strong moral views, and indeed ones whose content was thoroughly conventional, while believing that they were simply attitudes and policies with regard to conduct that he and other people held. Conversely, a man could reject all established morality while believing it to be an objective truth that it was evil or corrupt.

With another sort of misunderstanding moral scepticism would seem not so much pernicious as absurd. How could anyone deny that there is a difference between a kind action and a cruel one, or that a coward and a brave man behave differently in the face of danger? Of course, this is undeniable; but it is not to the point. The kinds of behaviour to which moral values and disvalues are ascribed are indeed part of the furniture of the world, and so are the natural, descriptive, differences between them; but not, perhaps, their differences in value. It is a hard fact that cruel actions differ from kind ones, and hence that we can learn, as in fact we all do, to distinguish them fairly well in practice, and to use the words "cruel" and "kind" with fairly clear descriptive meanings; but is it an equally hard fact that actions which are cruel in such a descriptive sense are to be condemned? The present issue is with regard to the objectivity specifically of value, not with regard to the objectivity of those natural, factual, differences on the basis of which differing values are assigned. . . .

Standards of Evaluation

One way of stating the thesis that there are no objective values is to say that value statements cannot be either true or false. But this formulation, too, lends itself to misinterpretation. For there are certain kinds of value statements which undoubtedly can be true or false, even if, in the sense I intend, there are no objective values. Evaluations of many sorts are commonly made in relation to agreed and assumed standards. The classing of wool, the grading of apples, the awarding of prizes at sheepdog trials, flower shows, skating and diving championships, and even the marking of examination papers are carried out in relation to standards of quality or merit which are peculiar to each particular subject-matter or type of contest, which may be explicitly laid down but which, even if they are nowhere explicitly stated, are fairly well understood and agreed by those who are recognized as judges or experts in each particular field. Given any sufficiently determinate standards, it will be an objective issue, a matter of truth and falsehood, how well any particular specimen measures up to those standards. Comparative judgements in particular will be capable of truth and falsehood: it will be a factual question whether this sheepdog has performed better than that one.

The subjectivist about values, then, is not denying that there can be objective evaluations relative to standards, and these are as possible in the aesthetic and moral fields as in any of those just mentioned. More than this, there is an objective distinction which applies in many such fields, and yet would itself be regarded as a peculiarly moral one: the distinction between justice and injustice. In one important sense of the word it is a paradigm case of injustice if a court declares someone to be guilty of an offence of which it knows him to be innocent. More generally, a finding is unjust if it is at variance with what the relevant law and the facts together require, and particularly if it is known by the court to be so. More generally still, any award of marks, prizes, or the like is unjust if it is at variance with the agreed standards for the contest in question: if one diver's performance in fact measures up better to the accepted standards for diving than another's, it will be unjust if the latter is awarded higher marks or the prize. In this way the justice or injustice of decisions relative to standards can be a thoroughly objective matter, though there may still be a subjective element in the interpretation or application of standards. But the statement that a certain decision is thus just or unjust will not be objectively prescriptive: in so far as it can be simply true it leaves open the question whether there is any objective requirement to do what is just and to refrain from what is unjust, and equally leaves open the practical decision to act in either way.

Recognizing the objectivity of justice in relation to standards, and of evaluative judgements relative to standards, then, merely shifts the question of the objectivity of values back to the standards themselves. The subjectivist may try to make his point by insisting that there is no objective validity about the choice of standards. Yet he would clearly be wrong if he said that the choice of even the most basic standards in any field was completely arbitrary. The standards used in sheepdog trials clearly bear some relation to the work that sheepdogs are kept to do, the standards for grading apples bear some relation to what people generally want in or like about apples, and so on. On the other hand, standards are not as a rule strictly validated by such purposes. The appropriateness of standards is neither fully determinate nor totally indeterminate in relation to independently specifiable aims or desires. But however determinate it is, the objective appropriateness of standards in relation to aims or desires is no more of a threat to the denial of objective values than is the objectivity of evaluation relative to standards. In fact it is logically no different from the objectivity of goodness relative to desires. Something may be called good simply in so far as it satisfies or is such as to satisfy a certain desire; but the objectivity of such relations of satisfaction does not constitute in our sense an objective value.

Hypothetical and Categorical Imperatives

We may make this issue clearer by referring to Kant's distinction between hypothetical and categorical imperatives, though what he called imperatives are more naturally expressed as "ought" statements than in the imperative mood. "If you want X, do Y" (or "You ought to do Y") will be a hypothetical imperative if it is based on the supposed fact that Y is, in the circumstances, the only (or the best) available means to X, that is, on a causal relation between Y and X. The reason for doing Y lies in its causal connection with the desired end, X; the oughtness is contingent upon the desire. But "You ought to do Y" will be a categorical imperative if you ought to do Y irrespective of any such desire for any end to which Y would contribute, if the oughtness is not thus contingent upon any desire. But this distinction needs to be handled with some care. . . .

A categorical imperative, then, would express a reason for acting which was unconditional in the sense of not being contingent upon any present desire of the agent to whose satisfaction the recommended action would contribute as a means—or more directly: "You ought to dance," if the implied reason is just that you want to dance or like dancing, is still a hypothetical imperative. Now Kant himself held that moral judgements are categorical imperatives, or perhaps are all applications of one categorical imperative, and it can plausibly be maintained at least that many moral judgements contain a categorically imperative element. So far as ethics is concerned, my thesis that there are no objective values is specifically the denial that any such categorically imperative element is objectively valid. The objective values which I am denying would be action-directing absolutely, not contingently (in the way indicated) upon the agent's desires and inclinations.

Another way of trying to clarify this issue is to refer to moral reasoning or moral arguments. In practice, of course, such reasoning is seldom fully explicit: but let us suppose that we could make explicit the reasoning that supports some evaluative conclusion, where this conclusion has some action-guiding force that is not contingent upon desires or purposes or chosen ends. Then what I am saying is that somewhere in the input to this argument—perhaps in one or more of the premisses, perhaps in some part of the form of the argument— there will be something which cannot be objectively validated—some premiss which is not capable of being simply true, or some form of argument which is not valid as a matter of general logic, whose authority or cogency is not objective, but is constituted by our choosing or deciding to think in a certain way.

The Claim to Objectivity

If I have succeeded in specifying precisely enough the moral values whose objectivity I am denying, my thesis may now seem to be trivially true. Of course, some will say, valuing, preferring, choosing, recommending, rejecting, condemning, and so on, are human activities, and there is no need to look for values that are prior to and logically independent of all such activities. There may be widespread agreement in valuing, and particular value-judgements are not in general arbitrary or isolated: they typically cohere with others, or can be criticized if they do not, reasons can be given for them, and so on: but if all that the subjectivist is maintaining is that desires, ends, purposes, and the like figure somewhere in the system of reasons, and that no ends or purposes are objective as opposed to being merely intersubjective, then this may be conceded without much fuss.

But I do not think that this should be conceded so easily. As I have said, the main tradition of European moral philosophy includes the contrary claim, that there are objective values of just the sort I have denied. . . . Kant in particular holds that the categorical imperative is not only categorical and imperative but objectively so: though a rational being gives the moral law to himself, the law that he thus makes is determinate and necessary. Aristotle begins the *Nicomachean Ethics* by saying that the good is that at which all things aim, and that ethics is part of a science which he calls "politics," whose goal is not knowledge but practice; yet he does not doubt that there can be *knowledge* of what is the good for man, nor, once he has identified this as well-being or happiness, *eudaimonia*, that it can be known, rationally determined, in what happiness consists; and it is plain that he thinks that this happiness is intrinsically desirable, not good simply because it is desired. . . . Even the sentimentalist Hutcheson defines moral goodness as "some quality apprehended in actions, which procures approbation. . . ." while saying that the moral sense by which we perceive virtue and vice has been given to us (by the Author of nature) to direct our actions. Hume indeed was on the other side, but he is still a witness to the dominance of the objectivist tradition, since he claims that when we "see that the distinction of vice and virtue is not founded merely on the relations of objects, nor is perceiv'd by reason," this "wou'd subvert all the vulgar systems of morality." . . .

The prevalence of this tendency to objectify values—and not only moral ones—is confirmed by a pattern of thinking that we find in existentialists and those influenced by them. The denial of objective values can carry with it an extreme emotional reaction, a feeling that nothing matters at all, that life has lost its purpose. Of course this does not follow; the lack of objective values is not a good reason for abandoning subjective concern or for ceasing to want anything. But the abandonment of a belief in objective values can cause, at least temporarily, a decay of subjective concern and sense of purpose. That it does so is evidence that the people in whom this reaction occurs have been tending to objectify their concerns and purposes, have been giving them a fictitious external authority. A claim to objectivity has been so strongly associated with their subjective concerns and purposes that the collapse of the former seems to undermine the latter as well.

This view, that conceptual analysis would reveal a claim to objectivity, is sometimes dramatically confirmed by philosophers who are officially on the other side. Bertrand Russell, for example, says that "ethical propositions should be expressed in the optative mood, not in the indicative"; he defends himself effectively against the charge of inconsistency in both holding ultimate ethical valuations to be subjective and expressing emphatic opinions on ethical questions. Yet at the end he admits:

> Certainly there *seems* to be something more. Suppose, for example, that some one were to advocate the introduction of bullfighting in this country. In opposing the proposal, I should *feel*, not only that I was expressing my desires, but that my desires in the matter are *right*, whatever that may mean. As a matter of argument, I can, I think, show that I am not guilty of any logical inconsistency in holding to the above interpretation of ethics and at the same time expressing strong ethical preferences. But in feeling I am not satisfied.

But he concludes, reasonably enough, with the remark: "I can only say that, while my own opinions as to ethics do not satisfy me, other people's satisfy me still less."

I conclude, then, that ordinary moral judgements include a claim to objectivity, an assumption that there are objective values in just the sense in which I am concerned to deny this. And I do not think it is going too far to say that this assumption has been incorporated in the basic, conventional, meanings of moral terms. Any analysis of the meanings of moral terms which omits this claim to objective, intrinsic, prescriptivity is to that extent incomplete. . . .

If second order ethics were confined, then, to linguistic and conceptual analysis, it ought to conclude that moral values at least are objective: that they are so is part of what our ordinary moral statements mean: the traditional moral concepts of the ordinary man as well as of the main line of western philosophers are concepts of objective value. But it is precisely for this reason that linguistic and conceptual analysis is not enough. The claim to objectivity, however ingrained in our language and thought, is not self-validating. It can and should be questioned. But the denial of objective values will have to be put forward not as the result of an analytic approach, but as an "error theory," a theory that although most people in making moral judgements implicitly claim, among other things, to be pointing to something objectively prescriptive, these claims are all false. It is this that makes the name "moral scepticism" appropriate.

But since this is an error theory, since it goes against assumptions ingrained in our thought and built into some of the ways in which language is used, since it conflicts with what is sometimes called common sense, it needs very solid support. It is not something we can accept lightly or casually and then quietly pass on. If we are to adopt this view, we must argue explicitly for it. Traditionally it has been supported by arguments of two main kinds, which I shall call the argument from relativity and the argument from queerness, but these can, as I shall show, be supplemented in several ways.

The Argument from Relativity

The argument from relativity has as its premiss the well-known variation in moral codes from one society to another and from one period to another, and also the differences in moral beliefs between different groups and classes within a complex community. Such variation is in itself merely a truth of descriptive morality, a fact of anthropology which entails neither first order nor second order ethical views. Yet it may indirectly support second order subjectivism: radical differences between first order moral judgements make it difficult to treat those judgements as apprehensions of objective truths. But it is not the mere occurrence of disagreements that tells against the objectivity of values. Disagreement on questions in history or biology or cosmology does not show that there are no objective issues in these fields for investigators to disagree about. But such scientific disagreement results from speculative inferences or explanatory hypotheses based on inadequate evidence, and it is hardly plausible to interpret moral disagreement in the same way. Disagreement about moral codes seems to reflect people's adherence to and participation in different ways of life. The causal connection seems to be mainly that way round: it is that people approve of monogamy because they participate in a monogamous way of life rather than that they participate in a monogamous way of life because they approve of monogamy. Of course, the standards may be an idealization of the way of life from which they arise: the monogamy in which people participate may be less complete, less rigid, than that of which it leads them to approve. This is not to say that moral judgements are purely conventional. Of course there have been and are moral heretics and moral reformers, people who have turned against the established rules and practices of their own communities for moral reasons, and often for moral reasons that we would endorse. But this can usually be understood as the extension, in ways which, though new and unconventional, seemed to them to be required for consistency, of rules to which they already adhered as arising out of an existing way of life. In short, the argument from relativity has some force simply because the actual variations in the moral codes are more readily explained by the hypothesis that they reflect ways of life than by the hypothesis that they express perceptions, most of them seriously inadequate and badly distorted, of objective values.

But there is a well-known counter to this argument from relativity; namely to say that the items for which objective validity is in the first place to be claimed are not specific moral rules or codes but very general basic principles which are recognized at least implicitly to some extent in all society—such principles as provide the foundations of what Sidgwick has called different methods of ethics: the principle of universalizability, perhaps, or the rule that one ought to conform to the specific rules of any way of life in which one takes part, from which one profits, and on which one relies, or some utilitarian principle of doing what tends, or seems likely, to promote the general happiness. It is easy to show that such general principles, married with differing concrete circumstances, different existing social patterns or different preferences, will beget different specific moral rules; and there is some plausibility in the claim that the specific rules thus generated will vary from community to community or from group to group in close agreement with the actual variations in accepted codes.

The argument from relativity can be only partly countered in this way. To take this line the moral objectivist has to say that it is only in these principles that the objective moral character attaches immediately to its descriptively specified ground or subject: other moral judgements are objectively valid or true, but only derivatively and contingently—if things had been otherwise, quite different sorts of actions would have been right. And despite the prominence in recent philosophical ethics of universalization, utilitarian principles, and the like, these are very far from constituting the whole of what is actually affirmed as basic in ordinary moral thought. Much of this is concerned rather with what Hare calls "ideals" or, less kindly, "fanaticism." That is, people judge that some things are good or right, and others are bad or wrong, not because—or at any rate not only because—they exemplify some general principle for which widespread implicit acceptance could be claimed, but because something about those things arouses certain responses immediately in them, though they would arouse radically and irresolvably different responses in others. "Moral sense" or "intuition" is an initially more plausible description of what supplies many of our basic moral judgements than "reason." With regard to all these starting points of moral thinking the argument from relativity remains in full force.

The Argument from Queerness

Even more important, however, and certainly more generally applicable, is the argument from queerness. This has two parts, one metaphysical, the other epistemological. If there were objective values, then they would be entities or qualities or relations of a very strange sort, utterly different from anything else in the universe. Correspondingly, if we were aware of them, it would have to be by some special faculty of moral perception or intuition, utterly different from our ordinary ways of knowing everything else. These points were recognized by Moore when he spoke of non-natural qualities, and by the intuitionists in their talk about a "faculty of moral intuition." Intuitionism has long been out of favour, and it is indeed easy to point out its implausibilities. What is not so often stressed, but is more important, is that the central thesis of intuitionism is one to which any objectivist view of values is in the end committed: intuitionism merely makes unpalatably plain what other forms of objectivism wrap up. Of course the suggestion that moral judgements are made or moral problems solved by just sitting down and having an ethical intuition is a travesty of actual moral thinking. But, however complex the real process, it will require (if it is to yield authoritatively prescriptive conclusions) some input of this distinctive sort, either premisses or forms of argument or both. When we ask the awkward question, how we can be aware of this authoritative prescriptivity, of the truth of these distinctively ethical premisses or of the cogency of this distinctively ethical pattern of reasoning, none of our ordinary accounts of sensory perception or introspection or the framing and confirming of explanatory hypotheses or inference or logical construction or conceptual analysis, or any combination of these, will provide a satisfactory answer; "a special sort of intuition" is a lame answer, but it is the one to which the clearheaded objectivist is compelled to resort.

Indeed, the best move for the moral objectivist is not to evade this issue, but to look for companions in guilt. For example, Richard Price argues that it is not moral knowledge alone that such an empiricism as those of Locke and Hume is unable to account for, but also our knowledge and even our ideas of essence, number, identity, diversity, solidity, inertia, substance, the necessary existence and infinite extension of time and space, necessity and possibility in general, power, and causation. If the understanding, which Price defines as the faculty within us that discerns truth, is also a source of new simple ideas of so many other sorts, may it not also be a power of immediately perceiving right and wrong, which yet are real characters of actions?

This is an important counter to the argument from queerness. The only adequate reply to it would be to show how, on empiricist foundations, we can construct an account of the ideas and beliefs and knowledge that we have of all these matters. I cannot even begin to do that here, though I have undertaken some parts of the task elsewhere. I can only state my belief that satisfactory accounts of most of these can be given in empirical terms. If some supposed metaphysical necessities or essences resist such treatment, then they too should be included, along with objective values, among the targets of the argument from queerness. . . .

Plato's Forms give a dramatic picture of what objective values would have to be. The Form of the Good is such that knowledge of it provides the knower with both a direction and an overriding motive; something's being good both tells the person who knows this to pursue it and makes him pursue it. An objective good would be sought by anyone who was acquainted with it, not because of any contingent fact that this person, or every person, is so constituted that he desires this end, but just because the end has to-be-pursuedness somehow built into it. Similarly, if there were objective principles of right and wrong, any wrong (possible) course of action would have not-to-be-doneness somehow built into it. Or we should have something like Clarke's necessary relations of fitness between situations and actions, so that a situation would have a demand for such-and-such an action somehow built into it. . . .

Another way of bringing out this queerness is to ask, about anything that is supposed to have some objective moral quality, how this is linked with its natural features. What is the connection between the natural fact that an action is a piece of deliberate cruelty—say, causing pain just for fun—and the moral fact that it is wrong? It cannot be an entailment, a logical or semantic necessity. Yet it is not merely that the two features occur together. The wrongness must somehow be "consequential" or "supervenient"; it is wrong because it is a piece of deliberate cruelty. But just what *in the world* is signified by this "because"? And how do we know the relation that it signifies, if this is something more than such actions being socially condemned, and condemned by us too, perhaps through our having absorbed attitudes from our social environment? It is not even sufficient to postulate a faculty which "sees" the wrongness: something must be postulated which can see at once the natural features that constitute the cruelty, and the wrongness, and the mysterious consequential link between the two. Alternatively, the intuition required might be the perception that wrongness is a higher order property belonging to certain natural properties; but what is this belonging of properties to other properties, and how can we discern it? How much simpler and more comprehensible the situation would be if we could replace the moral quality with some sort of subjective response which could be causally related to the detection of the natural features on which the supposed quality is said to be consequential. . . .

CHAPTER 4

The Virtues

Aristotle

Aristotle (384–322 B.C.) may be the most influential thinker of all time. His theory of physics reigned for a thousand years; his system of logic was dominant until the 19th century; Charles Darwin called him "the greatest biologist of all time"; and his theory of ethics still has many followers.

Aristotle was born in Stagira in northern Greece and moved to Athens when he was 17. There he became a pupil of Plato. Aristotle left Athens after Plato's death in 347 B.C.; four years later, he became tutor to the young boy who was to become Alexander the Great. From 334 B.C. until his death, he headed his own school in Athens.

The following selection, from Books I and II of Aristotle's *Nicomachean Ethics*, discusses two central themes in his moral philosophy: the nature of the good life, and what it means to be virtuous.

But what is happiness? If we consider what the function of man is, we find that happiness is a virtuous activity of the soul

But presumably to say that happiness is the supreme good seems a platitude, and some more distinctive account of it is still required. This might perhaps be achieved by grasping what is the function of man. If we take a flautist or a sculptor or any artist—or in general any class of men who have a specific function or activity—his goodness and proficiency is considered to lie in the performance of that function; and the same will be true of man, assuming that man has

---

Excerpts from *The Ethics of Aristotle,* trans. J. A. K. Thomson (London: Penguin Books, 1976), bks. 1, 2, pp. 75–80, 84, 91–92, 94, 100–102. Reprinted by permission of Routledge Ltd.

a function. But is it likely that whereas joiners and shoemakers have certain functions or activities, man as such has none, but has been left by nature a functionless being? Just as we can see that eye and hand and foot and every one of our members has some function, should we not assume that in like manner a human being has a function over and above these particular functions? What, then, can this possibly be? Clearly life is a thing shared also by plants, and we are looking for man's *proper* function; so we must exclude from our definition the life that consists in nutrition and growth. Next in order would be a sort of sentient life; but this too we see is shared by horses and cattle and animals of all kinds. There remains, then, a practical life of the rational part. (This has two aspects: one amenable to reason, the other possessing it and initiating thought.) As this life also has two meanings, we must lay down that we intend here life determined by activity, because this is accepted as the stricter sense. Now if the function of man is an activity of the soul in accordance with, or implying, a rational principle; and if we hold that the function of an individual and of a good individual of the same kind—e.g. of a harpist and of a good harpist, and so on generally— is generically the same, the latter's distinctive excellence being attached to the name of the function (because the function of the harpist is to play the harp, but that of the good harpist is to play it well); and if we assume that the function of man is a kind of life, viz., an activity or series of actions of the soul, implying a rational principle; and if the function of a good man is to perform these well and rightly; and if every function is performed well when performed in accordance with its proper excellence: if all this is so, the conclusion is that the good for man is an activity of soul in accordance with virtue, or if there are more kinds of virtue than one, in accordance with the best and most perfect kind.

There is a further qualification: in a complete lifetime. One swallow does not make a summer; neither does one day. Similarly neither can one day, or a brief space of time, make a man blessed and happy. . . .

Our view of happiness is supported by popular beliefs

viii. We must examine our principle not only as reached logically, from a conclusion and premises, but also in the light of what is commonly said about it; because if a statement is true all the data are in harmony with it, while if it is false they soon reveal a discrepancy.

Now goods have been classified under three heads, as (*a*) external, (*b*) of the soul, and (*c*) of the body. Of these we say that goods of the soul are good in the strictest and fullest sense, and we rank actions and activities of soul as goods of the soul; so that according to this view, which is of long standing and accepted by philosophers, our definition will be correct. We are right, too, in saying that the end consists in certain actions or activities, because this puts it among goods of the soul and not among external goods. Our definition is also supported by the belief that the happy man lives and fares well; because what we have described is virtually a kind of good life or prosperity. Again, our definition seems to include all the required constituents of happiness; for some think that it is virtue, others prudence, and others wisdom; others that it is these, or one of these, with the addition of pleasure, or not in total separation from it; and others further include favourable external conditions. Some of these views are popular beliefs of long standing; others are those of a few distinguished men. It is reasonable to suppose that neither group is entirely mistaken, but is right in some respect, or even in most.

Now our definition is in harmony with those who say that happiness is virtue, or a particular virtue; because an activity in accordance with virtue implies virtue. But presumably it makes no little difference whether we think of the supreme good as consisting in the *possession* or in the *exercise* of virtue: in a state of mind or in an activity. For it is possible for the *state* to be present in a person without effecting any good result (e.g. if he is asleep or quiescent in some other way), but not for the *activity:* he will necessarily act, and act well. Just as at the Olympic Games it is not the best-looking or the strongest men present that are crowned with wreaths, but the competitors (because it is from them that the winners come), so it is those who *act* that rightly win the honours and rewards in life.

Moreover, the life of such people is in itself pleasant. For pleasure is an experience of the soul, and each individual finds pleasure in that of which he is said to be fond. For example, a horse gives pleasure to one who is fond of horses, and a spectacle to one who is fond of sight-seeing. In the same way just acts give pleasure to a lover of justice, and virtuous conduct generally to the lover of virtue. Now most people find that the things which give them pleasure conflict, because they are not pleasant by nature; but lovers of beauty find pleasure in things that are pleasant by nature, and virtuous actions are of this kind, so that they are pleasant not only to this type of person but also in themselves. So their life does not need to have pleasure attached to it as a sort of accessory, but contains its own pleasure in itself. Indeed, we may go further and assert that anyone who does not delight in fine actions is not even a good man; for nobody would say that a man is just unless he enjoys acting justly, nor liberal unless he enjoys liberal actions, and similarly in all the other cases. If this is so, virtuous actions must be pleasurable in themselves. What is more, they are both good and fine, and each in the highest degree, assuming that the good man is right in his judgement of them; and his judgement is as we have described. So happiness is the best, the finest, the most pleasurable thing of all; and these qualities are not separated as the inscription at Delos suggests:

> Justice is loveliest, and health is best,
> But sweetest to obtain is heart's desire.

All these attributes belong to the best activities; and it is these, or the one that is best of them, that we identify with happiness.

Nevertheless it seems clear that happiness needs the addition of external goods, as we have said; for it is difficult if not impossible to do fine deeds without any resources. Many can only be done by the help of friends, or wealth, or political influence. There are also certain advantages, such as good ancestry or good children, or personal beauty, the lack of which mars our felicity; for a man is scarcely happy if he is very ugly to look at, or of low birth, or solitary and childless; and presumably even less so if he has children or friends who are quite worthless, or if he had good ones who are now dead. So, as we said, happiness seems to require this sort of prosperity too; which is why some identify it with good fortune, although others identify it with virtue. . . .

We are now in a position to define the happy man as "one who is active in accordance with complete virtue, and who is adequately furnished with external goods, and that not for some unspecified period but throughout a complete life." And probably we should add "destined both to live in this way and to die accordingly"; because the future is obscure to us, and happiness we maintain to be an *end* in every way utterly final and complete. . . .

Moral virtues, like crafts, are acquired by practice and habituation

i. Virtue, then, is of two kinds, intellectual and moral. Intellectual virtue owes both its inception and its growth chiefly to instruction, and for this very reason needs time and experience. Moral goodness, on the other hand, is the result of habit, from which it has actually got its name, being a slight modification of the word *ethos*. This fact makes it obvious that none of the moral virtues is engendered in us by nature, since nothing that is what it is by nature can be made to behave differently by habituation. For instance, a stone, which has a natural tendency downwards, cannot be habituated to rise, however often you try to train it by throwing it into the air; nor can you train fire to burn downwards; nor can anything else that has any other natural tendency be trained to depart from it. The moral virtues, then, are engendered in us neither *by* nor *contrary to* nature; we are constituted by nature to receive them, but their full development in us is due to habit.

Again, of all those faculties with which nature endows us we first acquire the potentialities, and only later effect their actualization. (This is evident in the case of the senses. It was not from repeated acts of seeing or hearing that we acquired the senses but the other way round: we had these senses before we used them; we did not acquire them as the result of using them.) But the virtues we do acquire by first exercising them, just as happens in the arts. Anything that we have to learn to do we learn by the actual doing of it: people become builders by building and instrumentalists by playing instruments. Similarly we become just by performing just acts, temperate by performing temperate ones, brave by performing brave ones. This view is supported by what happens in city-states. Legislators make their citizens good by habituation; this is the intention of every legislator, and those who do not carry it out fail of their object. This is what makes the difference between a good constitution and a bad one.

Again, the causes or means that bring about any form of excellence are the same as those that destroy it, and similarly with art; for it is as a result of playing the harp that people become good and bad harpists. The same principle applies to builders and all other craftsmen. Men will become good builders as a result of building well, and bad ones as a result of building badly. Otherwise there would be no need of anyone to teach them: they would all be *born* either good or bad. Now this holds good also of the virtues. It is the way that we behave in our dealings with other people that makes us just or unjust, and the way that we behave in the face of danger, accustoming ourselves to be timid or confident, that makes us brave or cowardly. Similarly with situations involving desires and angry feelings: some people become temperate and patient from one kind of conduct in such situations, others licentious and choleric from another. In a word, then, like activities produce like dispositions. Hence we must give our activities a certain quality, because it is their characteristics that determine the resulting dispositions. So it is a matter of no little importance what sort of habits we form from the earliest age—it makes a vast difference, or rather all the difference in the world. . . .

A cardinal rule: right conduct is incompatible with excess or deficiency in feelings and actions

First, then, we must consider this fact: that it is in the nature of moral qualities that they are destroyed by deficiency and excess, just as we can see (since we have to use the evidence of visible facts to throw light on those that are invisible) in the case of bodily health and strength. For both excessive and insufficient exercise destroy one's strength, and both eating and drinking too much or too little destroy health, whereas the right quantity produces, increases and preserves it. So it is the same with temperance, courage and the other virtues. The man who shuns and fears everything and stands up to nothing becomes a coward; the man who is afraid of nothing at all, but marches up to every danger, becomes foolhardy. Similarly the man who indulges in every pleasure and refrains from none becomes licentious; but if a man behaves like a boor and turns his back on every pleasure, he is a case of insensibility. Thus temperance and courage are destroyed by excess and deficiency and preserved by the mean. . . .

If, then, every science performs its function well only when it observes the mean and refers its products to it (which is why it is customary to say of well-executed works that nothing can be added to them or taken away, the implication being that excess and deficiency alike destroy perfection, while the mean preserves it)—if good craftsmen, as we hold, work with the mean in view; and if virtue, like nature, is more exact and more efficient than any art, it follows that virtue aims to hit the mean. By virtue I mean moral virtue since it is this that is concerned with feelings and actions, and these involve excess, deficiency and a mean. It is possible, for example, to feel fear, confidence, desire, anger, pity, and pleasure and pain generally, too much or too little; and both of these are wrong. But to have these feelings at the right times on the right grounds towards the right people for the right motive and in the right way is to feel them to an intermediate, that is to the best, degree; and this is the mark of virtue. Similarly there are excess and deficiency and a mean in the case of actions. But it is in the field of actions and feelings that virtue operates; and in them excess and deficiency are failings, whereas the mean is praised and recognized as a success: and these are both marks of virtue. Virtue, then, is a mean condition, inasmuch as it aims at hitting the mean.

Again, failure is possible in many ways (for evil, as the Pythagoreans represented it, is a form of the Unlimited, and good of the Limited), but success is only one. That is why the one is easy and the other difficult; it is easy to miss the target and difficult to hit it. Here, then, is another reason why excess and deficiency fall under evil, and the mean state under good:

> For men are bad in countless ways, but good in only one.

A provisional definition of virtue

So virtue is a purposive disposition, lying in a mean that is relative to us and determined by a rational principle, and by that which a prudent man would use to determine it. It is a mean between two kinds of vice, one of excess and the other of deficiency; and also for this reason, that whereas these vices fall short of or exceed the right measure in both feelings and actions, virtue discovers the mean and chooses it. Thus from the point of view of its essence and the definition of its real nature, virtue is a mean; but in respect of what is right and best, it is an extreme.

CHAPTER 5

*E*thics and Natural Law

Saint Thomas Aquinas

Saint Thomas Aquinas (1225–1274) is commonly regarded as the greatest of all Christian thinkers (after, perhaps, Saint Paul). Aquinas was born in Roccasecca, Italy, the son of a count. At 19, having attended the University of Naples, he decided to join the Dominicans, then a new order. This so displeased his family that they forcibly restrained him for a year—in effect, holding him prisoner—but finally, unable to break his will, they had to let him go. After further studies, he became a professor of theology, first in Rome and then in Paris. He was a prolific writer; it is said that, in order to get his words down on paper more rapidly, he would dictate to three or four secretaries at once.

Aquinas holds a special place among Christian theologians. He was declared a saint in 1323. In 1567, he was named a Doctor of the Church, making him one of five preeminent figures, along with Augustine, Ambrose, Jerome, and Gregory. But in the respect accorded his teachings, he outranks all the others. In 1879, Pope Leo XIII officially recognized Aquinas's preeminence among church thinkers.

The key to understanding morality, according to Aquinas, is to understand that God has created the world according to a rational plan. Moreover, God created man as a rational being in his own image so that man has the capacity to understand that plan. Thus, human beings can discern the rational order of the world. Furthermore, it is part of the rational order that "natural laws" determine the moral structure of the world, just as they determine its physical structure. Man can discover these moral laws through the use of his reason. Acting morally is, therefore, acting in accordance with the natural law.

Excerpted from Saint Thomas Aquinas, *Summa Theologica*, First Part of the Second Part. In *Basic Writings of St. Thomas Aquinas*, edited by Anton C. Pegis, vol. 2 (New York: Random House, 1945), pp. 749–53, 776–78. Reprinted by permission of the Estate of Anton C. Pegis.

Question 91

Second Article: Whether There Is in Us a Natural Law? . . . The *Gloss* on *Rom.* 2:14 *(When the Gentiles, who have not the law, do by nature those things that are of the law)* comments as follows: *Although they have no written law, yet they have the natural law, whereby each one knows, and is conscious of, what is good and what is evil.* . . . Law, being a rule and measure, can be in a person in two ways: in one way, as in him that rules and measures; in another way, as in that which is ruled and measured, since a thing is ruled and measured in so far as it partakes of the rule or measure. Therefore, since all things subject to divine providence are ruled and measured by the eternal law . . . it is evident that all things partake in some way in the eternal law, in so far as, namely, from its being imprinted on them, they derive their respective inclinations to their proper acts and ends. Now among all others, the rational creature is subject to divine providence in a more excellent way, in so far as it itself partakes of a share of providence, by being provident both for itself and for others. Therefore it has a share of the eternal reason, whereby it has a natural inclination to its proper act and end; and this participation of the eternal law in the rational creature is called the natural law. Hence the Psalmist, after saying *(Ps.* 4:6): *Offer up the sacrifice of justice,* as though someone asked what the works of justice are, adds: *Many say, Who showeth us good things?* in answer to which question he says: *The light of Thy countenance, O Lord, is signed upon us.* He thus implies that the light of natural reason, whereby we discern what is good and what is evil, which is the function of the natural law, is nothing else than an imprint on us of the divine light. It is therefore evident that the natural law is nothing else than the rational creature's participation of the eternal law.

Third Article: Whether There Is a Human Law? . . . Augustine distinguishes two kinds of law, the one eternal, the other temporal, which he calls human. . . . As we have stated above, a law is a dictate of the practical reason. . . . Accordingly, we conclude that, just as in the speculative reason, from naturally known indemonstrable principles we draw the conclusions of the various sciences, the knowledge of which is not imparted to us by nature, but acquired by the efforts of reason, so too it is that from the precepts of the natural law, as from common and indemonstrable principles, the human reason needs to proceed to the more particular determination of certain matters. These particular determinations, devised by human reason, are called human laws, provided that the other essential conditions of law be observed. . . . Therefore

Tully says in his *Rhetoric* that *justice has its source in nature; thence certain things came into custom by reason of their utility; afterwards these things which emanated from nature, and were approved by custom, were sanctioned by fear and reverence for the law.* . . . Just as on the part of the speculative reason, by a natural participation of divine wisdom, there is in us the knowledge of certain common principles, but not a proper knowledge of each single truth, such as that contained in the divine wisdom, so, too, on the part of the practical reason, man has a natural participation of the eternal law, according to certain common principles, but not as regards the particular determinations of individual cases, which are, however, contained in the eternal law. Hence the need for human reason to proceed further to sanction them by law.

Fourth Article: Whether There Was Any Need for a Divine Law? . . . Besides the natural and the human law it was necessary for the directing of human conduct to have a divine law. And this for four reasons. First, because it is by law that man is directed how to perform his proper acts in view of his last end. Now if man were ordained to no other end than that which is proportionate to his natural ability, there would be no need for man to have any further direction, on the part of his reason, in addition to the natural law and humanly devised law which is derived from it. But since man is ordained to an end of eternal happiness which exceeds man's natural ability, . . . therefore it was necessary that, in addition to the natural and the human law, man should be directed to his end by a law given by God.

Secondly, because, by reason of the uncertainty of human judgment, especially on contingent and particular matters, different people form different judgments on human acts; whence also different and contrary laws result. In order, therefore, that man may know without any doubt what he ought to do and what he ought to avoid, it was necessary for man to be directed in his proper acts by a law given by God, for it is certain that such a law cannot err.

Thirdly, because man can make laws in those matters of which he is competent to judge. But man is not competent to judge of interior movements, that are hidden, but only of exterior acts which are observable; and yet for the perfection of virtue it is necessary for man to conduct himself rightly in both kinds of acts. Consequently, human law could not sufficiently curb and direct interior acts, and it was necessary for this purpose that a divine law should supervene.

Fourthly, because, as Augustine says, human law cannot punish or forbid all evil deeds, since, while aiming at doing away with all evils, it would do away with many good things, and would hinder the advance of the common good, which is necessary for human living. In order, therefore, that no evil might remain unforbidden and unpunished, it was necessary for the divine law to supervene, whereby all sins are forbidden. . . .

Question 94

Third Article: Whether All the Acts of the Virtues Are Prescribed by the Natural Law? . . . We may speak of virtuous acts in two ways: first, in so far as they are virtuous; secondly, as such and such acts considered in their proper species. If, then, we are speaking of the acts of the virtues in so far as they are virtuous, thus all virtuous acts belong to the natural law. For it has been stated that to the natural law belongs everything to which a man is inclined according to his nature. Now each thing is inclined naturally to an operation that is suitable to it according to its form: *e.g.*, fire is inclined to give heat. Therefore, since the rational soul is the proper form of man, there is in every man a natural inclination to act according to reason; and this is to act according to virtue. Consequently, considered thus, all the acts of the virtues are prescribed by the natural law, since each one's reason naturally dictates to him to act virtuously. But if we speak of virtuous acts, considered in themselves, *i.e.*, in their proper species, thus not all virtuous acts are prescribed by the natural law. For many things are done virtuously, to which nature does not primarily incline, but which, through the inquiry of reason, have been found by men to be conducive to well-living. . . .

Temperance is about the natural concupiscences of food, drink and sexual matters, which are indeed ordained to the common good of nature, just as other matters of law are ordained to the moral common good. . . .

By human nature we may mean either that which is proper to man, and in this sense all sins, as being against reason, are also against nature, as Damascene states; or we may mean that nature which is common to man and other animals, and in this sense, certain special sins are said to be against nature: *e.g.*, contrary to sexual intercourse, which is natural to all animals, is unisexual lust, which has received the special name of the unnatural crime. . . .

Fourth Article: Whether the Natural Law Is the Same in All Men? . . . As we have stated above, to the natural law belong those things to which a man is inclined naturally; and among these it is proper to man to be inclined to act according to reason. Now it belongs to the reason to proceed from what is common to what is proper, as is stated in *Physics* i. The speculative reason, however, is differently situated, in this matter, from the practical reason. For, since the speculative reason is concerned chiefly with necessary things, which cannot be otherwise than they are, its proper conclusions, like the universal principles, contain the truth without fail. The practical reason, on the other hand, is concerned with contingent matters, which is the domain of human actions: and, consequently, although there is necessity in the common principles, the more we descend towards the particular, the more frequently we encounter defects. Accordingly, then, in speculative matters truth is the same in all men, both as to principles and as to conclusions; although the truth is not known to all as regards the conclusions, but only as regards the principles which are called *common notions*. But in matters of action, truth or practical rectitude is not the same for all as to what is particular, but only as to the common principles; and where there is the same rectitude in relation to particulars, it is not equally known to all.

It is therefore evident that, as regards the common principles whether of speculative or of practical reason, truth or rectitude is the same for all, and is equally known by all. But as to the proper conclusions of the speculative reason, the truth is the same for all, but it is not equally known to all. It is true for all that the three angles of a triangle are together equal to two right angles, although it is not known to all. But as to the proper conclusions of the practical reason, neither is the truth or rectitude the same for all, nor, where it is the same, is it equally known by all. Thus, it is right and true for all to act according to reason, and from this principle it follows, as a proper conclusion, that goods entrusted to another should be restored to their owner. Now this is true for the majority of cases. But it may happen in a particular case that it would be injurious, and therefore unreasonable, to restore goods held in trust; for instance, if they are claimed for the purpose of fighting against one's country. And this principle will be found to fail the more, according as we descend further towards the particular, *e.g.,* if one were to say that goods held in trust should be restored with such and such a guarantee, or in such and such a way; because the greater the number of conditions added, the greater the number of ways in which the principle may fail, so that it be not right to restore or not to restore.

Consequently, we must say that the natural law, as to the first common principles, is the same for all, both as to rectitude and as to knowledge. But as to certain more particular aspects, which are conclusions, as it were, of those common principles, it is the same for all in the majority of cases, both as to rectitude and as to knowledge; and yet in some few cases it may fail, both as to rectitude, by reason of certain obstacles (just as natures subject to generation and corruption fail in some few cases because of some obstacle), and as to knowledge, since in some the reason is perverted by passion, or evil habit, or an evil disposition of nature. Thus at one time theft, although it is expressly contrary to the natural law, was not considered wrong among the Germans, as Julius Caesar relates.

CHAPTER 6

The Social Contract

Thomas Hobbes

Thomas Hobbes (1588–1679), the foremost British philosopher of the
17th century, was the first to set out the Social Contract Theory in detail.
The son of a vicar, he was educated at Oxford and became a tutor in the
household of the Earl of Devonshire. This post permitted him to travel to
France and Italy, where he got to know such men as Francis Bacon and
Pierre Gassendi. Later he was appointed tutor to the future Charles II.
In his own lifetime, Hobbes was a prominent figure. His political views, as
well as his views about the mind, caused controversy, and he was accused
of atheism. Hobbes denied the charge, but some historians contend that
he was more of a skeptic than he was willing to admit.

At any rate, Hobbes proposed a view of morality that completely divorced it from religion. Morality, he said, should be seen as
the outcome of an agreement that rational, self-interested people
enter into for their own benefit. These agreed-upon rules make possible a peaceful, secure society. The alternative would be the "state of
nature," a war of all against all in which everyone would be vastly
worse off. The following selection from Hobbes's *Leviathan* sets out
the details of this argument.

Of the Natural Condition of Mankind as Concerning Their Felicity, and Misery

Nature hath made men so equal, in the faculties of the body, and
mind; as that though there be found one man sometimes manifestly
stronger in body, or of quicker mind than another; yet when all is
reckoned together, the difference between man, and man, is not so

Excerpted from Thomas Hobbes, *Leviathan* (1651), chs. 13, 14.

considerable, as that one man can thereupon claim to himself any benefit, to which another may not pretend, as well as he. For as to the strength of body, the weakest has strength enough to kill the strongest, either by secret machination, or by confederacy with others, that are in the same danger with himself.

And as to the faculties of the mind, setting aside the arts grounded upon words, and especially that skill of proceeding upon general, and infallible rules, called science; which very few have, and but in few things; as being not a native faculty, born with us; nor attained, as prudence, while we look after somewhat else, I find yet a greater equality amongst men, than that of strength. For prudence, is but experience; which equal time, equally bestows on all men, in those things they equally apply themselves unto. That which may perhaps make such equality incredible, is but a vain conceit of one's own wisdom, which almost all men think they have in a greater degree, than the vulgar; that is, than all men but themselves, and a few others, whom by fame, or for concurring with themselves, they approve. For such is the nature of men, that howsoever they may acknowledge many others to be more witty, or more eloquent, or more learned; yet they will hardly believe there be many so wise as themselves; for they see their own wit at hand, and other men's at a distance. But this proveth rather that men are in that point equal, than unequal. For there is not ordinarily a greater sign of the equal distribution of anything, than that every man is contented with his share.

From this equality of ability, ariseth equality of hope in the attaining of our ends. And therefore if any two men desire the same thing, which nevertheless they cannot both enjoy, they become enemies; and in the way to their end, which is principally their own conservation, and sometimes their delectation only, endeavor to destroy, or subdue one another. And from hence it comes to pass that where an invader hath no more to fear, than another man's single power; if one plant, sow, build, or possess a convenient seat, others may probably be expected to come prepared with forces united, to dispossess, and deprive him, not only of the fruit of his labour, but also of his life, or liberty. And the invader again is in the like danger of another.

And from this diffidence of one another, there is no way for any man to secure himself, so reasonable, as anticipation; that is, by force, or wiles, to master the persons of all men he can, so long, till he see no other power great enough to endanger him: and this is no more than his own conservation requireth, and is generally allowed. Also because there be some, that taking pleasure in contemplating their own power in the acts of conquest, which they pursue farther than their security requires; if others, that otherwise would be glad to be at ease within modest bounds, should not by invasion increase their power, they would not be able, long time, by standing only on their defence, to subsist. And by consequence, such augmentation of dominion over men being necessary to a man's conservation, it ought to be allowed him.

Again, men have no pleasure, but on the contrary a great deal of grief, in keeping company, where there is no power able to over-awe them all. For every man looketh that his companion should value him, at the same rate he sets upon himself: and upon all signs of contempt, or undervaluing, naturally endeavours, as far as he dares, (which amongst them that have no common power to keep them in quiet, is far enough to make them destroy each other), to extort a greater value from his contemners, by damage; and from others, by the example.

So that in the nature of man, we find three principal causes of quarrel. First, competition; secondly, diffidence; thirdly, glory.

The first, maketh men invade for gain; the second, for safety; and the third, for reputation. The first use violence, to make themselves masters of other men's persons, wives, children, and cattle; the second to defend them; the third, for trifles, as a word, a smile, a different opinion, and any other sign of undervalue, either direct in their persons, or by reflection in their kindred, their friends, their nation, their profession, or their name.

Hereby it is manifest, that during the time men live without a common power to keep them all in awe, they are in that condition which is called war; and such a war, as is of every man, against every man. For WAR, consisteth not in battle only, or the act of fighting; but in a tract of time, wherein the will to contend by battle is sufficiently known: and therefore the notion of *time*, is to be considered in the nature of war; as it is in the nature of weather. For as the nature of foul weather, lieth not in a shower or two of rain; but in an inclination thereto of many days together: so the nature of war, consisteth not in actual fighting; but in the known disposition thereto, during all the time there is no assurance to the contrary. All other time is PEACE.

Whatsoever therefore is consequent to a time of war, where every man is enemy to every man; the same is consequent to the time, wherein men live without other security, than what their own strength, and their own invention shall furnish them withal. In such condition, there is no place for industry; because the fruit thereof is uncertain: and consequently no culture of the earth; no navigation, nor use of the commodities that may be imported by sea; no commodious build-ing; no instruments of moving, and removing, such things as require much force; no knowledge of the face of the earth; no account of time; no arts; no letters; no society; and which is worst of all, continual fear, and danger of violent death; and the life of man, solitary, poor, nasty, brutish, and short.

It may seem strange to some man, that has not well weighed these things; that nature should thus dissociate, and render men apt to invade, and destroy one another: and he may therefore, not trust-ing to this inference, made from the passions, desire perhaps to have the same confirmed by experience. Let him therefore consider with himself, when taking a journey, he arms himself, and seeks to go well accompanied; when going to sleep, he locks his doors; when even in his house he locks his chests; and this when he knows there be laws, and public officers, armed, to revenge all injuries shall be done him; what opinion he has of his fellow-subjects, when he rides armed; of his fellow citizens, when he locks his doors; and of his children, and ser-vants, when he locks his chests. Does he not there as much accuse mankind by his actions, as I do by my words? But neither of us accuse man's nature in it. The desires, and other passions of man, are in themselves no sin. No more are the actions, that proceed from those passions, till they know a law that forbids them: which till laws be made they cannot know: nor can any law be made, till they have agreed upon the person that shall make it.

It may peradventure be thought, there was never such a time, nor condition of war as this; and I believe it was never generally so, over all the world: but there are many places, where they live so now. For the savage people in many places of America, except the govern-ment of small families, the concord whereof dependeth on natural lust, have no government at all; and live at this day in that brutish man-ner, as I said before. Howsoever, it may be perceived what manner of life there would be, where there were no common power to fear, by the manner of life, which men that have formerly lived under a peace-ful government use to degenerate into, in a civil war.

But though there had never been any time, wherein particular men were in a condition of war one against another; yet in all times, kings, and persons of sovereign authority, because of their indepen-dency, are in continual jealousies, and in the state and posture of glad-iators; having their weapons pointing, and their eyes fixed on one another; that is, their forts, garrisons, and guns upon the frontiers of their kingdoms; and continual spies upon their neighbours; which is a posture of war. But because they uphold thereby, the industry of their subjects; there does not follow from it, that misery, which accompanies the liberty of particular men.

To this war of every man, against every man, this also is consequent; that nothing can be unjust. The notions of right and wrong justice and injustice have there no place. Where there is no common power, there is no law: where no law, no injustice. Force, and fraud, are in war the two cardinal virtues. Justice, and injustice are none of the faculties neither of the body, nor mind. If they were, they might be in a man that were alone in the world, as well as his senses, and passions. They are qualities, that relate to men in society, not in solitude. It is consequent also to the same condition, that there be no propriety, no dominion, no *mine* and *thine* distinct; but only that to be every man's, that he can get; and for so long, as he can keep it. And thus much of the ill condition, which man by mere nature is actually placed in; though with a possibility to come out of it, consisting partly in the passions, partly in his reason.

The passions that incline men to peace, are fear of death; desire of such things as are necessary to commodious living; and a hope by their industry to obtain them. And reason suggesteth convenient articles of peace, upon which men may be drawn to agreement. These articles, are they, which otherwise are called the Laws of Nature: whereof I shall speak more particularly . . .

Of the First and Second Natural Laws, and of Contracts

The right of nature, which writers commonly call *jus naturale,* is liberty each man hath, to use his own power, as he will himself, for the preservation of his own nature; that is to say, of his own life; and consequently, of doing any thing, which in his own judgment, and reason, he shall conceive to be the aptest means thereunto.

By *liberty,* is understood, according to the proper signification of the word, the absence of external impediments: which impediments, may oft take away part of a man's power to do what he would; but cannot hinder him from using the power left him, according as his judgment, and reason shall dictate to him.

A *law of nature, lex naturalis,* is a precept or general rule, found out by reason, by which a man is forbidden to do that, which is destructive of his life, or taketh away the means of preserving the same; and to omit that, by which he thinketh it may be best preserved. For though they that speak of this subject, use to confound *jus,* and *lex, right* and *law:* yet they ought to be distinguished; because *right,* consisteth in liberty to do, or to forbare; whereas *law,* determineth, and bindeth to one of them: so that law, and right, differ as much, as obligation, and liberty; which in one and the same matter are inconsistent.

And because the condition of man, as hath been declared in the precedent chapter, is a condition of war of every one against every one: in which case every one is governed by his own reason; and there is nothing he can make use of, that may not be a help unto him, in preserving his life against his enemies; it followeth, that in such a condition, every man has a right to every thing; even to one another's body. And therefore, as long as this natural right of every man to every thing endureth, there can be no security to any man, how strong or wise soever he be, of living out the time, which nature ordinarily alloweth men to live, and consequently it is a precept, or general rule of reason, *that every man, ought to endeavour peace, as far as he has hope of obtaining it; and when he cannot obtain it, that he may seek, and use, all helps, and advantages of war.* The first branch of which rule, containeth the first, and fundamental law of nature; which is, *to seek peace, and follow it.* The second, the sum of the right of nature; which is, *by all means we can, to defend ourselves.*

From this fundamental law of nature, by which men are commanded to endeavour peace, is derived this second law; *that a man be willing, when others are so too, as far-forth, as for peace, and defence of himself he shall think it necessary, to lay down this right to all things; and be contented with so much liberty against other men, as he would allow other men against himself.* For as long as every man holdeth this right, of doing any thing he liketh; so long are all men in the condition of war. But if other men will not lay down their right, as well as he; then there is no reason for any one, to divest himself of his: for that were to expose himself to prey, which no man is bound to, rather than to dispose himself to peace. This is that law of the Gospel; *whatsoever you require that others should do to you, that do ye to them.* . . .

To *lay down* a man's *right* to any thing, is to *divest* himself of the *liberty,* of hindering another of the benefit of his own right to the same. For he that renounceth, or passeth away his right, giveth not to any other man a right which he had not before; because there is nothing to which every man had not right by nature: but only standeth out of his way, that he may enjoy his own original right, without hindrance from him; not without hindrance from another. So that the effect which redoundeth to one man, by another man's defect of right, is but so much diminution of impediments to the use of his own right original.

Right is laid aside, either by simply renouncing it; or by transferring it to another. By *simply renouncing;* when he cares not to whom the benefit thereof redoundeth. By *transferring;* when he intendeth the benefit thereof to some certain person, or persons. And when a man hath in either manner abandoned, or granted away his right; then he is said to be *obliged,* or *bound,* not to hinder those, to whom such right is granted, or abandoned, from the benefit of it: and that he *ought,* and it is his *duty,* not to make void that voluntary act of his own: and that such hindrance is *injustice,* and *injury,* as being *sine jure;* the right being before renounced, or transferred. So that *injury,* or *injustice,* in the controversies of the world, is somewhat like to that, which in the disputations of scholars is called *absurdity.* For as it is there called an absurdity, to contradict what one maintained in the beginning: so in the world, it is called injustice, and injury, voluntarily to undo that, which from the beginning he had voluntarily done. The way by which a man either simply renounceth, or transferreth his right, is a declaration, or signification, by some voluntary and sufficient sign, or signs, that he doth so renounce, or transfer; or hath so renounced, or transferred the same, to him that accepteth it. And these signs are either words only, or actions only; or, as it happeneth most often, both words, and actions. And the same are the *bonds,* by which men are bound, and obliged: bonds, that have their strength, not from their own nature, for nothing is more easily broken than a man's word, but from fear of some evil consequence upon that rupture.

Whensoever a man transferreth his right, or renounceth it; it is either in consideration of some right reciprocally transferred to himself; or for some other good he hopeth for thereby. For it is a voluntary act: and of the voluntary acts of every man the object is some *good to himself.* And therefore there be some rights, which no man can be understood by any words, or other signs to have abandoned, or transferred. As first a man cannot lay down the right of resisting them, that assault him by force, to take away his life; because he cannot be understood to aim thereby, at any good to himself. The same may be said of wounds, and chains, and imprisonment; both because there is no benefit consequent to such patience; as there is to the patience of suffering another to be wounded, or imprisoned: as also because a man cannot tell, when he seeth men proceed against him by violence, whether they intend his death or not. And lastly the motive, and end for which this renouncing, and transferring of right is introduced, is nothing else but the security of a man's person, in his life, and in the means of so preserving life, as not to be weary of it. And therefore if a man by words, or other signs, seems to despoil himself of the end, for which those signs were intended; he is not to be understood as if he meant it, or that it was his will; but that he was ignorant of how such words and actions were to be interpreted.

The mutual transferring of right, is that which men call *contract*. . . .

And though this may seem too subtle a deduction of the laws of nature, to be taken notice of by all men; whereof the most part are too busy in getting food, and the rest too negligent to understand; yet to leave all men inexcusable, they have been contracted into one easy sum, intelligible even to the meanest capacity; and that is, *Do not that to another, which thou wouldest not have done to thyself;* which sheweth him, that he has no more to do in learning the laws of nature, but, when weighing the actions of other men with his own, they seem too heavy, to put them into the other part of the balance, and his own into their place, that his passions, and self-love, may add nothing to the weight; and then there is none of these laws of nature that will not appear unto him very reasonable.

The laws of nature oblige *in foro interno;* that is to say, they bind to a desire they should take place: but *in foro externo;* that is, to the putting them in act, not always. For he that should be modest, and tractable, and perform all he promises, in such time, and place, where no man else should do so, should but make himself a prey to others, and procure his own certain ruin, contrary to the ground of all laws of nature, which tend to nature's preservation. And again, he that having sufficient security, that others shall observe the same laws towards him, observes them not himself, seeketh not peace but war; and consequently the destruction of his nature by violence.

And whatsoever laws bind *in foro interno,* may be broken, not only by a fact contrary to the law, but also by a fact according to it, in case a man think it contrary. For though his action in this case, be according to the law; yet his purpose was against the law; which, where the obligation is *in foro interno,* is a breach.

The laws of nature are immutable and eternal; for injustice, ingratitude, arrogance, pride, iniquity, acception of persons, and the rest, can never be made lawful. For it can never be that war shall preserve life, and peace destroy it.

The same laws, because they oblige only to a desire, and endeavour, I mean an unfeigned and constant endeavour, are easy to be observed. For in that they require nothing but endeavour, he that endeavoureth their performance, fulfilleth them; and he that fulfill-eth the law, is just.

And the science of them, is the true and only moral philosophy. For moral philosophy is nothing else but the science of what is *good,* and *evil,* in the conversation, and society of mankind. *Good,* and *evil,* are names that signify our appetites, and aversions; which in different tempers, customs, and doctrines of men, are different: and divers men, differ not only in their judgment, on the senses of what is pleas-ant, and unpleasant to the taste, smell, hearing, touch, and sight; but also of what is comfortable, or disagreeable to reason, in the actions of common life. Nay, the same man in divers times, differs from himself; and one time praiseth, that is, calleth good, what another time he dis-praiseth, and calleth evil: from whence arise disputes, controversies, and at last war. And therefore so long as a man is in the condition of mere nature, which is a condition of war, as private appetite is the mea-sure of good, and evil: and consequently all men agree on this, that peace is good, and therefore also the way, or means of peace, which, as I have shewed before, are *justice, gratitude, modesty, equity, mercy,* and the rest of the laws of nature, are good; that is to say; *moral virtues;* and their contrary *vices,* evil.

CHAPTER 7

Morality as Based on Sentiment

David Hume

The most influential advocate of Ethical Subjectivism was David Hume, the great Scottish philosopher of the 18th century. Born in Edinburgh in 1711, Hume was a precocious youth. He completed his greatest work, *A Treatise of Human Nature,* at the age of 25. Hume would go on to write many other important books on history, philosophy, religion, and politics. He held a variety of jobs, including librarian at Edinburgh University and first secretary of the British embassy in Paris, where he was a favorite of the French intellectuals. But when he applied for the post of professor of moral philosophy at Edinburgh, influential clergymen saw to it that his application was rejected.

The clergymen were appalled by Hume's ethical views. One of them, the bishop of Gloucester, wrote to Hume's publisher to complain about another of his books, the *Enquiry Concerning the Principles of Morals:* "You have often told me of this man's moral virtues," the bishop wrote. "He may have many, for aught I know; but let me observe to you, there are vices of the mind as well as of the body: and I think a wickeder mind, and more obstinately bent on public mischief, I never knew."

Apparently, the bishop believed that Ethical Subjectivism leads to a breakdown in public morals. This is a common complaint—it is argued that without objective standards of right and wrong, "anything goes," and all manner of mischief is permitted. But, Hume thought, this does not follow. Ethical Subjectivism is a theory about the *nature* of morality—it says that a person's moral judgments are an expression of his or her feelings—and it implies nothing about which moral beliefs should be accepted or rejected. Hume believed that our

---

Excerpted from David Hume, *A Treatise of Human Nature* (1740), bk. 3, pt. 1, sec. 1; and *An Inquiry Concerning the Principles of Morals* (1751), app. 1.

conduct should be directed by a general sentiment of beneficence toward all of humankind, and so he favored an enlightened morality of universal altruism. He did not, however, think this was a matter of reason. Instead, such a morality depends on whether, in fact, human beings have beneficent sentiments.

Those who affirm that virtue is nothing but a conformity to reason; that there are eternal fitnesses and unfitnesses of things, which are the same to every rational being that considers them; that the immutable measures of right and wrong impose an obligation, not only on human creatures, but also on the Deity himself: All these systems concur in the opinion, that morality, like truth, is discern'd merely by ideas, and by their juxta-position and comparison. In order, therefore, to judge of these systems, we need only consider, whether it be possible, from reason alone, to distinguish betwixt moral good and evil, or whether there must concur some other principles to enable us to make that distinction.

If morality had naturally no influence on human passions and actions, 'twere in vain to take such pains to inculcate it; and nothing wou'd be more fruitless than that multitude of rules and precepts, with which all moralists abound. Philosophy is commonly divided into *speculative* and *practical;* and as morality is always comprehended under the latter division, 'tis supposed to influence our passions and actions, and to go beyond the calm and indolent judgments of the understanding. And this is confirm'd by common experience, which informs us, that men are often govern'd by their duties, and are deter'd from some actions by the opinion of injustice, and impell'd to others by that of obligation.

Since morals, therefore, have an influence on the actions and affections, it follows, that they cannot be deriv'd from reason; and that because reason alone, as we have already prov'd, can never have any such influence. Morals excite passions, and produce or prevent actions. Reason of itself is utterly impotent in this particular. The rules of morality, therefore, are not conclusions of our reason.

. . . Take any action allow'd to be vicious: Wilful murder, for instance. Examine it in all lights, and see if you can find that matter of fact, or real existence, which you call *vice.* In whichever way you take it, you find only certain passions, motives, volitions and thoughts. There is no other matter of fact in the case. The vice entirely escapes you, as long as you consider the object. You never can find it, till you turn your reflexion into your own breast, and find a sentiment of disapprobation, which arises in you, towards this action. Here is a matter of fact; but 'tis the object of feeling, not of reason. It lies in yourself, not in the object. So that when you pronounce any action or character to be vicious, you mean nothing, but that from the constitution of your nature you have a feeling or sentiment of blame from the contemplation of it.

. . . I cannot forbear adding to these reasonings an observation, which may, perhaps, be found of some importance. In every system of morality, which I have hitherto met with, I have always remark'd, that the author proceeds for some time in the ordinary way of reasoning, and establishes the being of a God, or makes observations concerning human affairs; when of a sudden I am surpriz'd to find, that instead of the usual copulations of propositions, *is,* and *is not,* I meet with no proposition that is not connected with an *ought,* or an *ought not.* This change is imperceptible; but is, however, of the last consequence. For as this *ought,* or *ought not,* expresses some new relation or affirmation, 'tis necessary that it shou'd be observ'd and explain'd; and at the same time that a reason should be given, for what seems altogether inconceivable, how this new relation can be a deduction from others, which are entirely different from it. But as authors do not commonly use this precaution, I shall presume to recommend it to the readers; and am persuaded, that this small attention wou'd subvert all the vulgar systems of morality, and let us see, that the distinction of vice and virtue is not founded merely on the relations of objects, nor is perceiv'd by reason. . . .

Examine the crime of *ingratitude,* for instance, which has place wherever we observe good-will expressed and known, together with good-offices performed, on the one side, and a return of ill-will or indifference with ill-offices or neglect on the other: anatomize all these circumstances and examine, by your reason alone, in what consists the demerit or blame. You never will come to any issue or conclusion.

Reason judges either of *matter of fact* or of *relations.* Enquire then, *first,* where is that matter of fact which we here call *crime;* point it out, determine the time of its existence, describe its essence or nature, explain the sense or faculty to which it discovers itself. It resides in the mind of the person who is ungrateful. He must, therefore, feel it and be conscious of it. But nothing is there, except the passion of ill-will or absolute indifference. You cannot say that these, of themselves, always and in all circumstances are crimes. No, they are only crimes when directed towards persons who have before expressed and displayed good-will towards us. Consequently, we may infer that the crime of ingratitude is not any particular individual *fact,* but arises from a complication of circumstances which, being presented to the spectator, excites the *sentiment* of blame by the particular structure and fabric of his mind.

This representation, you say, is false. Crime, indeed, consists not in a particular *fact,* of whose reality we are assured by *reason,* but it consists in certain *moral relations,* discovered by reason, in the same manner as we discover by reason the truths of geometry or algebra. But what are the relations, I ask, of which you here talk? In the case stated above, I see first good-will and good-offices in one person, then ill-will and ill-offices in the other. Between these, there is a relation of *contrariety.* Does the crime consist in that relation? But suppose a person bore me ill-will or did me ill-offices, and I, in return, were indifferent towards him, or did him good offices. Here is the same relation of *contrariety,* and yet my conduct is often highly laudable. Twist and turn this matter as much as you will, you can never rest the morality on relation, but must have recourse to the decisions of sentiment.

When it is affirmed that two and three are equal to the half of ten, this relation of equality I understand perfectly. I conceive that, if ten be divided into two parts, of which one has as many units as the other, and if any of these parts be compared to two added to three, it will contain as many units as that compound number. But when you draw thence a comparison to moral relations, I own that I am altogether at a loss to understand you. A moral action, a crime, such as ingratitude, is a complicated object. Does the morality consist in the relation of its parts to each other? How? After what manner? Specify the relation: be more particular and explicit in your propositions, and you will easily see their falsehood.

No, say you, the morality consists in the relation of actions to the rule of right; and they are denominated good or ill, according as they agree or disagree with it. What then is this rule of right? In what does it consist? How is it determined? By reason, you say, which examines the moral relations of actions. So that moral relations are determined by the comparison of action to a rule. And that rule is determined by considering the moral relations of objects. Is not this fine reasoning?

All this is metaphysics, you cry. That is enough; there needs nothing more to give a strong presumption of falsehood. Yes, reply I, here are metaphysics surely; but they are all on your side, who advance an abstruse hypothesis which can never be made intelligible, nor quadrate with any particular instance or illustration. The hypothesis which we embrace is plain. It maintains that morality is determined by sentiment. It defines virtue to be *whatever mental action or quality gives to a spectator the pleasing sentiment of approbation;* and vice the contrary. We then proceed to examine a plain matter of fact, to wit, what actions have this influence. We consider all the circumstances in which these actions agree, and thence endeavour to extract some general observations with regard to these sentiments. If you call this metaphysics and find anything abstruse here, you need only conclude that your turn of mind is not suited to the moral sciences.

CHAPTER 8

Utilitarianism

John Stuart Mill

In the history of moral philosophy, the name of John Stuart Mill (1806–1873) is inevitably linked with that of Jeremy Bentham (1748–1832). Few philosophers have combined theory and practice as successfully as Bentham. A wealthy Londoner, he studied law but never became a lawyer, instead devoting himself to writing and working for social reform. He became the leader of a group of philosophical radicals known as the Benthamites, who campaigned for causes like prison reform and restrictions on the use of child labor. Bentham was a reformer but was not, as many reformers are, an "outsider." He was an effective member of the British establishment, and almost all the Benthamites' legislative proposals eventually became law.

Bentham was convinced that both law and morals must be based on a realistic, nonsupernatural conception of human beings. The first sentence of his greatest work, *The Principles of Morals and Legislation*, declares: "Nature has placed mankind under the governance of two sovereign masters, *pain* and *pleasure*." Some things give us pleasure, whereas other things cause us pain. This fundamental, rock-bottom fact explains why we behave as we do—we seek pleasure and avoid pain—and it explains why we judge some things to be good and others evil. Therefore, he reasoned, morality must consist in trying to bring about as much pleasure as possible, while striving to minimize pain.

Following up on this basic insight, Bentham argued that there is one ultimate moral principle, the Principle of Utility. It requires us, whenever we have to choose between alternative actions or social policies, to pick the one that provides the most happiness for everyone concerned.

One of Bentham's followers was James Mill, a distinguished Scottish philosopher, historian, and economist. James Mill's son, John Stuart, would become the leading advocate of utilitarian moral theory for the next generation.

The following material was excerpted from John Stuart Mill, *Utilitarianism* (1861).

It was no accident that John Stuart Mill became the next great Benthamite; James Mill educated his son with this in mind. He had the boy studying Greek and Latin at age 3, and by the time he entered his teens, John Stuart was already mastering the blend of subjects that the British call "political economy." He was 26 when Bentham died, and he knew the older man well. It would be a mistake, however, to regard John Stuart Mill as merely a follower of the master. Mill became a more distinguished thinker than Bentham, contributing to subjects that Bentham barely knew, such as the philosophy of science and the foundations of mathematical knowledge.

Unlike Bentham, the Mills were not wealthy, and John Stuart Mill earned his living in the office of the East India Company, as had his father. In 1830, he met and fell in love with Harriet Taylor, who, alas, was married with three children. Harriet was faithful to her husband until he died in 1849; two years later, she and Mill married. Probably as a result of her influence, Mill became a leader in the movement for women's rights and published *The Subjection of Women* in 1869.

The following excerpts are from Mill's book *Utilitarianism*, in which he develops some of the basic ideas of utilitarian moral theory.

II. What Utilitarianism Is

. . . The creed which accepts as the foundation of morals, Utility, or the Greatest Happiness Principle, holds that actions are right in proportion as they tend to promote happiness, wrong as they tend to produce the reverse of happiness. By happiness is intended pleasure, and the absence of pain; by unhappiness, pain, and the privation of pleasure. To give a clear view of the moral standard set up by the theory, much more requires to be said; in particular, what things it includes in the ideas of pain and pleasure; and to what extent this is left an open question. But these supplementary explanations do not affect the theory of life on which this theory of morality is grounded—namely, that pleasure, and freedom from pain, are the only things desirable as ends; and that all desirable things (which are as numerous in the utilitarian as in any other scheme) are desirable either for the pleasure inherent in themselves, or as means to the promotion of pleasure and the prevention of pain.

Now, such a theory of life excites in many minds, and among them in some of the most estimable in feeling and purpose, inveterate dislike. To suppose that life has (as they express it) no higher end than pleasure—no better and nobler object of desire and pursuit—they designate as utterly mean and grovelling; as a doctrine worthy only of swine, to whom the followers of Epicurus were, at a very early period, contemptuously likened; and modern holders of the doctrine are occasionally made the subject of equally polite comparisons by its German, French, and English assailants.

When thus attacked, the Epicureans have always answered, that it is not they, but their accusers, who represent human nature in a degrading light; since the accusation supposes human beings to be capable of no pleasures except those of which swine are capable. If this supposition were true, the charge could not be gainsaid, but would then be no longer an imputation; for if the sources of pleasure were precisely the same to human beings and to swine, the rule of life which is good enough for the one would be good enough for the other. The comparison of the Epicurean life to that of beasts is felt as degrading, precisely because a beast's pleasures do not satisfy a human being's conceptions of happiness. Human beings have faculties more elevated than the animal appetites, and when once made conscious of them, do not regard anything as happiness which does not include their gratification. I do not, indeed, consider the Epicureans to have been by any means faultless in drawing out their scheme of consequences from the utilitarian principle. To do this in any sufficient manner, many Stoic, as well as Christian elements require to be included. But there is no known Epicurean theory of life which does not assign to the pleasures of the intellect, of the feelings and imagination, and of the moral sentiments, a much higher value as pleasures than to those of mere sensation. It must be admitted, however, that utilitarian writers in general have placed the superiority of mental over bodily pleasures chiefly in the greater permanency, safety, uncostliness, & c., of the former—that is, in their circumstantial advantages rather than in their intrinsic nature. And on all these points utilitarians have fully proved their case; but they might have taken the other, and, as it may be called, higher ground, with entire consistency. It is quite compatible with the principle of utility to recognise the fact, that some *kinds* of pleasure are more desirable and more valuable than others. It would be absurd that while, in estimating all other things, quality is considered as well as quantity, the estimation of pleasures should be supposed to depend on quantity alone.

If I am asked, what I mean by difference of quality in pleasures, or what makes one pleasure more valuable than another, merely as a pleasure, except its being greater in amount, there is but one possible answer. Of two pleasures, if there be one to which all or almost all who have experience of both give a decided preference, irrespective of any feeling of moral obligation to prefer it, that is the more desirable pleasure. If one of the two is, by those who are competently acquainted with both, placed so far above the other that they prefer it, even though knowing it to be attended with a greater amount of discontent, and would not resign it for any quantity of the other pleasure which their nature is capable of, we are justified in ascribing to the preferred enjoyment a superiority in quality, so far outweighing quantity as to render it, in comparison, of small account.

Now it is an unquestionable fact that those who are equally acquainted with, and equally capable of appreciating and enjoying, both, do give a most marked preference to the manner of existence which employs their higher faculties. Few human creatures would consent to be changed into any of the lower animals, for a promise of the fullest allowance of a beast's pleasures; no intelligent human being would consent to be a fool, no instructed person would be an ignoramus, no person of feeling and conscience would be selfish and base, even though they should be persuaded that the fool, the dunce, or the rascal is better satisfied with his lot than they are with theirs. They would not resign what they possess more than he, for the most complete satisfaction of all the desires which they have in common with him. If they ever fancy they would, it is only in cases of unhappiness so extreme, that to escape from it they would exchange their lot for almost any other, however undesirable in their own eyes. A being of higher faculties requires more to make him happy, is capable probably of more acute suffering, and is certainly accessible to it at more points, than one of an inferior type; but in spite of these liabilities, he can never really wish to sink into what he feels to be a lower grade of existence. We may give what explanation we please of this unwillingness; we may attribute it to pride, a name which is given indiscriminately to some of the most and to some of the least estimable feelings of which mankind are capable; we may refer it to the love of liberty and personal independence, an appeal to which was with the Stoics one of the most effective means for the inculcation of it; to the love of power, or to the love of excitement, both of which do really enter into and contribute to it: but its most appropriate appellation is a sense of dignity, which all human beings possess in one form or other, and in some, though by no means in exact, proportion to their higher faculties, and which is so essential a part of the happiness of those in whom it is strong, that nothing which conflicts with it could be, otherwise than momentarily, an object of desire to them. Whoever supposes that this preference takes place at a sacrifice of happiness—that the superior being, in anything like the equal circumstances, is not happier than the inferior—confounds the two very different ideas, of happiness, and content. It is indisputable that the being whose capacities of enjoyment are low, has the greatest chance of having them fully satisfied; and a highly-endowed being will always feel that any happiness which he can look for, as the world is constituted, is imperfect. But he can learn to bear its imperfections, if they are at all bearable; and they will not make him envy the being who is indeed unconscious of the imperfections, but only because he feels not at all the good which those imperfections qualify. It is better to be a human being dissatisfied than a pig satisfied; better to be Socrates dissatisfied than a fool satisfied. And if the fool, or the pig, is of a different opinion, it is because they only know their own side of the question. The other party to the comparison knows both sides.

It may be objected, that many who are capable of the higher pleasures, occasionally, under the influence of temptation, postpone them to the lower. But this is quite compatible with a full appreciation of the intrinsic superiority of the higher. Men often, from infirmity of character, make their election for the nearer good, though they know it to be the less valuable; and this no less when the choice is between two bodily pleasures, than when it is between bodily and mental. They pursue sensual indulgences to the injury of health, though perfectly aware that health is the greater good. It may be further objected, that many who begin with youthful enthusiasm for everything noble, as they advance in years sink into indolence and selfishness. But I do not believe that those who undergo this very common change, voluntarily choose the lower description of pleasures in preference to the higher. I believe that before they devote themselves exclusively to the one, they have already become incapable of the other. Capacity for the nobler feelings is in most natures a very tender plant, easily killed, not only by hostile influences, but by mere want of sustenance; and in the majority of young persons it speedily dies away if the occupations to which their position in life has devoted them, and the society into which it has thrown them, are not favourable to keeping that higher capacity in exercise. Men lose their high aspirations as they lose their intellectual tastes, because they have not time or opportunity for indulging them; and they addict themselves to inferior pleasures, not because they deliberately prefer them, but because they are either the only ones to which they have access, or the only ones which they are any longer capable of enjoying. It may be questioned whether any one who has remained equally susceptible to both classes of pleasures, ever knowingly and calmly preferred the lower, though many, in all ages, have broken down in an ineffectual attempt to combine both.

From this verdict of the only competent judges, I apprehend there can be no appeal. On a question which is the best worth having of two pleasures, or which of two modes of existence is the most grateful to the feelings, apart from its moral attributes and from its consequences, the judgment of those who are qualified by knowledge of both, or, if they differ, that of the majority among them, must be admitted as final. And there needs be the less hesitation to accept this judgment respecting the quality of pleasures, since there is no other tribunal to be referred to even on the question of quantity. What means are there of determining which is the acutest of two pains, or the intensest of two pleasurable sensations, except the general suffrage of those who are familiar with both? Neither pains nor pleasures are homogeneous, and pain is always heterogeneous with pleasure. What is there to decide whether a particular pleasure is worth purchasing at the cost of a particular pain, except the feelings and judgment of the experienced? When, therefore, those feelings and judgment declare the pleasures derived from the higher faculties to be preferable *in kind*, apart from the question of intensity, to those of which the animal nature, disjoined from the higher faculties, is susceptible, they are entitled on this subject to the same regard.

I have dwelt on this point, as being a necessary part of a perfectly just conception of Utility or Happiness, considered as the directive rule of human conduct. But it is by no means an indispensable condition to the acceptance of the utilitarian standard; for that standard is not the agent's own greatest happiness, but the greatest amount of happiness altogether; and if it may possibly be doubted whether a noble character is always the happier for its nobleness, there can be no doubt that it makes other people happier, and that the world in general is immensely a gainer by it. Utilitarianism, therefore, could only attain its end by the general cultivation of nobleness of character, even if each individual were only benefitted by the nobleness of others, and his own, so far as happiness is concerned, were a sheer deduction from the benefit. But the bare enunciation of such an absurdity as this last, renders refutation superfluous.

According to the Greatest Happiness Principle, as above explained, the ultimate end, with reference to and for the sake of which all other things are desirable (whether we are considering our own good or that of other people), is an existence exempt as far as possible from pain, and as rich as possible in enjoyments, both in point of quantity and quality; the test of quality, and the rule for measuring it against quantity, being the preference felt by those who, in their opportunities of experience, to which must be added their habits of self-consciousness and self-observation, are best furnished with the means of comparison. This, being, according to the utilitarian opinion, the end of human action, is necessarily also the standard of morality; which may accordingly be defined, the rules and precepts for human conduct, by the observance of which an existence such as has been described might be, to the greatest extent possible, secured to all mankind; and not to them only, but, so far as the nature of things admits, to the whole sentient creation. . . .

I must again repeat, what the assailants of utilitarianism seldom have the justice to acknowledge, that the happiness which forms the utilitarian standard of what is right in conduct, is not the agent's own happiness, but that of all concerned. As between his own happiness and that of others, utilitarianism requires him to be as strictly impartial as a disinterested and benevolent spectator. In the golden rule of Jesus of Nazareth, we read the complete spirit of the ethics of utility. To do as one would be done by, and to love one's neighbour as oneself, constitute the ideal perfection of utilitarian morality. As the means of making the nearest approach to this ideal, utility would enjoin, first, that laws and social arrangements should place the happiness, or (as speaking practically it may be called) the interest, of every individual, as nearly as possible in harmony with the interest of the whole; and secondly, that education and opinion, which have so vast a power over human character, should so use that power as to establish in the mind of every individual an indissoluble association between his own happiness and the good of the whole; especially between his own happiness and the practice of such modes of conduct, negative and positive, as regard for the universal happiness prescribes: so that not only he may be unable to conceive the possibility of happiness to himself, consistently with conduct opposed to the general good, but also that a direct impulse to promote the general good may be in every individual one of the habitual motives of action, and the sentiments connected therewith may fill a large and prominent place in every human being's sentient existence. If the impugners of the utilitarian morality represented it to their own minds in this its true character, I know not what recommendation possessed by any other morality they could possibly affirm to be wanting to it: what more beautiful or more exalted developments of human nature any other ethical system can be supposed to foster, or what springs of action, not accessible to the utilitarian, such systems rely on for giving effect to their mandates. . . .

IV. Of What Sort of Proof the Principle of Utility Is Susceptible

It has already been remarked, that questions of ultimate ends do not admit of proof, in the ordinary acceptation of the term. To be incapable of proof by reasoning is common to all first principles; to the first premises of our knowledge, as well as to those of our conduct. But the former, being matters of fact, may be the subject of a direct appeal to the faculties which judge of fact—namely, our senses, and our internal consciousness. Can an appeal be made to the same faculties on questions of practical ends? Or by what other faculty is cognizance taken of them?

Questions about ends are, in other words, questions about what things are desirable. The utilitarian doctrine is, that happiness is desirable, and the only thing desirable, as an end; all other things being only desirable as means to that end. What ought to be required of this doctrine—what conditions is it requisite that the doctrine should fulfill—to make good its claim to be believed?

The only proof capable of being given that an object is visible, is that people actually see it. The only proof that a sound is audible, is that people hear it: and so of the other sources of our experience. In like manner, I apprehend, the sole evidence it is possible to produce that anything is desirable, is that people do actually desire it. If the end which the utilitarian doctrine proposes to itself were not, in theory and in practice, acknowledged to be an end, nothing could ever convince any person that it was so. No reason can be given why the general happiness is desirable, except that each person, so far as he believes it to be attainable, desires his own happiness. This, however, being a fact, we have not only all the proof which the case admits of, but all which it is possible to require, that happiness is a good: that each person's happiness is a good to that person, and the general happiness, therefore, a good to the aggregate of all persons. Happiness has made out its title as *one* of the ends of conduct, and consequently one of the criteria of morality.

But it has not, by this alone, proved itself to be the sole criterion. To do that, it would seem, by the same rule, necessary to show, not only that people desire happiness, but that they never desire anything else.

Now it is palpable that they do desire things which, in common language, are decidedly distinguished from happiness. They desire, for example, virtue, and the absence of vice, no less really than pleasure and the absence of pain. The desire of virtue is not as universal, but it is as authentic a fact, as the desire of happiness. And hence the opponents of the utilitarian standard deem that they have a right to infer that there are other ends of human action besides happiness, and that happiness is not the standard of approbation and disapprobation.

But does the utilitarian doctrine deny that people desire virtue, or maintain that virtue is not a thing to be desired? The very reverse. It maintains not only that virtue is to be desired, but that it is to be desired disinterestedly, for itself. Whatever may be the opinion of utilitarian moralists as to the original conditions by which virtue is made virtue; however they may believe (as they do) that actions and dispositions are only virtuous because they promote another end than virtue; yet this being granted, and it having been decided, from considerations of this description, what *is* virtuous, they not only place virtue at the very head of the things which are good as means to the ultimate end, but they also recognise as a psychological fact the possibility of its being, to the individual, a good in itself, without looking to any end beyond it; and hold, that the mind is not in a right state, not in a state comfortable to Utility, not in the state most conducive to the general happiness, unless it does love virtue in this manner—as a thing desirable in itself, even although, in the individual instance, it should not produce those other desirable consequences which it tends to produce, and on account of which it is held to be virtue. This opinion is not, in the smallest degree, a departure from the Happiness principle. The ingredients of happiness are very various, and each of them is desirable in itself, and not merely when considered as swelling an aggregate. The principle of utility does not mean that any given pleasure, as music, for instance, or any given exemption from pain, as for example health, are to be looked upon as a means to a collective something termed happiness, and to be desired on that account. They are desired and desirable in and for themselves; besides being means, they are a part of the end. Virtue, according to the utilitarian doctrine, is not naturally and originally part of the end, but it is capable of becoming so; and in those who love it disinterestedly it has become so, and is desired and cherished, not as a means to happiness, but as a part of their happiness.

To illustrate this farther, we may remember that virtue is not the only thing, originally a means, and which if it were not a means to anything else, would be and remain indifferent, but which by association with what it is a means to, comes to be desired for itself, and that too with the utmost intensity. What, for example, shall we say of the love of money? There is nothing originally more desirable about money than about any heap of glittering pebbles. Its worth is solely that of the things which it will buy; the desires for other things than itself, which it is a means of gratifying. Yet the love of money is not only one of the strongest moving forces of human life, but money is, in many cases, desired in and for itself; the desire to possess it is often stronger than the desire to use it, and goes on increasing when all the desires which point to ends beyond it, to be encompassed by it, are falling off. It may be then said truly, that money is desired not for the sake of an end, but as part of the end. From being a means to happiness, it has come to be itself a principal ingredient of the individual's conception of happiness. The same may be said of the majority of the great objects of human life—power, for example, or fame; except that to each of these there is a certain amount of immediate pleasure annexed, which has at least the semblance of being naturally inherent in them; a thing which cannot be said of money. Still, however, the strongest natural attraction, both of power and of fame, is the immense aid they give to the attainment of our other wishes; and it is the strong association thus generated between them and all our objects of desire, which gives to the direct desire of them the intensity it often assumes, so as in some characters to surpass in strength all other desires. In these cases the means have become a part of the end, and a more important part of it than any of the things which they are means to. What was once desired as an instrument for the attainment of happiness, has come to be desired for its own sake. In being desired for its own sake it is, however, desired as *part* of happiness. The person is made, or thinks he would be made, happy by its mere possession; and is made unhappy by failure to obtain it. The desire of it is not a different thing from the desire of happiness, any more than the love of music, or the desire of health. They are included in happiness. They are some of the elements of which the desire of happiness is made up. Happiness is not an abstract idea, but a concrete whole; and these are some of its parts. And the utilitarian standard sanctions and approves their being so. Life would be a poor thing, very ill provided with sources of happiness, if there were not this provision of nature, by which things originally indifferent, but conducive to, or otherwise associated with, the satisfaction of our primitive desires, become in themselves sources of pleasure more valuable than the primitive pleasures, both in permanency, in the space of human existence that they are capable of covering, and even in intensity.

Virtue, according to the utilitarian conception, is a good of this description. There was no original desire of it, or motive to it, save its conduciveness to pleasure, and especially to protection from pain. But through the association thus formed, it may be felt a good in itself, and desired as such with as great intensity as any other good; and with this difference between it and the love of money, of power, or of fame, that all of these may, and often do, render the individual noxious to the other members of the society to which he belongs, whereas there is nothing which makes him so much a blessing to them as the cultivation of the disinterested love of virtue. And consequently, the utilitarian standard, while it tolerates and approves those other acquired desires, up to the point beyond which they would be more injurious to the general happiness than promotive of it, enjoins and requires the cultivation of the love of virtue up to the greatest strength possible, as being above all things important to the general happiness.

It results from the preceding considerations, that there is in reality nothing desired except happiness. Whatever is desired otherwise than as a means to some end beyond itself, and ultimately to happiness, is desired as itself a part of happiness, and is not desired for itself until it has become so.

CHAPTER 9

The Categorical Imperative

Immanuel Kant

Immanuel Kant, whom many regard as the greatest modern philosopher, led an uneventful life. He was born in 1724 in Königsberg, East Prussia, and died there in 1804, never traveling more than a few miles from his home. He was a professor in the local university, popular with students, and a much-sought-after dinner guest, renowned for his entertaining style of conversation. He was also known for his regular habits: A bachelor, he arose each morning at the same time (4 A.M.), prepared his lectures, taught from 7 A.M. until noon, read until 4 P.M., took a walk, had dinner, and wrote until bedtime. This routine he repeated day after day, year after year. Yet despite his quiet habits, on the day he was buried, thousands of people followed his coffin, and the bells of all the churches tolled.

Kant's unorthodox views on religion caused the only controversy in his life. However, Kant was not an atheist. He was from a family of Pietists, who distrusted organized religion. In his later years, when he was rector of the university, it was his duty to lead the faculty procession to the university chapel for religious services; and he would, but upon reaching the chapel, he would stand aside and not enter. In 1786, having become the most famous philosopher in Germany, and having argued that God's existence cannot be proven, Kant was ordered to publish nothing more on the subject.

Today, "Kant scholarship" is an academic specialty unto itself; many scholars spend their whole lives trying to understand what Kant had to say, and every year new books appear arguing new interpretations of his philosophy. The multitude of interpretations is partly due to the richness of Kant's thought and to the difficulty of the topics he discussed. But it is also due to the fact that he was an exceedingly obscure writer.

Excerpted from Immanuel Kant, "Foundations of the Metaphysics of Morals" (1785) in *The Critique of Practical Reason and Other Writings in Moral Philosophy,* trans. Lewis White Beck (Chicago: University of Chicago Press, 1949), pp. 73–74, 80–83, 86–87. Reprinted with permission of the Estate of Lewis White Beck.

Kant would be remembered as a major figure for his work on metaphysics and human knowledge even if he had never written on ethics. But his ethical writings are among his most influential works. Kant believed that morality can be summed up in one ultimate principle, from which all our duties and obligations are derived. He called this principle the Categorical Imperative. According to the Categorical Imperative, to act morally is to act from motives that everyone, everywhere could live by.

The following selection is from Kant's *Foundations of the Metaphysics of Morals*, the most accessible presentation of his ethical theory.

All imperatives command either hypothetically or categorically. The former present the practical necessity of a possible action as a means to achieving something else which one desires (or which one may possibly desire). The categorical imperative would be one which presented an action as of itself objectively necessary, without regard to any other end.

Since every practical law presents a possible action as good and thus as necessary for a subject practically determinable by reason, all imperatives are formulas of the determination of action which is necessary by the principle of a will which is in any way good. If the action is good only as a means to something else, the imperative is hypothetical; but if it is thought of as good in itself, and hence as necessary in a will which of itself conforms to reason as the principle of this will, the imperative is categorical.

The imperative thus says what action possible to me would be good, and it presents the practical rule in relation to a will which does not forthwith perform an action simply because it is good, in part because the subject does not always know that the action is good and in part (when he does know it) because his maxims can still be opposed to the objective principles of practical reason.

The hypothetical imperative, therefore, says only that the action is good to some purpose, possible or actual. In the former case it is a problematical, in the latter an assertorical, practical principle. The categorical imperative, which declares the action to be of itself objectively necessary without making any reference to a purpose, i.e., without having any other end, holds as an apodictical (practical) principle. . . .

If I think of a hypothetical imperative as such, I do not know what it will contain until the condition is stated [under which it is an imperative].

But if I think of a categorical imperative, I know immediately what it contains. For since the imperative contains besides the law only the necessity of the maxim of acting in accordance with this law, while the law contains no condition to which it is restricted, there is nothing remaining in it except the universality of law as such to which the maxim of the action should conform; and in effect this conformity alone is represented as necessary by the imperative.

There is, therefore, only one categorical imperative. It is: Act only according to that maxim by which you can at the same time will that it should become a universal law.

Now if all imperatives of duty can be derived from this one imperative as a principle, we can at least show what we understand by the concept of duty and what it means, even though it remain undecided whether that which is called duty is an empty concept or not.

The universality of law according to which effects are produced constitutes what is properly called nature in the most general sense (as to form), i.e., the existence of things so far as it is determined by universal laws. [By analogy], then, the universal imperative of duty can be expressed as follows: Act as though the maxim of your action were by your will to become a universal law of nature.

We shall now enumerate some duties, adopting the usual division of them into duties to ourselves and to others and into perfect and imperfect duties.

1. A man who is reduced to despair by a series of evils feels a weariness with life but is still in possession of his reason sufficiently to ask whether it would not be contrary to his duty to himself to take his own life. Now he asks whether the maxim of his action could become a universal law of nature. His maxim, however, is: For love of myself, I make it my principle to shorten my life when by a longer duration it threatens more evil than satisfaction. But it is questionable whether this principle of self-love could become a universal law of nature. One immediately sees a contradiction in a system of nature, whose law would be to destroy life by the feeling whose special office is to impel the improvement of life. In this case it would not exist as nature; hence that maxim cannot obtain as a law of nature, and thus it wholly contradicts the supreme principle of all duty.

2. Another man finds himself forced by need to borrow money. He well knows that he will not be able to repay it, but he also sees that nothing will be loaned him if he does not firmly promise to repay it at a certain time. He desires to make such a promise, but he has enough conscience to ask himself whether it is not improper and opposed to duty to relieve his distress in such a way. Now, assuming he does decide to do so, the maxim of his action would be as follows: When I believe myself to be in need of money, I will borrow money and promise to repay it, although I know I shall never do so. Now this principle of self-love or of his own benefit may very well be compatible with his whole future welfare, but the question is whether it is right. He changes the pretension of self-love into a universal law and then puts the question: How would it be if my maxim became a universal law? He immediately sees that it could never hold as a universal law of nature and be consistent with itself; rather it must necessarily contradict itself. For the universality of a law which says that anyone who believes himself to be in need could promise what he pleased with the intention of not fulfilling it would make the promise itself and the end to be accomplished by it impossible; no one would believe what was promised to him but would only laugh at any such assertion as vain pretense.

3. A third finds in himself a talent which could, by means of some cultivation, make him in many respects a useful man. But he finds himself in comfortable circumstances and prefers indulgence in pleasure to troubling himself with broadening and improving his fortunate natural gifts. Now, however, let him ask whether his maxim of neglecting his gifts, besides agreeing with his propensity to idle amusement, agrees also with what is called duty. He sees that a system of nature could indeed exist in accordance with such a law, even though man (like the inhabitants of the South Sea Islands) should let his talents rust and resolve to devote his life merely to idleness, indulgence, and propagation—in a word, to pleasure. But he cannot possibly will that this should become a universal law of nature or that it should be implanted in us by a natural instinct. For, as a rational being, he necessarily wills that all his faculties should be developed, inasmuch as they are given to him for all sorts of possible purposes.

4. A fourth man, for whom things are going well, sees that others (whom he could help) have to struggle with great hardships, and he asks, "What concern of mine is it? Let each one be as happy as heaven wills, or as he can make himself; I will not take anything from him or even envy him; but to his welfare or to his assistance in time of need I have no desire to contribute." If such a way of thinking were a universal law of nature, certainly the human race could exist, and without doubt even better than in a state where everyone talks of sympathy and good will or even exerts himself occasionally to practice them while, on the other hand, he cheats when he can and betrays or otherwise violates the rights of man. Now although it is possible that a universal law of nature according to

that maxim could exist, it is nevertheless impossible to will that such a principle should hold everywhere as a law of nature. For a will which resolved this would conflict with itself, since instances can often arise in which he would need the love and sympathy of others, and in which he would have robbed himself, by such a law of nature springing from his own will, of all hope of the aid he desires.

The foregoing are a few of the many actual duties, or at least of duties we hold to be actual, whose derivation from the one stated principle is clear. We must be able to will that a maxim of our action become a universal law; this is the canon of the moral estimation of our action generally. Some actions are of such a nature that their maxim cannot even be *thought* as a universal law of nature without contradiction, far from it being possible that one could will that it should be such. In others this internal impossibility is not found though it is still impossible to *will* that their maxim should be raised to the universality of a law of nature, because such a will would contradict itself. We easily see that the former maxim conflicts with the stricter or narrower (imprescriptable) duty, the latter with broader (meritorious) duty. Thus all duties, so far as the kind of obligation (not the object of their action) is concerned, have been completely exhibited by these examples in their dependence on the one principle. . . .

Now, I say, man and, in general, every rational being exists as an end in himself and not merely as a means to be arbitrarily used by this or that will. In all his actions, whether they are directed to himself or to other rational beings, he must always be regarded at the same time as an end. All objects of inclinations have only a conditional worth, for if the inclinations and the needs founded on them did not exist, their object would be without worth. The inclinations themselves as the sources of needs, however, are so lacking in absolute worth that the universal wish of every rational being must be indeed to free himself completely from them. Therefore, the worth of any objects to be obtained by our actions is at all times conditional. Beings whose existence does not depend on our will but on nature, if they are not rational beings, have only a relative worth as means and are therefore called "things"; on the other hand, rational beings are designated "persons," because their nature indicates that they are ends in themselves, i.e., things which may not be used merely as means. Such a being is thus an object of respect and, so far, restricts all [arbitrary] choice. Such beings are not merely subjective ends whose existence as a result of our action has a worth for us but are objective ends, i.e., beings whose existence in itself is an end.

Such an end is one for which no other end can be substituted, to which these beings should serve merely as means. For, without them, nothing of absolute worth could be found, and if all worth is conditional and thus contingent, no supreme practical principle for reason could be found anywhere.

Thus if there is to be a supreme practical principle and a categorical imperative for the human will, it must be one that forms an objective principle of the will from the conception of that which is necessarily an end for everyone because it is an end in itself. Hence this objective principle can serve as a universal practical law. The ground of this principle is: rational nature exists as an end in itself. Man necessarily thinks of his own existence in this way; thus far it is a subjective principle of human actions. Also every other rational being thinks of his existence by means of the same rational ground which holds also for myself; thus it is at the same time an objective principle from which, as a supreme practical ground, it must be possible to derive all laws of the will. The practical imperative, therefore, is the following: Act so that you treat humanity, whether in your own person or in that of another, always as an end and never as a means only.

PART II

Essays about Moral Issues

CHAPTER 10

Why Abortion Is Immoral

Don Marquis

Abortion was not traditionally treated as a crime in Western law. Under English common law, abortion was tolerated even when performed late in the pregnancy, and in the United States, no laws prohibited it until well into the 19th century. When such laws were enacted, they were motivated by three concerns: a desire to discourage illicit sexual activity, the belief that abortion was an unsafe medical procedure, and the feeling that it is morally wrong to kill an unborn baby.

In the 20th century, every state passed laws forbidding abortion. However, these laws were struck down by the U.S. Supreme Court in its famous (some would say infamous) decision in *Roe v. Wade* (1973). In that decision, the Court held that laws outlawing abortion violate a woman's right to privacy. Since 1973, over a million abortions per year have been legally performed in the United States.

According to a 2005 Gallup Poll, 68% of Americans think that *Roe v. Wade* should not be overturned. However, the future of abortion in America is uncertain. At the moment, five Supreme Court justices out of nine are on record in support of *Roe:* Stevens, Kennedy, Souter, Ginsburg, and Breyer. But these justices, like the rest of us, will not live forever. Justice Stevens was born in 1920, and the rest were born in the 1930s. President George W. Bush, who opposes abortion, may be able to replace at least one of them. Nobody knows what the legal status of abortion will be in two years' time.

The crucial moral question about abortion is usually taken to be whether a fetus is a person, with a right to life. However, Don Marquis, a professor of philosophy at the University of Kansas, asks a somewhat different question: Do we have the same reasons not to kill a fetus that we have not to kill an adult? Killing adults, he says, is wrong because it deprives them of their future. But in killing a fetus,

Excerpts from Don Marquis, "Why Abortion Is Immoral," *The Journal of Philosophy*, vol. 86 (1989): 183–85, 189–92, 194. Reprinted by permission.

we are also depriving it of its future. Thus, it seems inconsistent to object to one but not the other.

The view that abortion is, with rare exceptions, seriously immoral has received little support in the recent philosophical literature. No doubt most philosophers affiliated with secular institutions of higher education believe that the anti-abortion position is either a symptom of irrational religious dogma or a conclusion generated by seriously confused philosophical argument. The purpose of this essay is to undermine this general belief. This essay sets out an argument that purports to show, as well as any argument in ethics can show, that abortion is, except possibly in rare cases, seriously immoral, that it is in the same moral category as killing an innocent adult human being. . . .

I

A sketch of standard anti-abortion and pro-choice arguments exhibits how those arguments possess certain symmetries that explain why partisans of those positions are so convinced of the correctness of their own positions, why they are not successful in convincing their opponents, and why, to others, this issue seems to be unresolvable. An analysis of the nature of this standoff suggests a strategy for surmounting it.

Consider the way a typical anti-abortionist argues. She will argue or assert that life is present from the moment of conception or that fetuses look like babies or that fetuses possess a characteristic such as a genetic code that is both necessary and sufficient for being human. Anti-abortionists seem to believe that (1) the truth of all of these claims is quite obvious, and (2) establishing any of these claims is sufficient to show that abortion is morally akin to murder.

A standard pro-choice strategy exhibits similarities. The pro-choicer will argue or assert that fetuses are not persons or that fetuses are not rational agents or that fetuses are not social beings. Pro-choicers seem to believe that (1) the truth of any of these claims is quite obvious, and (2) establishing any of these claims is sufficient to show that an abortion is not a wrongful killing.

In fact, both the pro-choice and the anti-abortion claims do seem to be true, although the "it looks like a baby" claim is more difficult to establish the earlier the pregnancy. We seem to have a standoff. How can it be resolved?

As everyone who has taken a bit of logic knows, if any of these arguments concerning abortion is a good argument, it requires not only some claim characterizing fetuses, but also some general moral principle that ties a characteristic of fetuses to having or not having the right to life or to some other moral characteristic that will generate the obligation or the lack of obligation not to end the life of a fetus. Accordingly, the arguments of the anti-abortionist and the pro-choicer need a bit of filling in to be regarded as adequate.

Note what each partisan will say. The anti-abortionist will claim that her position is supported by such generally accepted moral principles as "It is always prima facie seriously wrong to take a human life" or "It is always prima facie seriously wrong to end the life of a baby." Since these are generally accepted moral principles, her position is certainly not obviously wrong. The pro-choicer will claim that her position is supported by such plausible moral principles as "Being a person is what gives an individual intrinsic moral worth" or "It is only seriously prima facie wrong to take the life of a member of the human community." Since these are generally accepted moral principles, the pro-choice position is certainly not obviously wrong. Unfortunately, we have again arrived at a standoff.

Now, how might one deal with this standoff? The standard approach is to try to show how the moral principles of one's opponent lose their plausibility under analysis. It is easy to see how this is possible. On the one hand, the anti-abortionist will defend a moral principle concerning the wrongness of killing which tends to be broad in scope in order that even fetuses at an early stage of pregnancy will fall under it. The problem with broad principles is that they often embrace too much. In this particular instance, the principle "It is always prima facie wrong to take a human life" seems to entail that it is wrong to end the existence of a living human cancer-cell culture, on the grounds that the culture is both living and human. Therefore, it seems that the anti-abortionist's favored principle is too broad.

On the other hand, the pro-choicer wants to find a moral principle concerning the wrongness of killing which tends to be narrow in scope in order that fetuses will *not* fall under it. The problem with narrow principles is that they often do not embrace enough. Hence, the needed principles such as "It is prima facie seriously wrong to kill only persons" or "It is prima facie wrong to kill only rational agents" do not explain why it is wrong to kill infants or young children or the severely retarded or even perhaps the severely mentally ill. Therefore, we seem again to have a standoff. The anti-abortionist charges, not unreasonably, that pro-choice principles concerning killing are too narrow to be acceptable; the pro-choicer charges, not unreasonably, that anti-abortionist principles concerning killing are too broad to be acceptable. . . .

. . . All this suggests that a necessary condition of resolving the abortion controversy is a more theoretical account of the wrongness of killing. After all, if we merely believe, but do not understand, why killing adult human beings such as ourselves is wrong, how could we conceivably show that abortion is either immoral or permissible?

II

In order to develop such an account, we can start from the following unproblematic assumption concerning our own case: it is wrong to kill *us*. Why is it wrong? Some answers can be easily eliminated. It might be said that what makes killing us wrong is that a killing brutalizes the one who kills. But the brutalization consists of being inured to the performance of an act that is hideously immoral; hence, the brutalization does not explain the immorality. It might be said that what makes killing us wrong is the great loss others would experience due to our absence. Although such hubris is understandable, such an explanation does not account for the wrongness of killing hermits, or those whose lives are relatively independent and whose friends find it easy to make new friends.

A more obvious answer is better. What primarily makes killing wrong is neither its effect on the murderer nor its effect on the victim's friends and relatives, but its effect on the victim. The loss of one's life is one of the greatest losses one can suffer. The loss of one's life deprives one of all the experiences, activities, projects, and enjoyments that would otherwise have constituted one's future. Therefore, killing someone is wrong, primarily because the killing inflicts (one of) the greatest possible losses on the victim. To describe this as the loss of life can be misleading, however. The change in my biological state does not by itself make killing me wrong. The effect of the loss of my biological life is the loss to me of all those activities, projects, experiences, and enjoyments which would otherwise have constituted my future personal life. These activities, projects, experiences, and enjoyments are either valuable for their own sakes or are means to something else that is valuable for its own sake. Some parts of my future are not valued by me now, but will come to be valued by me as

I grow older and as my values and capacities change. When I am killed, I am deprived both of what I now value which would have been part of my future personal life, but also what I would come to value. Therefore, when I die, I am deprived of all of the value of my future. Inflicting this loss on me is ultimately what makes killing me wrong. This being the case, it would seem that what makes killing *any* adult human being prima facie seriously wrong is the loss of his or her future.[1]

How should this rudimentary theory of the wrongness of killing be evaluated? It cannot be faulted for deriving an "ought" from an "is," for it does not. The analysis assumes that killing me (or you, reader) is prima facie seriously wrong. The point of the analysis is to establish which natural property ultimately explains the wrongness of the killing, given that it is wrong. A natural property will ultimately explain the wrongness of killing, only if (1) the explanation fits with our intuitions about the matter and (2) there is no other natural property that provides the basis for a better explanation of the wrongness of killing. This analysis rests on the intuition that what makes killing a particular human or animal wrong is what it does to that particular human or animal. What makes killing wrong is some natural effect or other of the killing. Some would deny this. For instance, a divine-command theorist in ethics would deny it. Surely this denial is, however, one of those features of divine-command theory which renders it so implausible.

The claim that what makes killing wrong is the loss of the victim's future is directly supported by two considerations. In the first place, this theory explains why we regard killing as one of the worst of crimes. Killing is especially wrong, because it deprives the victim of more than perhaps any other crime. In the second place, people with AIDS or cancer who know they are dying believe, of course, that dying is a very bad thing for them. They believe that the loss of a future to them that they would otherwise have experienced is what makes their premature death a very bad thing for them. A better theory of the wrongness of killing would require a different natural property associated with killing which better fits with the attitudes of the dying. What could it be?

The view that what makes killing wrong is the loss to the victim of the value of the victim's future gains additional support when some of its implications are examined. In the first place, it is incompatible with the view that it is wrong to kill only beings who are biologically human. It is possible that there exists a different species from another planet whose members have a future like ours. Since having a future like that is what makes killing someone wrong, this theory entails that it would be wrong to kill members of such a species. Hence, this theory is opposed to the claim that only life that is biologically human has great moral worth, a claim which many anti-abortionists have seemed to adopt. This opposition, which this theory has in common with personhood theories, seems to be a merit of the theory.

In the second place, the claim that the loss of one's future is the wrong-making feature of one's being killed entails the possibility that the futures of some actual nonhuman mammals on our own planet are sufficiently like ours that it is seriously wrong to kill them also. Whether some animals do have the same right to life as human beings depends on adding to the account of the wrongness of killing some additional account of just what it is about my future or the futures of other adult human beings which makes it wrong to kill us. No such additional account will be offered in this essay. Undoubtedly, the provision of such an account would be a very difficult matter. Undoubtedly, any such account would be quite controversial. Hence, it surely should not reflect badly on this sketch of an elementary theory of the wrongness of killing that it is indeterminate with respect to some very difficult issues regarding animal rights.

In the third place, the claim that the loss of one's future is the wrong-making feature of one's being killed does not entail, as sanctity of human life theories do, that active euthanasia is wrong. Persons who are severely and incurably ill, who face a future of pain and despair, and who wish to die will not have suffered a loss if they are killed. It is, strictly speaking, the value of a human's future which makes killing wrong in this theory. This being so, killing does not necessarily wrong some persons who are sick and dying. Of course, there may be other reasons for a prohibition of active euthanasia, but that is another matter. Sanctity-of-human-life theories seem to hold that active euthanasia is seriously wrong even in an individual case where there seems to be good reason for it independently of public policy considerations. This consequence is most implausible, and it is a plus for the claim that the loss of a future of value is what makes killing wrong that it does not share this consequence.

In the fourth place, the account of the wrongness of killing defended in this essay does straightforwardly entail that it is prima facie seriously wrong to kill children and infants, for we do presume that they have futures of value. Since we do believe that it is wrong to kill defenseless little babies, it is important that a theory of the wrongness of killing easily account for this. Personhood theories of the wrongness of killing, on the other hand, cannot straightforwardly account for the wrongness of killing infants and young children. Hence, such theories must add special ad hoc accounts of the wrongness of killing the young. The plausibility of such ad hoc theories seems to be a function of how desperately one wants such theories to work. The claim that the primary wrong-making feature of a killing is the loss to the victim of the value of its future accounts for the wrongness of killing young children and infants directly; it makes the wrongness of such acts as obvious as we actually think it is. This is a further merit of this theory. Accordingly, it seems that this value of a future-like-ours theory of the wrongness of killing shares strengths of both sanctity-of-life and personhood accounts while avoiding weaknesses of both. In addition, it meshes with a central intuition concerning what makes killing wrong.

The claim that the primary wrong-making feature of a killing is the loss to the victim of the value of its future has obvious consequences for the ethics of abortion. The future of a standard fetus includes a set of experiences, projects, activities, and such which are identical with the futures of adult human beings and are identical with the futures of young children. Since the reason that is sufficient to explain why it is wrong to kill human beings after the time of birth is a reason that also applies to fetuses, it follows that abortion is prima facie seriously morally wrong.

This argument does not rely on the invalid inference that, since it is wrong to kill persons, it is wrong to kill potential persons also. The category that is morally central to this analysis is the category of having a valuable future like ours; it is not the category of personhood. The argument to the conclusion that abortion is prima facie seriously morally wrong proceeded independently of the notion of person or potential person or any equivalent. Someone may wish to start with this analysis in terms of the value of a human future, conclude that abortion is, except perhaps in rare circumstances, seriously morally wrong, infer that fetuses have the right to life, and then call fetuses "persons" as a result of their having the right to life. Clearly, in this case, the category of person is being used to state the *conclusion* of the analysis rather than to generate the *argument* of the analysis. . . .

Of course, this value of a future-like-ours argument, if sound, shows only that abortion is prima facie wrong, not that it is wrong in any and all circumstances. Since the loss of the future to a standard fetus, if killed, is, however, at least as great a loss as the loss of the future to a standard adult human being who is killed, abortion, like ordinary killing, could be justified only by the most compelling reasons. The loss of one's life is almost the greatest misfortune that can happen to one. Presumably abortion could be justified in some circumstances, only if the loss consequent on failing to abort would be at least as great. Accordingly, morally permissible abortions will be rare indeed unless, perhaps, they occur so early in pregnancy that a fetus is not yet definitely an individual. Hence, this argument should be taken as showing that abortion is presumptively very seriously wrong, where the presumption is very strong—as strong as the presumption that killing another adult human being is wrong.

Note

1. I have been most influenced on this matter by Jonathan Glover, *Causing Death and Saving Lives* (New York: Penguin, 1977), ch. 3; and Robert Young, "What Is So Wrong with Killing People?" *Philosophy* I.IV, 210 (1979), 515–28.

CHAPTER 11

A Defense of Abortion

Judith Jarvis Thomson

For the sake of argument, Judith Jarvis Thomson grants that a fetus is a person, with a right to life, from the moment of conception. Can we conclude from that assumption that abortion is immoral? The answer turns out to be surprisingly complicated. Thomson's discussion not only throws light on the abortion issue, it illuminates the nature of rights.

Readers of this essay who are unfamiliar with Henry Fonda may instead think of Orlando Bloom, Colin Farrell, or Josh Hartnett. The philosophical point involving Fonda will be the same.

Judith Jarvis Thomson is a professor of philosophy at the Massachusetts Institute of Technology (MIT). Her most recent book is *Goodness and Advice* (2003).

Most opposition to abortion relies on the premise that the fetus is a human being, a person, from the moment of conception. . . .

. . . I think that the premise is false, that the fetus is not a person from the moment of conception. A newly fertilized ovum, a newly implanted clump of cells, is no more a person than an acorn is an oak tree. But I shall not discuss any of this. For it seems to me to be of great interest to ask what happens if, for the sake of argument, we allow the premise. How, precisely, are we supposed to get from there to the conclusion that abortion is morally impermissible? Opponents of abortion commonly spend most of their time establishing that the fetus is a person, and hardly any time explaining the step from there to the impermissibility of abortion. Perhaps they think the step too simple and obvious to require much comment. . . . Whatever the explanation,

Excerpted from Judith Jarvis Thomson, "A Defense of Abortion," *Philosophy and Public Affairs*, Vol. 1, No. 1 (Autumn, 1971), pp. 47–66. Reprinted by permission.

I suggest that the step they take is neither easy nor obvious, that it calls for closer examination than it is commonly given, and that when we do give it this closer examination we shall feel inclined to reject it.

I propose, then, that we grant that the fetus is a person from the moment of conception. How does the argument go from here? Something like this, I take it. Every person has a right to life. So the fetus has a right to life. No doubt the mother has a right to decide what shall happen in and to her body; everyone would grant that. But surely a person's right to life is stronger and more stringent than the mother's right to decide what happens in and to her body, and so outweighs it. So the fetus may not be killed; an abortion may not be performed.

It sounds plausible. But now let me ask you to imagine this. You wake up in the morning and find yourself back to back in bed with an unconscious violinist. A famous unconscious violinist. He has been found to have a fatal kidney ailment, and the Society of Music Lovers has canvassed all the available medical records and found that you alone have the right blood type to help. They have therefore kidnapped you, and last night the violinist's circulatory system was plugged into yours, so that your kidneys can be used to extract poisons from his blood as well as your own. The director of the hospital now tells you, "Look, we're sorry the Society of Music Lovers did this to you—we would never have permitted it if we had known. But still, they did it, and the violinist now is plugged into you. To unplug you would be to kill him. But never mind, it's only for nine months. By then he will have recovered from his ailment, and can safely be unplugged from you." Is it morally incumbent on you to accede to this situation? No doubt it would be very nice of you if you did, a great kindness. But do you *have* to accede to it? What if it were not nine months, but nine years? Or longer still? What if the director of the hospital says, "Tough luck, I agree, but you've now got to stay in bed, with the violinist plugged into you, for the rest of your life. Because remember this. All persons have a right to life, and violinists are persons. Granted you have a right to decide what happens in and to your body, but a person's right to life outweighs your right to decide what happens in and to your body. So you cannot ever be unplugged from him." I imagine you would regard this as outrageous, which suggests that something really is wrong with that plausible-sounding argument I mentioned a moment ago.

In this case, of course, you were kidnapped; you didn't volunteer for the operation that plugged the violinist into your kidneys.

Can those who oppose abortion on the ground I mentioned make an exception for a pregnancy due to rape? Certainly. They can say that persons have a right to life only if they didn't come into existence because of rape; or they can say that all persons have a right to life, but that some have less of a right to life than others, in particular, that those who came into existence because of rape have less. But these statements have a rather unpleasant sound. Surely the question of whether you have a right to life at all, or how much of it you have, shouldn't turn on the question of whether or not you are the product of a rape. And in fact the people who oppose abortion on the ground I mentioned do not make this distinction, and hence do not make an exception in case of rape.

Nor do they make an exception for a case in which the mother has to spend the nine months of her pregnancy in bed. They would agree that would be a great pity, and hard on the mother; but all the same, all persons have a right to life, the fetus is a person, and so on. I suspect, in fact, that they would not make an exception for a case in which, miraculously enough, the pregnancy went on for nine years, or even the rest of the mother's life.

Some won't even make an exception for a case in which continuation of the pregnancy is likely to shorten the mother's life; they regard abortion as impermissible even to save the mother's life. Such cases are nowadays very rare, and many opponents of abortion do not accept this extreme view. All the same, it is a good place to begin: a number of points of interest come out in respect to it.

1. Let us call the view that abortion is impermissible even to save the mother's life "the extreme view." I want to suggest first that it does not issue from the argument I mentioned earlier without the addition of some fairly powerful premises. Suppose a woman has become pregnant, and now learns that she has a cardiac condition such that she will die if she carries the baby to term. What may be done for her? The fetus, being a person, has a right to life, but as the mother is a person too, so has she a right to life. Presumably they have an equal right to life. How is it supposed to come out that an abortion may not be performed? If mother and child have an equal right to life, shouldn't we perhaps flip a coin? Or should we add to the mother's right to life her right to decide what happens in and to her body, which everybody seems to be ready to grant—the sum of her rights now outweighing the fetus' right to life?

The most familiar argument here is the following. We are told that performing the abortion would be directly killing the child, whereas doing nothing would not be killing the mother, but only letting her die. Moreover, in killing the child, one would be killing an innocent person, for the child has committed no crime, and is not aiming at his mother's death. And then there are a variety of ways in which this might be continued. (1) But as directly killing an innocent person is always and absolutely impermissible, an abortion may not be performed. Or, (2) as directly killing an innocent person is murder, and murder is always and absolutely impermissible, an abortion may not be performed. Or, (3) as one's duty to refrain from directly killing an innocent person is more stringent than one's duty to keep a person from dying, an abortion may not be performed. Or, (4) if one's only options are directly killing an innocent person or letting a person die, one must prefer letting the person die, and thus an abortion may not be performed.

Some people seem to have thought that these are not further premises which must be added if the conclusion is to be reached, but that they follow from the very fact that an innocent person has a right to life. But this seems to me to be a mistake, and perhaps the simplest way to show this is to bring out that while we must certainly grant that innocent persons have a right to life, the theses in (1) through (4) are all false. Take (2), for example. If directly killing an innocent person is murder, and thus is impermissible, then the mother's directly killing the innocent person inside her is murder, and thus is impermissible. But it cannot seriously be thought to be murder if the mother performs an abortion on herself to save her life. It cannot seriously be said that she *must* refrain, that she *must* sit passively by and wait for her death. Let us look again at the case of you and the violinist. There you are, in bed with the violinist, and the director of the hospital says to you, "It's all most distressing, and I deeply sympathize, but you see this is putting an additional strain on your kidneys, and you'll be dead within the month. But you *have* to stay where you are all the same. Because unplugging you would be directly killing an innocent violinist, and that's murder, and that's impermissible." If anything in the world is true, it is that you do not commit murder, you do not do what is impermissible, if you reach around to your back and unplug yourself from that violinist to save your life.

The main focus of attention in writings on abortion has been on what a third party may or may not do in answer to a request from a woman for an abortion. This is in a way understandable. Things being as they are, there isn't much a woman can safely do to abort herself. So the question asked is what a third party may do, and what the mother may do, if it is mentioned at all, is deduced, almost as an after-thought, from what it is concluded that third parties may do. But it seems to me that to treat the matter in this way is to refuse to grant to the mother that very status of person which is so firmly insisted on for the fetus. For we cannot simply read off what a person may do from what a third party may do. Suppose you find yourself trapped in a tiny house with a growing child. I mean a very tiny house, and a rapidly growing child—you are already up against the wall of the house and in a few minutes you'll be crushed to death. The child on the other hand won't be crushed to death; if nothing is done to stop him from growing he'll be hurt, but in the end he'll simply burst open the house and walk out a free man. Now I could well understand it if a bystander were to say, "There's nothing we can do for you. We cannot choose between your life and his, we cannot be the ones to decide who is to live, we cannot intervene." But it cannot be concluded that you too can do nothing, that you cannot attack it to save your life. However innocent the child may be, you do not have to wait passively while it crushes you to death. Perhaps a pregnant woman is vaguely felt to have the status of house, to which we don't allow the right of self-defense. But if the woman houses the child, it should be remembered that she is a person who houses it.

I should perhaps stop to say explicitly that I am not claiming that people have a right to do anything whatever to save their lives. I think, rather, that there are drastic limits to the right of self-defense. If some-one threatens you with death unless you torture someone else to death, I think you have not the right, even to save your life, to do so. But the case under consideration here is very different. In our case there are only two people involved, one whose life is threatened, and one who threatens it. Both are innocent: the one who is threatened is not threat-ened because of any fault, the one who threatens does not threaten because of any fault. For this reason we may feel that we bystanders can-not intervene. But the person threatened can.

In sum, a woman surely can defend her life against the threat to it posed by the unborn child, even if doing so involves its death. And this shows not merely that the theses in (1) through (4) are false; it shows also that the extreme view of abortion is false, and so we need not canvass any other possible ways of arriving at it from the argument I mentioned at the outset.

2. The extreme view could of course be weakened to say that while abortion is permissible to save the mother's life, it may not be performed by a third party, but only by the mother herself. But this cannot be right either. For what we have to keep in mind is that the mother and the unborn child are not like two tenants in a small house which has, by an unfortunate mistake, been rented to both: the mother *owns* the house. The fact that she does adds to the offensiveness of deducing that the mother can do nothing from the supposition that third parties can do nothing. But it does more than this: it casts a bright light on the supposition that third parties can do nothing. Certainly it lets us see that a third party who says "I cannot choose between you" is fooling himself if he thinks this is impartiality. If Jones has found and fastened on a certain coat, which he needs to keep him from freezing, but which Smith also needs to keep him from freezing, then it is not impartiality that says "I cannot choose between you" when Smith owns the coat. Women have said again and again "This body is *my* body!" and they have reason to feel angry, reason to feel that it has been like shouting into the wind. Smith, after all, is hardly likely to bless us if we say to him, "Of course it's your coat, anybody would grant that it is. But no one may choose between you and Jones who is to have it.". . .

I suppose that in some views of human life the mother's body is only on loan to her, the loan not being one which gives her any prior claim to it. One who held this view might well think it impartiality to say "I cannot choose." But I shall simply ignore this possibility. My own view is that if a human being has any just, prior claim to anything at all, he has a just, prior claim to his own body. And perhaps this needn't be argued for here anyway, since, as I mentioned, the arguments against abortion we are looking at do grant that the woman has a right to decide what happens in and to her body.

But although they do grant it, I have tried to show that they do not take seriously what is done in granting it. I suggest the same thing will reappear even more clearly when we turn away from cases in which the mother's life is at stake, and attend, as I propose we now do, to the vastly more common cases in which a woman wants an abortion for some less weighty reason than preserving her own life.

3. Where the mother's life is not at stake, the argument I mentioned at the outset seems to have a much stronger pull. "Everyone has a right to life, so the unborn person has a right to life." And isn't the child's right to life weightier than anything other than the mother's own right to life, which she might put forward as ground for an abortion?

This argument treats the right to life as if it were unproblematic. It is not, and this seems to me to be precisely the source of the mistake.

For we should now, at long last, ask what it comes to, to have a right to life. In some views having a right to life includes having a right to be given at least the bare minimum one needs for continued life. But suppose that what in fact *is* the bare minimum a man needs for continued life is something he has no right at all to be given? If I am sick unto death, and the only thing that will save my life is the touch of Henry Fonda's cool hand on my fevered brow, then all the same, I have no right to be given the touch of Henry Fonda's cool hand on my fevered brow. It would be frightfully nice of him to fly in from the West Coast to provide it. It would be less nice, though no doubt well meant, if my friends flew out to the West Coast and carried Henry Fonda back with them. But I have no right at all against anybody that he should do this for me. Or again, to return to the story I told earlier, the fact that for continued life that violinist needs the continued use of your kidneys does not establish that he has a right to be given the continued use of your kidneys. He certainly has no right against you that *you* should give him continued use of your kidneys. For nobody has any right to use your kidneys unless you give him such a right; and nobody has the right against you that you shall give him this right—if you do allow him to go on using your kidneys, this is a kindness on your part, and not something he can claim from you as his due. Nor has he any right against anybody else that *they* should give him continued use of your kidneys. Certainly he had no right against the Society of Music Lovers that they should plug him into you in the first place. And if you now start to unplug yourself, having learned that you will otherwise have to spend nine years in bed with him, there is nobody in the world who must try to prevent you, in order to see to it that he is given something he has a right to be given.

Some people are rather stricter about the right to life. In their view, it does not include the right to be given anything, but amounts to, and only to, the right not to be killed by anybody. But here a related difficulty arises. If everybody is to refrain from killing that violinist, then everybody must refrain from doing a great many different sorts of things. Everybody must refrain from slitting his throat, everybody must refrain from shooting him—and everybody must refrain from unplugging you from him. But does he have a right against everybody that they shall refrain from unplugging you from him? To refrain from doing this is to allow him to continue to use your kidneys. It could be argued that he has a right against us that *we* should allow him to continue to use your kidneys. That is, while he had no right against us that we should give him the use of your kidneys, it might be argued that he anyway has a right against us that we shall not now intervene and deprive him of the use of your kidneys. I shall come back to third-party interventions later. But certainly the violinist has no right against you that *you* shall allow him to continue to use your kidneys. As I said, if you do allow him to use them, it is a kindness on your part, and not something you owe him.

. . . I would stress that I am not arguing that people do not have a right to life—quite to the contrary, it seems to me that the primary control we must place on the acceptability of an account of rights is that it should turn out in that account to be a truth that all persons have a right to life. I am arguing only that having a right to life does not guarantee having either a right to be given the use of or a right to be allowed continued use of another person's body—even if one needs it for life itself. So the right to life will not serve the opponents of abortion in the very simple and clear way in which they seem to have thought it would.

4. There is another way to bring out the difficulty. In the most ordinary sort of case, to deprive someone of what he has a right to is to treat him unjustly. Suppose a boy and his small brother are jointly given a box of chocolates for Christmas. If the older boy takes the box and refuses to give his brother any of the chocolates, he is unjust to him, for the brother has been given a right to half of them. But suppose that, having learned that otherwise it means nine years in bed with that violinist, you unplug yourself from him. You surely are not being unjust to him, for you gave him no right to use your kidneys, and no one else can have given him any such right. But we have to notice that in unplugging yourself, you are killing him; and violinists, like everybody else, have a right to life, and thus in the view we were considering just now, the right not to be killed. So here you do what he supposedly has a right you shall not do, but you do not act unjustly to him in doing it.

The emendation which may be made at this point is this: the right to life consists not in the right not to be killed, but rather in the right not to be killed unjustly. This runs a risk of circularity, but never mind: it would enable us to square the fact that the violinist has a right to life with the fact that you do not act unjustly toward him in unplugging yourself, thereby killing him. For if you do not kill him unjustly, you do not violate his right to life, and so it is no wonder you do him no injustice.

But if this emendation is accepted, the gap in the argument against abortion stares us plainly in the face: it is by no means enough to show that the fetus is a person, and to remind us that all persons have a right to life—we need to be shown also that killing the fetus violates its right to life, i.e., that abortion is unjust killing. And is it?

I suppose we may take it as a datum that in a case of pregnancy due to rape the mother has not given the unborn person a right to the use of her body for food and shelter. Indeed, in what pregnancy could it be supposed that the mother has given the unborn person such a right? It is not as if there were unborn persons drifting about the world, to whom a woman who wants a child says "I invite you in."

But it might be argued that there are other ways one can have acquired a right to the use of another person's body than by having been invited to use it by that person. Suppose a woman voluntarily indulges in intercourse, knowing of the chance it will issue in pregnancy, and then she does become pregnant; is she not in part responsible for the presence, in fact the very existence, of the unborn person inside her? No doubt she did not invite it in. But doesn't her partial responsibility for its being there itself give it a right to the use of her body? If so, then her aborting it would be more like the boy's taking away the chocolates, and less like your unplugging yourself from the violinist—doing so would be depriving it of what it does have a right to, and thus would be doing it an injustice.

And then, too, it might be asked whether or not she can kill it even to save her own life: If she voluntarily called it into existence, how can she now kill it, even in self-defense?

The first thing to be said about this is that it is something new. Opponents of abortion have been so concerned to make out the independence of the fetus, in order to establish that it has a right to life, just as its mother does, that they have tended to overlook the possible support they might gain from making out that the fetus is *dependent* on the mother, in order to establish that she has a special kind of responsibility for it, a responsibility that gives it rights against her which are not possessed by any independent person—such as an ailing violinist who is a stranger to her.

On the other hand, this argument would give the unborn person a right to its mother's body only if her pregnancy resulted from a voluntary act, undertaken in full knowledge of the chance a pregnancy might result from it. It would leave out entirely the unborn person whose existence is due to rape. Pending the availability of some further argument, then, we would be left with the conclusion that unborn persons whose existence is due to rape have no right to the use of their mothers' bodies, and thus that aborting them is not depriving them of anything they have a right to and hence is not unjust killing.

And we should also notice that it is not at all plain that this argument really does go even as far as it purports to. For there are cases and cases, and the details make a difference. If the room is stuffy, and I therefore open a window to air it, and a burglar climbs in, it would be absurd to say, "Ah, now he can stay, she's given him a right to the use of her house—for she is partially responsible for his presence there, having voluntarily done what enabled him to get in, in full knowledge that there are such things as burglars, and that burglars burgle." It would be still more absurd to say this if I had had bars installed outside my windows, precisely to prevent burglars from getting in, and a burglar got in only because of a defect in the bars. It remains equally absurd if we imagine it is not a burglar who climbs in, but an innocent person who blunders or falls in. Again, suppose it were like this: people-seeds drift about in the air like pollen, and if you open your windows, one may drift in and take root in your carpets or upholstery. You don't want children, so you fix up your windows with fine mesh screens, the very best you can buy. As can happen, however, and on very, very rare occasions does happen, one of the screens is defective; and a seed drifts in and takes root. Does the person-plant who now develops have a right to the use of your house? Surely not— despite the fact that you voluntarily opened your windows, you knowingly kept carpets and upholstered furniture, and you knew that screens were sometimes defective. Someone may argue that you are responsible for its rooting, that it does have a right to your house, because after all you *could* have lived out your life with bare floors and furniture, or with sealed windows and doors. But this won't do— for by the same token anyone can avoid a pregnancy due to rape by having a hysterectomy, or anyway by never leaving home without a (reliable!) army.

It seems to me that the argument we are looking at can establish at most that there are *some* cases in which the unborn person has a right to the use of its mother's body, and therefore *some* cases in which abortion is unjust killing. There is room for much discussion and argument as to precisely which, if any. But I think we should sidestep this issue and leave it open, for at any rate the argument certainly does not establish that all abortion is unjust killing.

5. There is room for yet another argument here, however. We surely must all grant that there may be cases in which it would be morally indecent to detach a person from your body at the cost of his life. Suppose you learn that what the violinist needs is not nine years of your life, but only one hour: all you need do to save his life is to spend one hour in that bed with him. Suppose also that letting him use your kidneys for that one hour would not affect your health in the slightest. Admittedly you were kidnapped. Admittedly you did not give anyone permission to plug him into you. Nevertheless it seems to me plain you *ought* to allow him to use your kidneys for that hour—it would be indecent to refuse.

Again, suppose pregnancy lasted only an hour, and constituted no threat to life or health. And suppose that a woman becomes pregnant as a result of rape. Admittedly she did not voluntarily do anything to bring about the existence of a child. Admittedly she did nothing at all which would give the unborn person a right to the use of her body. All the same it might well be said, as in the newly emended violinist story, that she *ought* to allow it to remain for that hour—that it would be indecent in her to refuse.

Now some people are inclined to use the term "right" in such a way that it follows from the fact that you ought to allow a person to use your body for the hour he needs, that he has a right to use your body for the hour he needs, even though he has not been given that right by any person or act. They may say that it follows also that if you refuse, you act unjustly toward him. This use of the term is perhaps so common that it cannot be called wrong; nevertheless it seems to me to be an unfortunate loosening of what we would do better to keep a tight rein on. Suppose that box of chocolates I mentioned earlier had not been given to both boys jointly, but was given only to the older boy. There he sits, stolidly eating his way through the box, his small brother watching enviously. Here we are likely to say "You ought not to be so mean. You ought to give your brother some of those chocolates." My own view is that it just does not follow from the truth of this that the brother has any right to any of the chocolates. If the boy refuses to give his brother any, he is greedy, stingy, callous—but not unjust. I suppose that the people I have in mind will say it does follow that the brother has a right to some of the chocolates, and thus that the boy does act unjustly if he refuses to give his brother any. But the effect of saying this is to obscure what we should keep distinct, namely the difference between the boy's refusal in this case and the boy's refusal in the earlier case, in which the box was given to both boys jointly, and in which the small brother thus had what was from any point of view clear title to half.

A further objection to so using the term "right" that from the fact that A ought to do a thing for B, it follows that B has a right against A that A do it for him, is that it is going to make the question of whether or not a man has a right to a thing turn on how easy it is to provide him with it; and this seems not merely unfortunate, but morally unacceptable. Take the case of Henry Fonda again. I said earlier that I had no right to the touch of his cool hand on my fevered brow, even though I needed it to save my life. I said it would be frightfully nice of him to fly in from the West Coast to provide me with it, but that I had no right against him that he should do so. But suppose he isn't on the West Coast. Suppose he has only to walk across the room, place a hand briefly on my brow—and lo, my life is saved. Then surely he ought to do it, it would be indecent to refuse. Is it to be said "Ah, well, it follows that in this case she has a right to the touch of his hand on her brow, and so it would be an injustice in him to refuse"? So that I have a right to it when it is easy for him to provide it, though no right when it's hard? It's rather a shocking idea that anyone's rights should fade away and disappear as it gets harder and harder to accord them to him.

So my own view is that even though you ought to let the violinist use your kidneys for the one hour he needs, we should not conclude that he has a right to do so—we should say that if you refuse, you are, like the boy who owns all the chocolates and will give none away, self-centered and callous, indecent in fact, but not unjust. And similarly, that even supposing a case in which a woman pregnant due to rape ought to allow the unborn person to use her body for the hour he needs, we should not conclude that he has a right to do so; we should conclude that she is self-centered, callous, indecent, but not unjust, if she refuses. The complaints are no less grave; they are just different. However, there is no need to insist on this point. If anyone does wish to deduce "he has a right" from "you ought," then all the same he must surely grant that there are cases in which it is not morally required of you that you allow that violinist to use your kidneys, and in which he does not have a right to use them, and in which you do not do him an injustice if you refuse. And so also for mother and unborn child. Except in such cases as the unborn person has a right to demand it—and we were leaving open the possibility that there may be such cases—nobody is morally *required* to make large sacrifices, of health, of all other interests and concerns, of all other duties and commitments, for nine years, or even for nine months, in order to keep another person alive.

6. We have in fact to distinguish between two kinds of Samaritan: the Good Samaritan and what we might call the Minimally Decent Samaritan. The story of the Good Samaritan, you will remember, goes like this:

> A certain man went down from Jerusalem to Jericho, and fell among thieves, which stripped him of his raiment, and wounded him, and departed, leaving him half dead.
>
> And by chance there came down a certain priest that way; and when he saw him, he passed by on the other side.
>
> And likewise a Levite, when he was at the place, came and looked on him, and passed by on the other side.
>
> But a certain Samaritan, as he journeyed, came where he was; and when he saw him he had compassion on him.
>
> And went to him, and bound up his wounds, pouring in oil and wine, and set him on his own beast, and brought him to an inn, and took care of him.
>
> And on the morrow, when he departed, he took out two pence, and gave them to the host, and said unto him, "Take care of him; and whatsoever thou spendest more, when I come again, I will repay thee."   (Luke 10:30–35)

The Good Samaritan went out of his way, at some cost to himself, to help one in need of it. We are not told what the options were, that is, whether or not the priest and the Levite could have helped by doing less than the Good Samaritan did, but assuming they could have, then the fact they did nothing at all shows they were not even Minimally Decent Samaritans, not because they were not Samaritans, but because they were not even minimally decent.

These things are a matter of degree, of course, but there is a difference, and it comes out perhaps most clearly in the story of Kitty Genovese, who, as you will remember, was murdered while thirty-eight people watched or listened, and did nothing at all to help her. A Good Samaritan would have rushed out to give direct assistance against the murderer. Or perhaps we had better allow that it would have been a Splendid Samaritan who did this, on the ground that it would have involved a risk of death for himself. But the thirty-eight not only did not do this, they did not even trouble to pick up a phone to call the police. Minimally Decent Samaritanism would call for doing at least that, and their not having done it was monstrous.

After telling the story of the Good Samaritan, Jesus said "Go, and do thou likewise." Perhaps he meant that we are morally required to act as the Good Samaritan did. Perhaps he was urging people to do more than is morally required of them. At all events it seems plain that it was not morally required of any of the thirty-eight that he rush out to give direct assistance at the risk of his own life, and that it is not morally required of anyone that he give long stretches of his life—nine years or nine months—to sustaining the life of a person who has no special right (we were leaving open the possibility of this) to demand it.

Indeed, with one rather striking class of exceptions, no one in any country in the world is *legally* required to do anywhere near as much as this for anyone else. The class of exceptions is obvious. My main concern here is not the state of the law in respect to abortion, but it is worth drawing attention to the fact that in no state in this country is any man compelled by law to be even a Minimally Decent Samaritan to any person; there is no law under which charges could be brought against the thirty-eight who stood by while Kitty Genovese died. By contrast, in most states in this country women are compelled by law to be not merely Minimally Decent Samaritans, but Good Samaritans to unborn persons inside them. This doesn't by itself settle anything one way or the other, because it may well be argued that there should be laws in this country—as there are in many European countries—compelling at least Minimally Decent Samaritanism. But it does show that there is a gross injustice in the existing state of the law. And it shows also that the groups currently working against liberalization of abortion laws, in fact working toward having it declared unconstitutional for a state to permit abortion, had better start working for the adoption of Good Samaritan laws generally, or earn the charge that they are acting in bad faith.

I should think, myself, that Minimally Decent Samaritan laws would be one thing, Good Samaritan laws quite another, and in fact highly improper. But we are not here concerned with the law. What we should ask is not whether anybody should be compelled by law to be a Good Samaritan, but whether we must accede to a situation in which somebody is being compelled—by nature, perhaps—to be a Good Samaritan. We have, in other words, to look now at third-party interventions. I have been arguing that no person is morally required to make large sacrifices to sustain the life of another who has no right to demand them, and this even where the sacrifices do not include life itself; we are not morally required to be Good Samaritans or anyway Very Good Samaritans to one another. But what if a man cannot extricate himself from such a situation? What if he appeals to us to extricate him? It seems to me plain that there are cases in which we can, cases in which a Good Samaritan would extricate him. There you are, you were kidnapped, and nine years in bed with that violinist lie ahead of you. You have your own life to lead. You are sorry, but you simply cannot see giving up so much of your life to the sustaining of his. You cannot extricate yourself, and ask us to do so. I should have thought that—in light of his having no right to the use of your body—it was obvious that we do not have to accede to your being forced to give up so much. We can do what you ask. There is no injustice to the violinist in our doing so.

7. Following the lead of the opponents of abortion, I have throughout been speaking of the fetus merely as a person, and what I have been asking is whether or not the argument we began with, which proceeds only from the fetus' being a person, really does establish its conclusion. I have argued that it does not.

But of course there are arguments and arguments, and it may be said that I have simply fastened on the wrong one. It may be said that what is important is not merely the fact that the fetus is a person, but that it is a person for whom the woman has a special kind of responsibility issuing from the fact that she is its mother. And it might be argued that all my analogies are therefore irrelevant—for you do not have that special kind of responsibility for that violinist, Henry Fonda does not have that special kind of responsibility for me. And our attention might be drawn to the fact that men and women both *are* compelled by law to provide support for their children.

I have in effect dealt (briefly) with this argument in section 4 above; but a (still briefer) recapitulation now may be in order. Surely we do not have any such "special responsibility" for a person unless we have assumed it, explicitly or implicitly. If a set of parents do not try to prevent pregnancy, do not obtain an abortion, and then at the time of birth of the child do not put it out for adoption, but rather take it home with them, then they have assumed responsibility for it, they have given it rights, and they cannot *now* withdraw support from it at the cost of its life because they now find it difficult to go on providing for it. But if they have taken all reasonable precautions against having a child, they do not simply by virtue of their biological relationship to the child who comes into existence have a special responsibility for it. They may wish to assume responsibility for it, or they may not wish to. And I am suggesting that if assuming responsibility for it would require large sacrifices, then they may refuse. A Good Samaritan would not refuse—or anyway, a Splendid Samaritan, if the sacrifices that had to be made were enormous. But then so would a Good

Samaritan assume responsibility for that violinist; so would Henry Fonda, if he is a Good Samaritan, fly in from the West Coast and assume responsibility for me.

8. My argument will be found unsatisfactory on two counts by many of those who want to regard abortion as morally permissible. First, while I do argue that abortion is not impermissible, I do not argue that it is always permissible. There may well be cases in which carrying the child to term requires only Minimally Decent Samaritanism of the mother, and this is a standard we must not fall below. I am inclined to think it a merit of my account precisely that it does *not* give a general yes or a general no. It allows for and supports our sense that, for example, a sick and desperately frightened fourteen-year-old schoolgirl, pregnant due to rape, may *of course* choose abortion, and that any law which rules this out is an insane law. And it also allows for and supports our sense that in other cases resort to abortion is even positively indecent. It would be indecent in the woman to request an abortion, and indecent in a doctor to perform it, if she is in her seventh month, and wants the abortion just to avoid the nuisance of postponing a trip abroad. The very fact that the arguments I have been drawing attention to treat all cases of abortion, or even all cases of abortion in which the mother's life is not at stake, as morally on a par ought to have made them suspect at the outset.

Secondly, while I am arguing for the permissibility of abortion in some cases, I am not arguing for the right to secure the death of the unborn child. It is easy to confuse these two things in that up to a certain point in the life of the fetus it is not able to survive outside the mother's body; hence removing it from her body guarantees its death. But they are importantly different. I have argued that you are not morally required to spend nine months in bed, sustaining the life of that violinist; but to say this is by no means to say that if, when you unplug yourself, there is a miracle and he survives, you then have a right to turn round and slit his throat. You may detach yourself even if this costs him his life; you have no right to be guaranteed his death, by some other means, if unplugging yourself does not kill him. There are some people who will feel dissatisfied by this feature of my argument. A woman may be utterly devastated by the thought of a child, a bit of herself, put out for adoption and never seen or heard of again. She may therefore want not merely that the child be detached from her, but more, that it die. Some opponents of abortion are inclined to regard this as beneath contempt—thereby showing insensitivity to what is surely a powerful source of despair.

All the same, I agree that the desire for the child's death is not one which anybody may gratify, should it turn out to be possible to detach the child alive.

At this place, however, it should be remembered that we have only been pretending throughout that the fetus is a human being from the moment of conception. A very early abortion is surely not the killing of a person, and so is not dealt with by anything I have said here.

CHAPTER 12

Will Cloning Harm People?

Gregory E. Pence

When Ian Wilmut and his colleagues in Scotland announced in 1997 that they had successfully cloned an adult sheep, everyone started thinking about human cloning, and there was an immediate clamor for laws— and even international treaties—to forbid it. Intellectuals produced some outlandish arguments to justify a prohibition. Will the clone have the same soul as the original? What is to stop rich people from cloning themselves? Do we want "rooms full of human clones, silently growing spare parts for the person from whom they had been copied"? It would be the worst thing in human history, said one critic; the people originated by cloning would be our slaves. Another added that such people might not be moral agents. All of these arguments had their intended effect; today, around 90% of Americans think that cloning is morally wrong.

But of course, cloning only reproduces a common occurrence in nature. A person who was conceived by cloning is the genetic duplicate of someone else, but so are monozygotic twins. No one thinks something terrible has happened when twins are born. The obvious question is this: If there is nothing bad about having twins "naturally," why should it be wrong to use cloning techniques to bring about the delayed birth of a twin? Gregory E. Pence, who teaches medical ethics at the University of Alabama at Birmingham, argues that it is not wrong.

The most important moral objection to originating a human by cloning is the claim that the resulting person may be unnecessarily harmed, either by something in the process of cloning or by the unique expectations placed upon the resulting child. This essay considers this kind of objection.

From Gregory E. Pence, "Will Cloning Harm People?" in *Flesh of My Flesh*, ed. Gregory E. Pence (Lanham, MD: Rowman & Littlefield, 1998). Reprinted by permission of Rowman & Littlefield.

By now the word "cloning" has so many bad associations from science fiction and political demagoguery that there is no longer any good reason to continue to use it. A more neutral phrase, meaning the same thing, is "somatic cell nuclear transfer" (SCNT), which refers to the process by which the genotype of an adult, differentiated cell can be used to create a new human embryo by transferring its nucleus to an enucleated human egg. The resulting embryo can then be gestated to create a baby who will be a delayed twin of its genetic ancestor.

For purposes of clarity and focus, I will only discuss the simple case where a couple wants to originate a single child by SCNT and not the cases of multiple origination of the same genotype. I will also not discuss questions of who would regulate reproduction of genotypes and processes of getting consent to reproduce genotypes.

Parallels with In Vitro Fertilization: Repeating History?

Any time a new method of human reproduction may occur, critics try to prevent it by citing possible harm to children. The implicit premise: before it is allowed, any new method must prove that only healthy children will be created. Without such proof, the new method amounts to "unconsented to" experimentation on the unborn. So argued the late conservative, Christian bioethicist Paul Ramsey in the early 1970s about in vitro fertilization (IVF).

Of course, ordinary sexual reproduction does not guarantee healthy children every time. Nor can a person consent until he is born. Nor can he really consent until he is old enough to understand consent. The requirement of "consent to be born" is silly.

Jeremy Rifkin, another critic of IVF in the early 1970s, seemed to demand that new forms of human reproduction be risk-free. Twenty years later, Rifkin predictably bolted out the gate to condemn human cloning, demanding its world-wide ban, with penalties for transgressions as severe as those for rape and murder: "It's a horrendous crime to make a Xerox of someone," he declared ominously. "You're putting a human into a genetic straitjacket. For the first time, we've taken the principles of industrial design—quality control, predictability—and applied them to a human being."

Daniel Callahan, a philosopher who had worked in the Catholic tradition and who founded the Hastings Center for research in medical ethics, argued in 1978 that the first case of IVF was "probably unethical" because there was no possible guarantee that Louise Brown would be normal. Callahan added that many medical breakthroughs are unethical because we cannot know (using the philosopher's strong sense of "know") that the first patient will not be harmed. Two decades later, he implied that human cloning would also be unethical: "We live in a culture that likes science and technology very much. If someone wants something, and the rest of us can't prove they are going to do devastating harm, they are going to do it."

Leon Kass, former chair of President George W. Bush's Council on Bioethics, argued strenuously in 1971 that babies created by artificial fertilization might be deformed: "It doesn't matter how many times the baby is tested while in the mother's womb," he averred, "they will never be certain the baby won't be born without defect."

What these critics overlooked is that no reasonable approach to life avoids all risks. Nothing in life is risk-free, including having children. Even if babies are born healthy, they do not always turn out as hoped. Taking such chances is part of becoming a parent.

Without some risk, there is no progress, no advance. Without risk, pioneers don't cross prairies, astronauts don't walk on the moon, and Freedom Riders don't take buses to integrate the South. The past critics of assisted reproduction demonstrated a psychologically normal but nevertheless unreasonable tendency to magnify the risk of a harmful but unlikely result. Such a result—even if very bad—still represents a very small risk. A baby born with a lethal genetic disease is an extremely bad but unlikely result; nevertheless, the risk shouldn't deter people from having children.

Humanity Will Not Be Harmed

Human SCNT is even more new and strange-sounding than in vitro fertilization (IVF). All that means is that it will take longer to get used to. Scaremongers have predicted terrible harm if children are born by SCNT, but in fact very little will change. Why is that?

First, to create a child by SCNT, a couple must use IVF, which is an expensive process, costing about $12,000 per attempt. Most American states do not require insurance companies to cover IVF, so IVF is mostly a cash-and-carry operation. Second, most IVF attempts are unsuccessful. The chances of any couple taking home a baby is quite low—only about 25%.

About 100,000 IVF babies have been born in America since the early 1980s. Suppose 50,000 such babies are born over the next decade. How many of these couples would want to originate a child by SCNT? Very few—at most, perhaps, a few hundred.

These figures are important because they tamp down many fears. As things now stand, originating humans by SCNT will never be common. Neither evolution nor old-fashioned human sex is in any way threatened. Nor is the family or human society. Most fears about human cloning stem from ignorance.

Similar fears linking cloning to dictatorship or the subjugation of women are equally ignorant. There are no artificial wombs (predictions, yes; realities, no—otherwise we could save premature babies born before 20 weeks). A healthy woman must agree to gestate any SCNT baby, and such a woman will retain her right to abort. Women's rights to abortion are checks on evil uses of any new reproductive technology.

New Things Make Us Fear
Harms Irrationally

SCNT isn't really so new or different. Consider some cases on a continuum. In the first, the human embryo naturally splits in the process of twinning and produces two genetically-identical twins. Mothers have been conceiving and gestating human twins for all of human history. Call the children who result from this process Rebecca and Susan.

In the second case a technique is used where a human embryo is deliberately twinned in order to create more embryos for implantation in a woman who has been infertile with her mate. Instead of a random quirk in the uterus, now a physician and an infertile couple use a tiny electric current to split the embryo. Two identical embryos are created. All embryos are implanted and, as sometimes happens, rather than no embryo implanting successfully or only one, both embryos implant. Again, Rebecca and Susan are born.

In the third case, one of the twinned embryos is frozen (Susan) along with other embryos from the couple and the other embryo is implanted. In this case, although several embryos were implanted, only the one destined to be Rebecca is successful. Again, Rebecca is born.

Two years pass, and the couple desires another child. Some of their frozen embryos are thawed and implanted in the mother. The couple knows that one of the implanted embryos is the twin of Rebecca. In this second round of reproductive assistance, the embryo destined to be Susan successfully implants and a twin is born. Now Susan and Rebecca exist as twins, but born two years apart. Susan is the delayed twin of Rebecca. (Rumors abound that such births have already occurred in American infertility clinics.)

Suppose now that the "embryo that could become Susan" was twinned, and the "non-Susan" embryo is frozen. The rest of the details are then the same as the last scenario, but now two more years pass and the previously-frozen embryo is now implanted, gestated, and born. Susan and Rebecca now have another identical sister, Samantha. They would be identical triplets, born two and four years apart. In contrast to SCNT, where the mother's contribution of mitochondrial genes introduces small variations in nearly-identical genotypes, these embryos would have identical genomes.

Next, suppose that the embryo that could have been Rebecca miscarried and never became a child. The twinned embryo that could become Susan still exists. So the parents implant this embryo and Susan is born. Query to National Bioethics Advisory Commission: have the parents done something illegal? A child has been born who was originated by reproducing an embryo with a unique genotype. Remember, the embryo-that-could-become Rebecca existed first. So Susan only exists as a "clone" of the non-existent Rebecca.

Now, as bioethicist Leroy Walters emphasizes, let us consider an even thornier but more probable scenario. Suppose we took the embryo-that-could-become Susan and transferred its nucleus to an enucleated egg of Susan's mother. Call the person who will emerge from this embryo "Suzette," because she is like Susan but different, because of her new mitochondrial DNA. Although the "Susan" embryo was created sexually, Suzette's origins are through somatic cell nuclear transfer. It is not clear that this process is illegal. The NBAC *Report* avoids taking a stand on this kind of case.

Now compare all the above cases to originating Susan asexually by SCNT from the genotype of the adult Rebecca. Susan would again have a nearly-identical genome with Rebecca (identical except for mitochondrial DNA contributed by the gestating woman). Here we have nearly identical female genotypes, separated in time, created by choice. But how is this so different from choosing to have a delayed twin-child? Originating a child by SCNT is not a breakthrough in kind but a matter of degree along a continuum involving twins and a special kind of reproductive choice.

Comparing the Harms
of Human Reproduction

The question of multiple copies of one genome and its special issues of harm are ones that will not be discussed in this essay, but one asymmetry in our moral intuitions should be noticed.

The increasing use of fertility drugs has expanded many times the number of humans born who are twins, triplets, quadruplets, quintuplets, sextuplets, and even (in November of 1997 to the McCaugheys of Iowa) septuplets. If an entire country can rejoice about seven humans who are gestated in the same womb, raised by the same parents, and simultaneously created randomly from the same two sets of chromosomes, why should the same country fear deliberately originating copies of the same genome, either at once or over time? Our intuitions are even more skewed when we rejoice in the statistically-unlikely case of the seven healthy McCaughey children and ignore the far more likely cases where several of the multiply-gestated fetuses are disabled or dead.

People exaggerate the fears of the unknown and downplay the very real dangers of the familiar. In a very important sense, driving a car each day is far more dangerous to children than the new form of human reproduction under discussion here. Many, many people are hurt and killed every day in automobile wrecks, yet few people consider not driving.

In SCNT, there are possible dangers of telomere shortening, inheritance of environmental effects on adult cells passed to embryonic cells, and possible unknown dangers. Mammalian animal studies must determine if such dangers will occur in human SCNT origination. Once such studies prove that there are no special dangers of SCNT, the crucial question will arise: how safe must we expect human SCNT to be before we allow it?

In answering this question, it is very important to ask about the baseline of comparison. How safe is ordinary, human sexual reproduction? How safe is assisted reproduction? Who or what counts as a subject of a safety calculation about SCNT?

At least 40% of human embryos fail to implant in normal sexual reproduction. Although this fact is not widely known, it is important because some discussions tend to assume that every human embryo becomes a human baby unless some extraordinary event occurs such as abortion. But this is not true. Nature seems to have a genetic filter, such that malformed embryos do not implant. About 50% of the rejected embryos are chromosomally abnormal, meaning that if they were somehow brought to term, the resulting children would be mutants or suffer genetic dysfunction.

A widely-reported but misleading aspect of Ian Wilmut's work was that it took 277 embryos to produce one live lamb. In fact, Wilmut started with 277 eggs, fused nuclei with them to create embryos, and then allowed them to become the best 29 embryos, which were allowed to gestate further. He had three lambs almost live, with one true success, Dolly. Subsequent work may easily bring the efficiency rate to 25%. When the calves "Charlie" and "George" were born in 1998, four live-born calves were created from an initial batch of only 50 embryos.

Wilmut's embryo-to-birth ratio only seems inefficient or unsafe because the real inefficiency rate of accepted forms of human assisted reproduction is so little known. In in vitro fertilization, a woman is given drugs to stimulate superovulation so that physicians can remove as many eggs as possible. Previously, several embryos were implanted during each cycle. Many couples attempt IVF three times, so each couple may use nine or more embryos. (Today, in 2006, most clinics implant no more than two embryos at a time.) As noted, only about 25% of couples undergoing such attempts ever take home a baby.

Consider what these numbers mean when writ large. Take 100 couples attempting assisted reproduction, each undergoing (on average) three attempts. Suppose there are unusually good results and that 30% of these couples eventually take home a baby. Because more than one embryo may implant, assume that among these 30 couples, half have non-identical twins. But what is the efficiency rate here? Assuming a low number of three embryos implanted each time for the 300 attempts, it will take 900 embryos to produce 45 babies, for an efficiency rate of 1 in 20.

Nor is it true that all the loss of human potential occurred at the embryonic stage. Unfortunately, some of these pregnancies will end in miscarriages of fetuses, some well along in the second trimester.

Nevertheless, such loss of embryos and fetuses is almost universally accepted as morally permissible. Why is that? Because the infertile parents are trying to conceive their own children, because everyone thinks that is a good motive, and because few people object to the loss of embryos and fetuses *in this context of trying to conceive babies*. Seen in this light, what Wilmut did, starting out with a large number of embryos to get one successful lamb at birth, is not so novel or different from what now occurs in human assisted reproduction.

Subjects and Nonsubjects of Harm

One premise that seems to figure in discussions of the safety of SCNT and other forms of assisted reproduction is that loss of human embryos morally matters. That premise should be rejected.

As the above discussion shows, loss of human embryos is a normal part of human conception and, without this process, humanity might suffer much more genetic disease. This process essentially involves the loss of human embryos as part of the natural state of things. Indeed, some researchers believe that for every human baby successfully born, there has been at least one human embryo lost along the way.

In vitro fertilization is widely-accepted as a great success in modern medicine. As said, over 100,000 American babies have been born this way. But calculations indicate that as many as a million human embryos may have been used in creating such successes.

Researchers often create embryos for subsequent cycles of implantation, only to learn that a pregnancy has been achieved and that such stored embryos are no longer needed. Thousands of such embryos can be stored indefinitely in liquid nitrogen. No one feels any great urgency about them and, indeed, many couples decline to pay fees to preserve their embryos.

The above considerations point to the obvious philosophical point that embryos are not persons with rights to life. Like an acorn, their value is all potential, little actual. Faced with a choice between paying a thousand dollars to keep two thousand embryos alive for a year in storage, or paying for an operation to keep a family pet alive for another year, no one will choose to pay for the embryos. How people actually act says much about their real values.

Thus an embryo cannot be harmed by being brought into existence and then being taken out of existence. An embryo is generally considered such until nine weeks after conception, when it is called a "fetus" (when it is born, it is called a "baby"). Embryos are not sentient and cannot experience pain. They are thus not the kind of subjects that can be harmed or benefitted.

As such, whether it takes one embryo to create a human baby or a hundred does not matter morally. It may matter aesthetically, financially, emotionally, or in time spent trying to reproduce, but it does not matter morally. As such, new forms of human reproduction such as IVF and SCNT that involve significant loss of embryos cannot be morally criticized on this charge.

Finally, because embryos don't count morally, they could be tested in various ways to eliminate defects in development or genetic mishaps. Certainly, if four or five SCNT embryos were implanted, only the healthiest one should be brought to term. As such, the risk of abnormal SCNT babies could be minimized. . . .

Psychological Harm to the Child

Another concern is about psychological harm to a child originated by SCNT. According to this objection, choosing to have a child is not like choosing a car or house. It is a moral decision because another being is affected. Having a child should be a careful, responsible choice and focused on what's best for the child. Having a child originated by SCNT is not morally permissible because it is not best for the child.

The problem with this argument is the last six words of the last sentence, which assumes bad motives on the part of parents. Unfortunately, SCNT is associated with bad motives in science fiction, but until we have evidence that it will be used this way, why assume the worst about people?

Certainly, if someone deliberately brought a child into the world with the intention of causing him harm, that would be immoral. Unfortunately, the concept of harm is a continuum and some people have very high standards, such that not providing a child a stay-at-home parent constitutes harming the child. But there is nothing about SCNT per se that is necessarily linked to bad motives. True, people would have certain expectations of a child created by SCNT, but parents-to-be already have certain expectations about children.

Too many parents are fatalistic and just accept whatever life throws at them. The very fact of being a parent for many people is something they must accept (because abortion was not a real option). Part of this acceptance is to just accept whatever genetic combination comes at birth from the random assortment of genes.

But why is such acceptance a good thing? It is a defeatist attitude in medicine against disease; it is a defeatist attitude toward survival when one's culture or country is under attack; and it is a defeatist attitude toward life in general. "The expectations of parents will be too high!" critics repeat. "Better to leave parents in ignorance and to leave their children as randomness decrees." The silliness of that view is apparent as soon as it is made explicit.

If we are thinking about harm to the child, an objection that comes up repeatedly might be called the argument for an open future.

"In the case of cloning," it is objected, "the expectations are very specifically tied to the life of another person. So in a sense, the child's future is denied to him because he will be expected to be like his ancestor. But part of the wonder of having children is surprise at how they turn out. As such, some indeterminacy should remain a part of childhood. Human SCNT deprives a person of an open future because when we know how his previous twin lived, we will know how the new child will live."

It is true that the adults choosing this genotype rather than that one must have some expectations. There has to be some reason for choosing one genotype over another. But these expectations are only half based in fact. As we know, no person originated by SCNT will be identical to his ancestor because of mitochondrial DNA, because of his different gestation, because of his different parents, because of his different time in history, and perhaps, because of his different country and culture. Several famous pairs of conjoined twins, such as Eng and Chang, with both identical genotypes and identical uterine/childhood environments, have still had different personalities. To assume that a SCNT child's future is not open is to assume genetic reductionism.

Moreover, insofar as parents have specific expectations about children created by SCNT, such expectations will likely be no better or worse than the normal expectations by parents of children created sexually. As said, there is nothing about SCNT per se that necessitates bad motives on the part of parents.

Notice that most of the expected harm to the child stems *from the predicted, prejudicial attitudes of other people to the SCNT child.* ("Would you want to be a cloned child? Can you imagine being called a freak and having only one genetic parent?") As such, it is important to remember that social expectations are *merely* social expectations. They are malleable and can change quickly. True, parents might initially have expectations that are too high and other people might regard such children with prejudice. But just as such inappropriate attitudes faded after the first cases of in vitro fertilization, they will fade here too.

Ron James, the Scottish millionaire who funded much of Ian Wilmut's research, points out that social attitudes change fast. Before the announcement of Dolly, polls showed that people thought that cloning animals and gene transfer to animals were "morally problematic," whereas germ-line gene therapy fell in the category of "just wrong." Two months after the announcement of Dolly, and after much discussion of human cloning, people's attitudes had shifted to seeing as morally permissible both animal cloning and gene transfer in humans, whereas germ-line gene therapy had shifted to being merely "morally problematic."

James Watson, the co-discoverer of the double helix, once opposed in vitro fertilization by claiming that prejudicial attitudes of other people would harm children created this way. The prejudice was really in Watson, because the way that he was stirring up fear was doing more to create the prejudice than any normal human reaction. Similarly, Leon Kass's long essay in *The New Republic,* where he calls human asexual reproduction "repugnant" and a "horror," creates exactly the kind of prejudiced reaction that he predicts. Rather than make a priori, self-fulfilling prophecies, wouldn't it be better to be empirical about such matters? To be more optimistic about the reactions of ordinary parents?

Children created by SCNT would not *look* any different from other children. Nobody at age two looks like he does at age 45 and, except for his parents, nobody knows what the 45-year-old man looked like at age two. And since ordinary children often look like their parents, no one would be able to tell a SCNT child from others until he had lived a decade.

Kass claims that a child originated by SCNT will have "a troubled psychic identity" because he or she will be "utterly" confused about his social, genetic, and kinship ties. At worst, this child will be like a child of "incest" and may, if originated as a male from the father, have the same sexual feelings towards the wife as the father. An older male might in turn have strong sexual feelings toward a young female with his wife's genome.

Yet if this were so, any husband of any married twin might have an equally troubled psychic identity because he might have the same sexual feelings toward the twin as his wife. Instead, those in relationships with twins claim that the individuals are very different.

Much of the above line of criticism simply begs the question and assumes that humans created by SCNT will be greeted by stigma or experience confusion. It is hard to understand why, once one gets beyond the novelty, because a child created asexually would know *exactly* who his ancestor was. No confusion there. True, prejudicial expectations could damage children, but why make public policy based on that?

Besides, isn't this kind of argument hypocritical in our present society? Where no one is making any serious effort to ban divorce, despite the overwhelming evidence that divorce seriously damages children, even teenage children. It is always far easier to concentrate on the dramatic, far-off harm than the ones close-at-hand. When we are really concerned about minimizing harm to children, we will pass laws requiring all parents wanting to divorce to go through counseling sessions or to wait a year. We will pass a federal law compelling child-support from fathers who flee to other states, and make it impossible to renew a professional license or get paid in a public institution in another state until all child-support is paid. After that is done, then we can non-hypocritically talk about how much our society cares about not harming children who may be originated in new ways.

In conclusion, the predicted harms of SCNT to humans are wildly exaggerated, lack a comparative baseline, stem from irrational fears of the unknown, overlook greater dangers of familiar things, and are often based on the armchair psychological speculation of amateurs. Once studies prove SCNT as safe as normal sexual reproduction in non-human mammals, the harm objection will disappear. Given other arguments that SCNT could substantially benefit many children, the argument that SCNT would harm children is a weak one that needs to be weighed against its many potential benefits.

CHAPTER 13

Is Homosexuality Unnatural?

Burton M. Leiser

Western attitudes toward homosexuality have been shaped largely by Christianity; and within the Christian tradition, homosexuality has been condemned time and again. Saint Paul declared that "idolaters, thieves, homosexuals, drunkards, and robbers" cannot inherit the Kingdom of God. But why? What is so bad about them? Subsequent theologians decided it was because homosexuality is *unnatural,* and this concept became the key term in the debate. Saint Thomas Aquinas held that morality is a matter of acting in accordance with "the laws of nature," and he cited "unisexual lust" as a particularly noxious "sin against nature" (see selection 5).

Today there are only four countries in the world where gay marriage is legal: Belgium, Canada, The Netherlands, and Spain. In the United States, gay marriage is legal only in Massachusetts, while six states allow same-sex civil unions. When people debate the merits of gay marriage, their opinions are often shaped by whether they think that homosexuality, in general, is unnatural and therefore wrong.

Burton M. Leiser is a professor of philosophy at Pace University in New York. In the following selection, he discusses the claim that gay sex is "unnatural." As he points out, this term can have several different meanings, and it is important to distinguish them in order to assess the traditional argument against homosexuality.

Theologians and other moralists have said homosexual acts violate the "natural law," and that they are therefore immoral and ought to be prohibited by the state.

From Burton M. Leiser, *Liberty, Justice, and Morals: Contemporary Value Conflicts,* 3rd ed., pp. 51–57, © 1986. Reprinted by permission of Prentice-Hall, Inc., Upper Saddle River, NJ.

The word *nature* has a built-in ambiguity that can lead to serious misunderstandings. When something is said to be "natural" or in conformity with "natural law" or the "law of nature," this may mean either (1) that it is in conformity with the descriptive laws of nature, or (2) that it is not artificial, that man has not imposed his will or his devices upon events or conditions as they exist or would have existed without such interference.

1. *The descriptive laws of nature.* The laws of nature, as these are understood by the scientist, differ from the laws of man. The former are purely descriptive, where the latter are prescriptive. When a scientist says that water boils at 212° Fahrenheit or that the volume of a gas varies directly with the heat that is applied to it and inversely with the pressure, he means merely that as a matter of recorded and observable fact, pure water under standard conditions always boils at precisely 212° Fahrenheit and that as a matter of observed fact, the volume of a gas rises as it is heated and falls as pressure is applied to it. These "laws" merely *describe* the manner in which physical substances *actually behave.* They differ from municipal and federal laws in that they *do not prescribe behavior.* Unlike man-made laws, natural laws are not passed by any legislator or group of legislators; they are not proclaimed or announced; they impose no obligation upon anyone or anything; their violation entails no penalty, and there is no reward for following them or abiding by them. When a scientist says that the air in a tire obeys the laws of nature that govern gases, he does *not* mean that the air, having been informed that it *ought* to behave in a certain way, behaves appropriately under the right conditions. He means, rather, that as a matter of fact, the air in a tire *will* behave like all other gases. In saying that Boyle's law governs the behavior of gases, he means merely that gases do, as a matter of fact, behave in accordance with Boyle's law, and that Boyle's law enables one to predict accurately what will happen to a given quantity of a gas as its pressure is raised; he does *not* mean to suggest that some heavenly voice has proclaimed that all gases should henceforth behave in accordance with the terms of Boyle's law and that a ghostly policeman patrols the world, ready to mete out punishments to any gases that violate the heavenly decree. In fact, according to the scientist, it does not make sense to speak of a natural law being violated. For if there were a true exception to a so-called law of nature, the exception would require a change in the description of those phenomena, and the law would have been shown to be no law at all. The laws of nature are revised as scientists discover new phenomena that require new refinements in their descriptions of the way things actually happen. In this respect they differ fundamentally from human laws, which are revised periodically by legislators who are not so interested in *describing* human behavior as they are in *prescribing* what human behavior *should* be.

2. *The artificial as a form of the unnatural.* On occasion when we say that something is not natural, we mean that it is a product of human artifice. A typewriter is not a natural object, in this sense, for the substances of which it is composed have been removed from their natural state— the state in which they existed before men came along—and have been transformed by a series of chemical and physical and mechanical processes into other substances. They have been rearranged into a whole that is quite different from anything found in nature. In short, a typewriter is an artificial object. In this sense, clothing is not natural, for it has been transformed considerably from the state in which it was found in nature; and wearing clothing is also not natural, in this sense, for in one's natural state, before the application of anything artificial, before any human interference with things as they are, one is quite naked. Human laws, being artificial conventions designed to exercise a degree of control over the natural inclinations and propensities of men, may in this sense be considered to be unnatural.

When theologians and moralists speak of homosexuality, contraception, abortion, and other forms of human behavior as being unnatural and say that for that reason such behavior must be considered to be wrong, in what sense are they using the word *unnatural?* Are they saying that homosexual behavior and the use of contraceptives are contrary to the scientific laws of nature, are they saying that they are artificial forms of behavior, or are they using the terms *natural* and *unnatural* in some third sense?

They cannot mean that homosexual behavior (to stick to the subject presently under discussion) violates the laws of nature in the first sense, for, as has been pointed out, in *that* sense it is impossible to violate the laws of nature. Those laws, being merely descriptive of what actually does happen, would have to *include* homosexual behavior if such behavior does actually take place. Even if the defenders of the theological view that homosexuality is unnatural were to appeal to a statistical analysis by pointing out that such behavior is not normal from a statistical point of view, and therefore not what the laws of nature require, it would be open to their critics to reply that any descriptive law of nature must account for and incorporate all statistical deviations, and that the laws of nature, in this sense, do not *require* anything. These critics might also note that the best statistics available reveal that about half of all American males engage in homosexual activity at some time in their lives, and that a very large percentage of American males have exclusively homosexual relations for a fairly extensive period of time; from which it would follow that such behavior is natural, for them, at any rate, in this sense of the word *natural*.

If those who say that homosexual behavior is unnatural are using the term *unnatural* in the second sense as artificial, it is difficult to understand their objection. That which is artificial is often far better than what is natural. Artificial homes seem, at any rate, to be more suited to human habitation and more conducive to longer life and better health than are caves and other natural shelters. There are distinct advantages to the use of such unnatural (artificial) amenities as clothes, furniture, and books. Although we may dream of an idyllic return to nature in our more wistful moments, we would soon discover, as Thoreau did in his attempt to escape from the artificiality of civilization, that needles and thread, knives and matches, ploughs and nails, and countless other products of human artifice are essential to human life. We would discover, as Plato pointed out in the *Republic*, that no man can be truly self-sufficient. Some of the by-products of industry are less than desirable, but neither industry nor the products of industry are intrinsically evil, even though both are unnatural in this sense of the word.

Interference with nature is not evil in itself. Nature, as some writers have put it, must be tamed. In some respects man must look upon it as an enemy to be conquered. If nature were left to its own devices, without the intervention of human artifice, men would be consumed by disease, they would be plagued by insects, they would be chained to the places where they were born with no means of swift communication or transport, and they would suffer the discomforts and the torments of wind and weather and flood and fire with no practical means of combating any of them. Interfering with nature, doing battle with nature, using human will and reason and skill to thwart what might otherwise follow from the conditions that prevail in the world is a peculiarly human enterprise, one that can hardly be condemned merely because it does what is not natural.

Homosexual behavior can hardly be considered to be unnatural in this sense. There is nothing artificial about such behavior. On the contrary, it is quite natural, in this sense, to those who engage in it. And even if it were not, even if it were quite artificial, this is not in itself a ground for condemning it.

It would seem, then, that those who condemn homosexuality as an unnatural form of behavior must mean something else by the word *unnatural,* something not covered by either of the preceding definitions. A third possibility is this:

3. *Anything uncommon or abnormal is unnatural.* If this is what is meant by those who condemn homosexuality on the ground that it is unnatural, it is quite obvious that their condemnation cannot be accepted without further argument. The fact that a given form of behavior is uncommon provides no justification for condemning it. Playing viola in a string quartet may be an uncommon form of human behavior. Yet there is no reason to suppose that such uncommon behavior is, by virtue of its uncommonness, deserving of condemnation or ethically or morally wrong. On the contrary, many forms of behavior are praised precisely because they are so uncommon. Great artists, poets, musicians, and scientists are uncommon in this sense; but clearly the world is better off for having them, and it would be absurd to condemn them or their activities for their failure to be common and normal. If homosexual behavior is wrong, then, it must be for some reason other than its unnaturalness in this sense of the word.

4. *Any use of an organ or an instrument that is contrary to its principal purpose or function is unnatural.* Every organ and every instrument—perhaps even every creature—has a function to perform, one for which it is particularly designed. Any use of those instruments and organs that is consonant with their purposes is natural and proper, but any use that is inconsistent with their principal functions is unnatural and improper, and to that extent, evil or harmful. Human teeth, for example, are admirably designed for their principal functions—biting and chewing the kinds of food suitable for human consumption. But they are not particularly well suited for prying the caps from beer bottles. If they are used for that purpose, which is not natural to them, they are likely to crack or break under the strain. The abuse of one's teeth leads to their destruction and to a consequent deterioration in one's overall health. If they are used only for their proper function, however, they may continue to serve well for many years. Similarly, a given drug may have a proper function. If used in the furtherance of that end, it can preserve life and restore health. But if it is abused and employed for purposes for which it was never intended, it may cause serious harm and even death. The natural uses of things are good and proper, but their unnatural uses are bad and harmful.

What we must do, then, is to find the proper use, or the true purpose, of each organ in our bodies. Once we have discovered that, we will know what constitutes the natural use of each organ and what constitutes an unnatural, abusive, and potentially harmful employment of the various parts of our bodies. If we are rational, we will be careful to confine behavior to the proper functions and to refrain from unnatural behavior. According to those philosophers who follow this line of reasoning, the way to discover the proper use of any organ is to determine what it is peculiarly suited to do. The eye is suited for seeing, the ear for hearing, the nerves for transmitting impulses from one part of the body to another, and so on.

What are the sex organs peculiarly suited to do? Obviously, they are peculiarly suited to enable men and women to reproduce their own kind. No other organ in the body is capable of fulfilling that function. It follows, according to those who follow the natural-law line, that the proper or natural function of the sex organs is reproduction, and that strictly speaking, any use of those organs for other purposes is unnatural, abusive, potentially harmful, and therefore wrong. The sex organs have been given to us in order to enable us to maintain the continued existence of mankind on this earth. All perversions—including masturbation, homosexual behavior, and heterosexual intercourse that deliberately frustrates the design of the sexual organs—are unnatural and bad. As Pope Pius XI once said, "Private individuals have no other power over the members of their bodies than that which pertains to their natural ends."

But the problem is not so easily resolved. Is it true that every organ has one and only one proper function? A hammer may have been designed to pound nails, and it may perform that particular job best. But it is not sinful to employ a hammer to crack nuts if you have no other more suitable tool immediately available. The hammer, being a relatively versatile tool, may be employed in a number of ways. It has no one proper or natural function. A woman's eyes are well adapted to seeing, it is true. But they seem also to be well adapted to flirting. Is a woman's use of her eyes for the latter purpose sinful merely because she is not using them, at that moment, for their "primary" purpose of seeing? Our sexual organs are uniquely adapted for procreation, but that is obviously not the only function for which they are adapted. Human beings may—and do—use those organs for a great many other purposes, and it is difficult to see why any *one* use should be considered to be the only proper one. The sex organs seem to be particularly well adapted to give their owners and others intense sensations of pleasure. Unless one believes that pleasure itself is bad, there seems to be little reason to believe that the use of the sex organs for the production of pleasure in oneself or in others is evil. In view of the peculiar design of these organs, with their great concentration of nerve endings, it would seem that they were designed (if they *were* designed) with that very goal in mind, and that their use for such purposes would be no more unnatural than their use for the purpose of procreation.

Nor should we overlook the fact that human sex organs may be and are used to express, in the deepest and most intimate way open to man, the love of one person for another. Even the most ardent opponents of "unfruitful" intercourse admit that sex does serve this function. They have accordingly conceded that a man and his wife may have intercourse even though she is pregnant, or past the age of child bearing, or in the infertile period of her menstrual cycle.

Human beings are remarkably complex and adaptable creatures. Neither they nor their organs can properly be compared to hammers or to other tools. The analogy quickly breaks down. The generalization that a given organ or instrument has one and only one proper function does not hold up, even with regard to the simplest manufactured tools, for, as we have seen, a tool may be used for more than one purpose—less effectively than one especially designed for a given task, perhaps, but properly and certainly not *sinfully*. A woman may use her eyes not only to see and to flirt, but also to earn money— if she is, for example, an actress or a model. Though neither of the latter functions seems to have been a part of the original design, if one may speak sensibly of *design* in this context, of the eye, it is difficult to see why such a use of the eyes of a woman should be considered sinful, perverse, or unnatural. Her sex organs have the unique capacity of producing ova and nurturing human embryos, under the right conditions; but why should any other use of those organs, including their use to bring pleasure to their owner or to someone else, or to manifest love to another person, or even, perhaps, to earn money, be regarded as perverse, sinful, or unnatural? Similarly, a man's sexual organs possess the unique capacity of causing the generation of another human being, but if a man chooses to use them for pleasure, or for the expression of love, or for some other purpose—so long as he does not interfere with the rights of some other person—the fact that his sex organs do have their unique capabilities does not constitute a convincing justification for condemning their other uses as being perverse, sinful, unnatural, or criminal. If a man "perverts" himself by wiggling his ears for the entertainment of his neighbors instead of using them exclusively for their "natural" function of hearing, no one thinks of consigning him to prison. If he abuses his teeth by using them to pull staples from memos—a function for which teeth were clearly not designed—he is not accused of being immoral, degraded, and degenerate. The fact that people *are* condemned for using their sex organs for their own pleasure or profit, or for that of others, may be more revealing about the prejudices and taboos of our society than it is about our perception of the true nature or purpose of our bodies.

In this connection, it may be worthwhile to note that with the development of artificial means of reproduction (that is, test tube babies), the sex organs may become obsolete for reproductive purposes but would still contribute greatly to human pleasure. In addition, studies of animal behavior and anthropological reports indicate that such nonreproductive sex acts as masturbation, homosexual intercourse, and mutual fondling of genital organs are widespread, both among human beings and among lower animals. Under suitable circumstances, many animals reverse their sex roles, males assuming the posture of females and presenting themselves to others for intercourse, and females mounting other females and going through all the actions of a male engaged in intercourse. Many peoples all around the world have sanctioned and even ritualized homosexual relations. It would seem that an excessive readiness to insist that human sex organs are designed only for reproductive purposes and therefore ought to be used only for such purposes must be based upon a very narrow conception that is conditioned by our own society's peculiar history and taboos.

To sum up, then, the proposition that any use of an organ that is contrary to its principal purpose or function is unnatural assumes that organs *have* a principal purpose or function, but this may be denied on the ground that the purpose or function of a given organ may vary according to the needs or desires of its owner. It may be denied on the ground that a given organ may have more than one principal purpose or function, and any attempt to call one use or another the only natural one seems to be arbitrary, if not question-begging. Also, the proposition suggests that what is unnatural is evil or depraved. This goes beyond the pure description of things, and enters into the problem of the evaluation of human behavior, which leads us to the fifth meaning of *natural.*

5. *That which is natural is good, and whatever is unnatural is bad.* When one condemns homosexuality or masturbation or the use of contraceptives on the ground that it is unnatural, one implies that whatever is unnatural is bad, wrongful, or perverse. But as we have seen, in some senses of the word, the unnatural (the artificial) is often very good, whereas that which is natural (that which has not been subjected to human artifice or improvement) may be very bad indeed. Of course, interference with nature may be bad. Ecologists have made us more aware than we have ever been of the dangers of unplanned and uninformed interference with nature. But this is not to say that *all* interference with nature is bad. Every time a man cuts down a tree to make room for a home for himself, or catches a fish to feed himself or his family, he is interfering with nature. If men did not interfere with nature, they would have no homes, they could eat no fish, and, in fact, they could not survive. What, then, can be meant by those who say that whatever is natural is good and whatever is unnatural is bad? Clearly, they cannot have intended merely to reduce the word *natural* to a synonym of *good, right,* and *proper,* and *unnatural* to a synonym of *evil, wrong, improper, corrupt,* and *depraved.* If that were all they had intended to do, there would be very little to discuss as to whether a given form of behavior might be proper even though it is not in strict conformity with someone's views of what is natural; for *good* and *natural* being synonyms, it would follow inevitably that whatever is good must be natural, and vice versa, by definition. This is certainly not what the opponents of homosexuality have been saying when they claim that homosexuality, being unnatural, is evil. For if it were, their claim would be quite empty. They would be saying merely that homosexuality, being evil, is evil—a redundancy that could as easily be reduced to the simpler assertion that homosexuality is evil. This assertion, however, is not an argument. Those who oppose homosexuality and other sexual "perversions" on the ground that they are "unnatural" are saying that there is some objectively identifiable quality in such behavior that is unnatural; and that that quality, once it has been identified by some kind of scientific observation, can be seen to be detrimental to those who engage in such behavior, or to those around them; and that *because* of the harm (physical, mental, moral, or spiritual) that results from engaging in any behavior possessing the attribute of unnaturalness, such behavior must be considered to be wrongful, and should be discouraged by society. "Unnaturalness" and "wrongfulness" are not synonyms, then, but different concepts. The problem with which we are wrestling is that we are unable to find a meaning for *unnatural* that enables us to arrive at the conclusion that homosexuality is unnatural or that if homosexuality is unnatural, it is therefore wrongful behavior. We have examined four common meanings of *natural* and *unnatural,* and have seen that none of them performs the task that it must perform if the advocates of this argument are to prevail.

CHAPTER 14

9/11 and Starvation

Mylan Engel, Jr.

Regrettable things, even tragic things, happen all the time. Which of these things do we choose to care about? This is a complicated question in the field of moral psychology. One fact is that people tend to care more about *concentrated* harms than *diffuse* harms. A traffic wreck involving 20 cars may grab our attention, while 10 separate wrecks, each involving 2 cars, may not. Also, people tend to care more about the striking and unpredictable than about the commonplace and familiar. An outbreak of the West Nile virus makes the news, but nobody notices as 36,000 Americans die each year from the flu.

Mylan Engel, Jr., is a professor of philosophy at Northern Illinois University.

You probably remember many of the tragic events of September 11, 2001. Nineteen terrorists hijacked four commercial airliners, crashing two of them into the World Trade Center towers, one into the Pentagon, and one in a field in Pennsylvania. Two thousand nine hundred and eighty-six innocent individuals died needlessly. People around the world stared at their televisions in horror and disbelief as the news media aired clips of the attack 'round the clock. The tragedy immediately roused President Bush to declare "War on terrorism." Volunteers from all across America traveled to New York at their own expense to aid in the rescue and clean-up efforts. Charitable contributions poured into the American Red Cross, which in turn wrote checks totaling $143.4 million in emergency aid (averaging $45,837 per family). The U.S. government put together a $5 billion relief package that will

Mylan Engel, Jr., "Taking Hunger Seriously," *Croatian Journal of Philosophy*, Vol. IV, No. 10, 2004. Reprinted by permission.

provide $1.6 million to each of the victim's families. The U.S. has spent billions more on its military efforts to root out Osama bin Laden and his al-Qaeda terrorist network. As the dust from the 9/11 attacks has finally settled, it is safe to say that Americans are now taking terrorism seriously.

Here are some of the tragic events that took place on 9/11 that you probably don't recall. On that infamous day, over 33,000 innocent children under the age of five died *senseless, needless* deaths—18,000 died from malnutrition and another 15,300 died of untreated poverty-related disease. It must be stressed that almost all of these deaths were *unnecessary*. They could have *easily been prevented*. The U.S. alone grows enough grain and soybeans to feed the world's human population several times over. Given this overabundance of food, the lives of those children who starved to death on 9/11 could have easily been saved, had we only diverted a relatively modest portion of this food to them. As for the disease-related deaths, nineteen percent of the 33,000 children who lost their lives on 9/11 died from the dehydrating effects of chronic diarrhea. Almost all of these 6,350 diarrheal dehydration deaths could have been prevented by administering each child a single packet of oral rehydration salts (cost per packet: 15 cents). Another nineteen percent of these children died from acute respiratory infections, most of whom could have been saved with a course of antibiotics (cost: 25 cents). Most of the 2,300 children who died from measles could have been saved with vitamin A therapy (cost per capsule: less than 10 cents). What makes the deaths of these children particularly tragic is that virtually all of them were readily preventable. They only occurred because otherwise good people did nothing to prevent them.

Despite the fact that the number of innocent children who died needlessly on 9/11 was ten times greater than the number of innocent people who lost their lives in the 9/11 terrorist attack, compassionate conservative President Bush did not declare war on hunger or on poverty. The U.S. Government did not immediately institute a multi-billion dollar relief package for the world's absolutely poor. People did not make out generous checks to famine relief organizations. The media did not so much as mention the tragedy of so many young innocent lives lost. And, as if 9/11 wasn't enough for us to deal with, on 9/12 another 33,000 innocent children under the age of five died unnecessarily, and another 33,000 on 9/13. In the twenty-two months that have transpired since the 9/11 tragedy, over 22 million innocent children under the age of five have died needlessly. By any objective measure, the tragedy of the 9/11 attack pales in comparison to the tragedy of world hunger and famine-related disease. Each year the latter claims 3,800 times more innocent lives than the 9/11 attack. Despite the magnitude of the tragedy of global hunger and childhood malnutrition, the overwhelming majority of affluent and moderately affluent people, including most philosophers, send no money to famine relief organizations. Of the 4 million people who receive solicitations from UNICEF each year, less than one percent donate anything at all. For most of us, world hunger doesn't even register a blip on our moral radar screens, much less present itself as a serious moral problem requiring action on our part. . . .

CHAPTER 15

The Singer Solution to World Poverty

Peter Singer

In 1972, a young Australian philosopher, Peter Singer, published an article titled "Famine, Affluence, and Morality" in the very first volume of *Philosophy and Public Affairs*. This new journal was part of a movement that changed philosophy. For most of the 20th century, moral philosophers had concentrated on abstract questions of ethical theory; they rarely wrote about practical issues. After 1970, however, "applied ethics" became a lively part of the subject, and Peter Singer became its best-known writer.

In "Famine, Affluence, and Morality," Singer argued that it is indefensible for affluent people to spend money on luxuries while the less fortunate are starving. If we can prevent something bad from happening, he said, without sacrificing anything of comparable moral importance, then we ought to do so. But death by starvation is bad; and we can prevent many people from dying of starvation by sacrificing our luxuries, which are not as important. Therefore, we ought to do so.

This simple argument caused quite a stir among moral philosophers. It seems to imply that we in the rich countries are leading immoral lives. Most of us find that hard to believe. The argument seems too demanding; it seems to require too much of us. Yet it is hard to refute.

In 1999, Singer moved to the United States to become DeCamp Professor of Bioethics at Princeton. By this time, his books on animal rights and bioethics had caused much controversy, and conservative groups protested his appointment. Articles and editorials appeared in the national press, most of them attacking Singer. At the height of the

From Peter Singer, "The Singer Solution to World Poverty," *The New York Times Magazine,* September 5, 1999. © Peter Singer, 1999.

debate, *The New York Times* invited Singer to explain his views about our duty to aid others, and he wrote the following article, which appeared in the *Times Magazine.*

In the Brazilian film *Central Station,* Dora is a retired schoolteacher who makes ends meet by sitting at the station writing letters for illiterate people. Suddenly she has an opportunity to pocket $1,000. All she has to do is persuade a homeless 9-year-old boy to follow her to an address she has been given. (She is told he will be adopted by wealthy foreigners.) She delivers the boy, gets the money, spends some of it on a television set, and settles down to enjoy her new acquisition. Her neighbor spoils the fun, however, by telling her that the boy was too old to be adopted—he will be killed and his organs sold for transplantation. Perhaps Dora knew this all along, but after her neighbor's plain speaking, she spends a troubled night. In the morning Dora resolves to take the boy back.

Suppose Dora had told her neighbor that it is a tough world, other people have nice new TVs too, and if selling the kid is the only way she can get one, well, he was only a street kid. She would then have become, in the eyes of the audience, a monster. She redeems herself only by being prepared to bear considerable risks to save the boy.

At the end of the movie, in cinemas in the affluent nations of the world, people who would have been quick to condemn Dora if she had not rescued the boy go home to places far more comfortable than her apartment. In fact, the average family in the United States spends almost one-third of its income on things that are no more necessary to them than Dora's new TV was to her. Going out to nice restaurants, buying new clothes because the old ones are no longer stylish, vacationing at beach resorts—so much of our income is spent on things not essential to the preservation of our lives and health. Donated to one of a number of charitable agencies, that money could mean the difference between life and death for children in need.

All of which raises a question: In the end, what is the ethical distinction between a Brazilian who sells a homeless child to organ peddlers and an American who already has a TV and upgrades to a better one—knowing that the money could be donated to an organization that would use it to save the lives of kids in need?

Of course, there are several differences between the two situations that could support different moral judgments about them. For one thing, to be able to consign a child to death when he is standing right in front of you takes a chilling kind of heartlessness; it is much easier to ignore an appeal for money to help children you will never meet. Yet for a utilitarian philosopher like myself—that is, one who judges whether acts are right or wrong by their consequences—if the upshot of the American's failure to donate the money is that one more kid dies on the streets of a Brazilian city, then it is, in some sense, just as bad as selling the kid to the organ peddlers. But one doesn't need to embrace my utilitarian ethic to see that, at the very least, there is a troubling incongruity in being so quick to condemn Dora for taking the child to the organ peddlers while, at the same time, not regarding the American consumer's behavior as raising a serious moral issue.

In his 1996 book, *Living High and Letting Die,* the New York University philosopher Peter Unger presented an ingenious series of imaginary examples designed to probe our intuitions about whether it is wrong to live well without giving substantial amounts of money to help people who are hungry, malnourished, or dying from easily treatable illnesses like diarrhea. Here's my paraphrase of one of these examples:

Bob is close to retirement. He has invested most of his savings in a very rare and valuable old car, a Bugatti, which he has not been able to insure. The Bugatti is his pride and joy. In addition to the pleasure he gets from driving and caring for his car, Bob knows that its rising market value means that he will always be able to sell it and live comfortably after retirement. One day when Bob is out for a drive, he parks the Bugatti near the end of a railway siding and goes for a walk up the track. As he does so, he sees that a runaway train, with no one aboard, is running down the railway track. Looking farther down the track, he sees the small figure of a child very likely to be killed by the runaway train. He can't stop the train and the child is too far away to warn of the danger, but he can throw a switch that will divert the train down the siding where his Bugatti is parked. Then nobody will be killed—but the train will destroy his Bugatti. Thinking of his joy in owning the car and the financial security it represents, Bob decides not to throw the switch. The child is killed. For many years to come, Bob enjoys owning his Bugatti and the financial security it represents.

Bob's conduct, most of us will immediately respond, was gravely wrong. Unger agrees. But then he reminds us that we, too, have opportunities to save the lives of children. We can give to organizations like UNICEF or Oxfam America. How much would we have to give one of these organizations to have a high probability of saving the life of a child threatened by easily preventable diseases? (I do not believe that children are more worth saving than adults, but since no one can argue that children have brought their poverty on themselves, focusing on them simplifies the issues.) Unger called up some experts and used the information they provided to offer some plausible estimates that include the cost of raising money, administrative expenses, and the cost of delivering aid where it is most needed. By his calculation, $200 in donations would help transform a sickly 2-year-old into a healthy 6-year-old—offering safe passage through childhood's most dangerous years. To show how practical philosophical argument can be, Unger even tells his readers that they can easily donate funds by using their credit card and calling one of these toll-free numbers: (800) 367-5437 for UNICEF; (800) 693-2687 for Oxfam America.

Now you, too, have the information you need to save a child's life. How should you judge yourself if you don't do it? Think again about Bob and his Bugatti. Unlike Dora, Bob did not have to look into the eyes of the child he was sacrificing for his own material comfort. The child was a complete stranger to him and too far away to relate to in an intimate, personal way. Unlike Dora, too, he did not mislead the child or initiate the chain of events imperiling him. In all these respects, Bob's situation resembles that of people able but unwilling to donate to overseas aid and differs from Dora's situation.

If you still think that it was very wrong of Bob not to throw the switch that would have diverted the train and saved the child's life, then it is hard to see how you could deny that it is also very wrong not to send money to one of the organizations listed above. Unless, that is, there is some morally important difference between the two situations that I have overlooked.

Is it the practical uncertainties about whether aid will really reach the people who need it? Nobody who knows the world of overseas aid can doubt that such uncertainties exist. But Unger's figure of $200 to save a child's life was reached after he had made conservative assumptions about the proportion of the money donated that will actually reach its target.

One genuine difference between Bob and those who can afford to donate to overseas aid organizations but don't is that only Bob can save the child on the tracks, whereas there are hundreds of millions of people who can give $200 to overseas aid organizations. The problem is that most of them aren't doing it. Does this mean that it is all right for you not to do it?

Suppose that there were more owners of priceless vintage cars—Carol, Dave, Emma, Fred, and so on, down to Ziggy—all in exactly the same situation as Bob, with their own siding and their own switch, all sacrificing the child in order to preserve their own cherished car. Would that make it all right for Bob to do the same? To answer this question affirmatively is to endorse follow-the-crowd ethics—the kind of ethics that led many Germans to look away when the Nazi atrocities were being committed. We do not excuse them because others were behaving no better.

We seem to lack a sound basis for drawing a clear moral line between Bob's situation and that of any reader of this article with $200 to spare who does not donate it to an overseas aid agency. These readers seem to be acting at least as badly as Bob was acting when he chose to let the runaway train hurtle toward the unsuspecting child. In the light of this conclusion, I trust that many readers will reach for the phone and donate that $200. Perhaps you should do it before reading further.

Now that you have distinguished yourself morally from people who put their vintage cars ahead of a child's life, how about treating yourself and your partner to dinner at your favorite restaurant? But wait. The money you will spend at the restaurant could also help save the lives of children overseas! True, you weren't planning to blow $200 tonight, but if you were to give up dining out just for one month, you would easily save that amount. And what is one month's dining out, compared with a child's life? There's the rub. Since there are a lot of desperately needy children in the world, there will always be another child whose life you could save for another $200. Are you therefore obliged to keep giving until you have nothing left? At what point can you stop?

Hypothetical examples can easily become farcical. Consider Bob. How far past losing the Bugatti should he go? Imagine that Bob had got his foot stuck in the track of the siding, and if he diverted the train, then before it rammed the car it would also amputate his big toe. Should he still throw the switch? What if it would amputate his foot? His entire leg?

As absurd as the Bugatti scenario gets when pushed to extremes, the point it raises is a serious one: only when the sacrifices become very significant indeed would most people be prepared to say that Bob does nothing wrong when he decides not to throw the switch. Of course, most people could be wrong; we can't decide moral issues by taking opinion polls. But consider for yourself the level of sacrifice that you would demand of Bob, and then think about how much money you would have to give away in order to make a sacrifice that is roughly equal to that. It's almost certainly much, much more than $200. For most middle-class Americans, it could easily be more like $200,000.

Isn't it counterproductive to ask people to do so much? Don't we run the risk that many will shrug their shoulders and say that morality, so conceived, is fine for saints but not for them? I accept that we are unlikely to see, in the near or even medium-term future, a world in which it is normal for wealthy Americans to give the bulk of their wealth to strangers. When it comes to praising or blaming people for what they do, we tend to use a standard that is relative to some conception of normal behavior. Comfortably off Americans who give, say, 10 percent of their income to overseas aid organizations are so far ahead of most of their equally comfortable fellow citizens that I wouldn't go out of my way to chastise them for not doing more. Nevertheless, they should be doing much more, and they are in no position to criticize Bob for failing to make the much greater sacrifice of his Bugatti.

At this point various objections may crop up. Someone may say: "If every citizen living in the affluent nations contributed his or her share, I wouldn't have to make such a drastic sacrifice, because long before such levels were reached, the resources would have been there to save the lives of all those children dying from lack of food or medical care. So why should I give more than my fair share?" Another, related objection is that the government ought to increase its overseas aid allocations, since that would spread the burden more equitably across all taxpayers.

Yet the question of how much we ought to give is a matter to be decided in the real world—and that, sadly, is a world in which we know that most people do not, and in the immediate future will not, give substantial amounts to overseas aid agencies. We know, too, that at least in the next year, the United States government is not going to meet even the very modest target, recommended by the United Nations, of 0.7 percent of gross national product; at the moment it lags far below that, at 0.09 percent, not even half of Japan's 0.22 percent or a tenth of Denmark's 0.97 percent. Thus, we know that the money we can give beyond that theoretical "fair share" is still going to save lives that would otherwise be lost. While the idea that no one need do more than his or her fair share is a powerful one, should it prevail if we know that others are not doing their fair share and that children will die preventable deaths unless we do more than our fair share? That would be taking fairness too far.

Thus, this ground for limiting how much we ought to give also fails. In the world as it is now, I can see no escape from the conclusion that each one of us with wealth surplus to his or her essential needs should be giving most of it to help people suffering from poverty so dire as to be life-threatening. That's right: I'm saying that you shouldn't buy that new car, take that cruise, redecorate the house, or get that pricey new suit. After all, a $1,000 suit could save five children's lives.

So how does my philosophy break down in dollars and cents? An American household with an income of $50,000 spends around $30,000 annually on necessities, according to the Conference Board, a nonprofit economic research organization. Therefore, for a household bringing in $50,000 a year, donations to help the world's poor should be as close as possible to $20,000. The $30,000 required for necessities holds for higher incomes as well. So a household making $100,000 could write a yearly check for $70,000. Again, the formula is simple: whatever money you're spending on luxuries, not necessities, should be given away.

Now, evolutionary psychologists tell us that human nature just isn't sufficiently altruistic to make it plausible that many people will sacrifice so much for strangers. On the facts of human nature, they might be right, but they would be wrong to draw a moral conclusion from those facts. If it is the case that we ought to do things that, predictably, most of us won't do, then let's face that fact head-on. Then, if we value the life of a child more than going to fancy restaurants, the next time we dine out we will know that we could have done something better with our money. If that makes living a morally decent life extremely arduous, well, then that is the way things are. If we don't do it, then we should at least know that we are failing to live a morally decent life— not because it is good to wallow in guilt but because knowing where we should be going is the first step toward heading in that direction.

When Bob first grasped the dilemma that faced him as he stood by that railway switch, he must have thought how extraordinarily unlucky he was to be placed in a situation in which he must choose between the life of an innocent child and the sacrifice of most of his savings. But he was not unlucky at all. We are all in that situation.

CHAPTER 16

Utilitarianism and Integrity

Bernard Williams

Utilitarianism is the theory that we should always try to bring about as much happiness as possible. It is hard to argue with the value of being happy, but critics are quick to point out that we value many things in addition to happiness.

Sir Bernard Williams (1929–2003), one of the great critics of utilitarianism, held professorships at both Cambridge University and Oxford University. In this selection, he considers two difficult test cases for the utilitarian theory.

(1) George, who has just taken his Ph.D. in chemistry, finds it extremely difficult to get a job. He is not very robust in health, which cuts down the number of jobs he might be able to do satisfactorily. His wife has to go out to work to support them, which itself causes a great deal of strain, since they have small children and there are severe problems about looking after them. The results of all this, especially on the children, are damaging. An older chemist, who knows about this situation, says that he can get George a decently paid job in a certain laboratory, which pursues research into chemical and biological warfare. George says that he cannot accept this, since he is opposed to chemical and biological warfare. The older man replies that he is not too keen on it himself, come to that, but after all George's refusal is not going to make the job or the laboratory go away; what is more, he happens to know that if George refuses the job, it will certainly go to a contemporary of George's who is not inhibited by any such scruples and

Bernard Williams, "A Critique of Utilitarianism," *Utilitarianism*, Cambridge University Press, 1973. Reprinted with the permission of Cambridge University Press.

is likely if appointed to push along the research with greater zeal than George would. Indeed, it is not merely concern for George and his family, but (to speak frankly and in confidence) some alarm about this other man's excess of zeal, which has led the older man to offer to use his influence to get George the job . . . George's wife, to whom he is deeply attached, has views (the details of which need not concern us) from which it follows that at least there is nothing particularly wrong with research into CBW. What should he do?

(2) Jim finds himself in the central square of a small South American town. Tied up against the wall are a row of twenty Indians, most terrified, a few defiant, in front of them several armed men in uniform. A heavy man in a sweat-stained khaki shirt turns out to be the captain in charge and, after a good deal of questioning of Jim which establishes that he got there by accident while on a botanical expedition, explains that the Indians are a random group of the inhabitants who, after recent acts of protest against the government, are just about to be killed to remind other possible protestors of the advantages of not protesting. However, since Jim is an honoured visitor from another land, the captain is happy to offer him a guest's privilege of killing one of the Indians himself. If Jim accepts, then as a special mark of the occasion, the other Indians will be let off. Of course, if Jim refuses, then there is no special occasion, and Pedro here will do what he was about to do when Jim arrived, and kill them all. Jim, with some desperate recollection of schoolboy fiction, wonders whether if he got hold of a gun, he could hold the captain, Pedro and the rest of the soldiers to threat, but it is quite clear from the set-up that nothing of that kind is going to work: any attempt at that sort of thing will mean that all the Indians will be killed, and himself. The men against the wall, and the other villagers, understand the situation, and are obviously begging him to accept. What should he do?

To these dilemmas, it seems to me that utilitarianism replies, in the first case, that George should accept the job, and in the second, that Jim should kill the Indian. Not only does utilitarianism give these answers but, if the situations are essentially as described and there are no further special factors, it regards them, it seems to me, as *obviously* the right answers. But many of us would certainly wonder whether, in (1), that could possibly be the right answer at all; and in the case of (2), even one who came to think that perhaps that was the answer, might well wonder whether it was obviously the answer. Nor is it just a question of the rightness or obviousness of these answers. It is also a question of what sort of considerations come into finding the answer.

A feature of utilitarianism is that it cuts out a kind of consideration which for some others makes a difference to what they feel about such cases: a consideration involving the idea, as we might first and very simply put it, that each of us is specially responsible for what *he* does, rather than for what other people do. This is an idea closely connected with the value of integrity. It is often suspected that utilitarianism, at least in its direct forms, makes integrity as a value more or less unintelligible. I shall try to show that this suspicion is correct. Of course, even if that is correct, it would not necessarily follow that we should reject utilitarianism; perhaps, as utilitarians sometimes suggest, we should just forget about integrity, in favour of such things as a concern for the general good. However, if I am right, we cannot merely do that, since the reason why utilitarianism cannot understand integrity is that it cannot coherently describe the relations between a man's projects and his actions.

Two Kinds of Remoter Effect

A lot of what we have to say about this question will be about the relations between my projects and other people's projects. But before we get on to that, we should first ask whether we are assuming too hastily what the utilitarian answers to the dilemmas will be. In terms of more direct effects of the possible decisions, there does not indeed seem much doubt about the answer in either case; but it might be said that in terms of more remote or less evident effects counterweights might be found to enter the utilitarian scales. Thus the effect on George of a decision to take the job might be invoked, or its effect on others who might know of his decision. The possibility of there being more beneficent labours in the future from which he might be barred or disqualified, might be mentioned; and so forth. Such effects—in particular, possible effects on the agent's character, and effects on the public at large—are often invoked by utilitarian writers dealing with problems about lying or promise-breaking, and some similar considerations might be invoked here.

There is one very general remark that is worth making about arguments of this sort. The certainty that attaches to these hypotheses about possible effects is usually pretty low; in some cases, indeed, the hypothesis invoked is so implausible that it would scarcely pass if it were not being used to deliver the respectable moral answer, as in the standard fantasy that one of the effects of one's telling a particular lie is to weaken the disposition of the world at large to tell the truth.

The demands on the certainty or probability of these beliefs as beliefs about particular actions are much milder than they would be on beliefs favouring the unconventional course. It may be said that this is as it should be, since the presumption must be in favour of the conventional course: but that scarcely seems a *utilitarian* answer, unless utilitarianism has already taken off in the direction of not applying the consequences to the particular act at all.

Leaving aside that very general point, I want to consider now two types of effect that are often invoked by utilitarians, and which might be invoked in connexion with these imaginary cases. The attitude or tone involved in invoking these effects may sometimes seem peculiar; but that sort of peculiarity soon becomes familiar in utilitarian discussions, and indeed it can be something of an achievement to retain a sense of it.

First, there is the psychological effect on the agent. Our descriptions of these situations have not so far taken account of how George or Jim will be after they have taken the one course or the other; and it might be said that if they take the course which seemed at first the utilitarian one, the effects on them will be in fact bad enough and extensive enough to cancel out the initial utilitarian advantages of that course. Now there is one version of this effect in which, for a utilitarian, some confusion must be involved, namely that in which the agent feels bad, his subsequent conduct and relations are crippled and so on, *because he thinks that he has done the wrong thing*—for if the balance of outcomes was as it appeared to be *before* invoking this effect, then he has not (from the utilitarian point of view) done the wrong thing. So that version of the effect, for a rational and utilitarian agent, could not possibly make any difference to the assessment of right and wrong. However, perhaps he is not a thoroughly rational agent, and is disposed to have bad feelings, whichever he decided to do. Now such feelings, which are from a strictly utilitarian point of view irrational—nothing, a utilitarian can point out, is advanced by having them—cannot, consistently, have any great weight in a utilitarian calculation. I shall consider in a moment an argument to suggest that they should have no weight at all in it. But short of that, the utilitarian could reasonably say that such feelings should not be encouraged, even if we accept their existence, and that to give them a lot of weight is to encourage them. Or, at the very best, even if they are straightforwardly and without any discount to be put into the calculation, their weight must be small: they are after all (and at best) one man's feelings.

That consideration might seem to have particular force in Jim's case. In George's case, his feelings represent a larger proportion of what is to be weighed, and are more commensurate in character with other items in the calculation. In Jim's case, however, his feelings might seem to be of very little weight compared with other things that are at stake. There is a powerful and recognizable appeal that can be made on this point: as that a refusal by Jim to do what he has been invited to do would be a kind of self-indulgent squeamishness. That is an appeal which can be made by other than utilitarians—indeed, there are some uses of it which cannot be consistently made by utilitarians, as when it essentially involves the idea that there is something dishonourable about such self-indulgence. But in some versions it is a familiar, and it must be said a powerful, weapon of utilitarianism. One must be clear, though, about what it can and cannot accomplish. The most it can do, so far as I can see, is to invite one to consider how seriously, and for what reasons, one feels that what one is invited to do is (in these circumstances) wrong, and in particular, to consider that question from the utilitarian point of view. When the agent is not seeing the situation from a utilitarian point of view, the appeal cannot force him to do so; and if he does come round to seeing it from a utilitarian point of view, there is virtually nothing left for the appeal to do. If he does not see it from a utilitarian point of view, he will not see his resistance to the invitation, and the unpleasant feelings he associates with accepting it, *just* as disagreeable experiences of his; they figure rather as emotional expressions of a thought that to accept would be wrong. He may be asked, as by the appeal, to consider whether he is right, and indeed whether he is fully serious, in thinking that. But the assertion of the appeal, that he is being self-indulgently squeamish, will not itself answer that question, or even help to answer it, since it essentially tells him to regard his feelings just as unpleasant experiences of his, and he cannot, by doing that, answer the question they pose when they are precisely not so regarded, but are regarded as indications of what he thinks is right and wrong. If he does come round fully to the utilitarian point of view then of course he will regard these feelings just as unpleasant experiences of his. And once Jim—at least—has come to see them in that light, there is nothing left for the appeal to do, since *of course* his feelings, so regarded, are of virtually no weight at all in relation to the other things at stake. The "squeamishness" appeal is not an argument which adds in a hitherto neglected consideration. Rather, it is an invitation to consider the situation, and one's own feelings, from a utilitarian point of view.

The reason why the squeamishness appeal can be very unsettling, and one can be unnerved by the suggestion of self-indulgence in going against utilitarian considerations, is not that we are utilitarians who are uncertain what utilitarian value to attach to our moral feelings, but that we are partially at least not utilitarians, and cannot regard our moral feelings merely as objects of utilitarian value. Because our moral relation to the world is partly given by such feelings, and by a sense of what we can or cannot "live with," to come to regard those feelings from a purely utilitarian point of view, that is to say, as happenings outside one's moral self, is to lose a sense of one's moral identity; to lose, in the most literal way, one's integrity. . . .

CHAPTER 17

The Morality of Euthanasia

James Rachels

James Rachels (1941–2003) was a professor of philosophy at the University of Alabama at Birmingham. He wrote six books, including *Problems from Philosophy* (2005). Here he defends the "argument from mercy." Euthanasia, he thinks, is justified when death is the only way to escape awful pain. In Rachels' main example, the pain is suffered by someone dying from cancer.

James Rachels himself died of cancer in 2003. At the end of his life, nothing persuaded him to change his view of euthanasia. But he did wonder whether the argument from mercy would require less intentional killing than he had thought. Often a humane death comes about when a patient is given more and more pain medication, administered in order to relieve pain. The intention to kill may be unnecessary.

The single most powerful argument in support of euthanasia is the argument from mercy. It is also an exceptionally simple argument, at least in its main idea, which makes one uncomplicated point. Terminally ill patients sometimes suffer pain so horrible that it is beyond the comprehension of those who have not actually experienced it. Their suffering can be so terrible that we do not like even to read about it or think about it; we recoil even from the descriptions of such agony. The argument from mercy says euthanasia is justified because it provides an end to *that*.

The great Irish satirist Jonathan Swift took eight years to die, while, in the words of Joseph Fletcher, "His mind crumbled to pieces."

From James Rachels, "Euthanasia," in *Matters of Life and Death*, 2nd ed., ed. Tom Regan, pp. 49–52. Copyright © 1986.

At times the pain in his blinded eyes was so intense he had to be restrained from tearing them out with his own hands. Knives and other potential instruments of suicide had to be kept from him. For the last three years of his life, he could do nothing but sit and drool: and when he finally died it was only after convulsions that lasted thirty-six hours.

Swift died in 1745. Since then, doctors have learned how to eliminate much of the pain that accompanies terminal illness, but the victory has been far from complete. So, here is a more modern example.

Stewart Alsop was a respected journalist who died in 1975 of a rare form of cancer. Before he died, he wrote movingly of his experiences as a terminal patient. Although he had not thought much about euthanasia before, he came to approve of it after rooming briefly with someone he called Jack:

> The third night that I roomed with Jack in our tiny double room in the solid-tumor ward of the cancer clinic of the National Institutes of Health in Bethesda, Md., a terrible thought occurred to me.
>
> Jack had a melanoma in his belly, a malignant solid tumor that the doctors guessed was about the size of a softball. The cancer had started a few months before with a small tumor in his left shoulder, and there had been several operations since. The doctors planned to remove the softball-sized tumor, but they knew Jack would soon die. The cancer had metastasized—it had spread beyond control.
>
> Jack was good-looking, about 28, and brave. He was in constant pain, and his doctor had prescribed an intravenous shot of a synthetic opiate—a pain-killer, or analgesic—every four hours. His wife spent many of the daylight hours with him, and she would sit or lie on his bed and pat him all over, as one pats a child, only more methodically, and this seemed to help control the pain. But at night, when his pretty wife had left (wives cannot stay overnight at the NIH clinic) and darkness fell, the pain would attack without pity.
>
> At the prescribed hour, a nurse would give Jack a shot of the synthetic analgesic, and this would control the pain for perhaps two hours or a bit more. Then he would begin to moan, or whimper, very low, as though he didn't want to wake me. Then he would begin to howl, like a dog.
>
> When this happened, either he or I would ring for a nurse, and ask for a pain-killer. She would give him some codeine or the like by mouth, but it never did any real good—it affected him no more than half an aspirin might affect a man who had just broken his arm. Always the nurse would explain as encouragingly as she

could that there was not long to go before the next intravenous shot—"Only about 50 minutes now." And always poor Jack's whimpers and howls would become more loud and frequent until at last the blessed relief came.

The third night of this routine, the terrible thought occurred to me. "If Jack were a dog," I thought, "what would be done with him?" The answer was obvious: the pound, and chloroform. No human being with a spark of pity could let a living thing suffer so, to no good end.

The NIH clinic is, of course, one of the most modern and best-equipped hospitals we have. Jack's suffering was not the result of poor treatment in some backward rural facility; it was the inevitable product of his disease, which medical science was powerless to prevent.

I have quoted Alsop at length not for the sake of indulging in gory details but to give a clear idea of the kind of suffering we are talking about. We should not gloss over these facts with euphemistic language or squeamishly avert our eyes from them. For only by keeping them firmly and vividly in mind can we appreciate the full force of the argument from mercy: If a person prefers—and even begs for—death as the only alternative to lingering on *in this kind of torment,* only to die anyway after a while, then surely it is not immoral to help this person die sooner. As Alsop put it, "No human being with a spark of pity could let a living thing suffer so, to no good end."

The Utilitarian Version of the Argument

In connection with this argument, the utilitarians deserve special mention. They argued that actions and social policies should be judged right or wrong *exclusively* according to whether they cause happiness or misery; and they argued that when judged by this standard, euthanasia turns out to be morally acceptable. The utilitarian argument may be elaborated as follows:

(1) Any action or social policy is morally right if it serves to increase the amount of happiness in the world or to decrease the amount of misery. Conversely, an action or social policy is morally wrong if it serves to decrease happiness or to increase misery.

(2) The policy of killing, at their own request, hopelessly ill patients who are suffering great pain would decrease the

amount of misery in the world. (An example could be Alsop's friend Jack.)

(3) Therefore, such a policy would be morally right.

The first premise of this argument, (1), states the Principle of Utility, which is the basic utilitarian assumption. Today most philosophers think that this principle is wrong, because they think that the promotion of happiness and the avoidance of misery are not the *only* morally important things. Happiness, they say, is only one among many values that should be promoted: freedom, justice, and a respect for people's rights are also important. To take one example: people *might* be happier if there were no freedom of religion, for if everyone adhered to the same religious beliefs, there would be greater harmony among people. There would be no unhappiness caused within families by Jewish girls marrying Catholic boys, and so forth. Moreover, if people were brainwashed well enough, no one would mind not having freedom of choice. Thus happiness would be increased. But, the argument continues, even if happiness *could* be increased this way, it would not be right to deny people freedom of religion, because people have a right to make their own choices. Therefore, the first premise of the utilitarian argument is unacceptable.

There is a related difficulty for utilitarianism, which connects more directly with the topic of euthanasia. Suppose a person is leading a miserable life—full of more unhappiness than happiness—but does *not* want to die. This person thinks that a miserable life is better than none at all. Now I assume that we would all agree that the person should not be killed; that would be plain, unjustifiable murder. Yet it *would* decrease the amount of misery in the world if we killed this person—it would lead to an increase in the balance of happiness over unhappiness—and so it is hard to see how, on strictly utilitarian grounds, it could be wrong. Again, the Principle of Utility seems to be an inadequate guide for determining right and wrong. So we are on shaky ground if we rely on *this* version of the argument from mercy for a defense of euthanasia.

Doing What Is in Everyone's Best Interests

Although the foregoing utilitarian argument is faulty, it is nevertheless based on a sound idea. For even if the promotion of happiness and avoidance of misery are not the *only* morally important things, they are still very important. So, when an action or a social policy would decrease misery, that is *a* very strong reason in its favor. In the cases of voluntary euthanasia we are now considering, great suffering is eliminated, and since the patient requests it, there is no question of violating individual rights. That is why, regardless of the difficulties of the Principle of Utility, the utilitarian version of the argument still retains considerable force.

I want now to present a somewhat different version of the argument from mercy, which is inspired by utilitarianism but which avoids the difficulties of the foregoing version by not making the Principle of Utility a premise of the argument. I believe that the following argument is sound and proves that active euthanasia *can* be justified:

> **(1)** If an action promotes the best interests of *everyone* concerned and violates *no one's* rights, then that action is morally acceptable.
>
> **(2)** In at least some cases, active euthanasia promotes the best interests of everyone concerned and violates no one's rights.
>
> **(3)** Therefore, in at least some cases, active euthanasia is morally acceptable.

It would have been in everyone's best interests if active euthanasia had been employed in the case of Stewart Alsop's friend Jack. First, and most important, it would have been in Jack's own interests, since it would have provided him with an easier, better death, without pain. (Who among us would choose Jack's death, if we had a choice, rather than a quick painless death?) Second, it would have been in the best interests of Jack's wife. Her misery, helplessly watching him suffer, must have been almost unbearable. Third, the hospital staff's best interests would have been served, since if Jack's dying had not been prolonged, they could have turned their attention to other patients whom they could have helped. Fourth, other patients would have benefited, since medical resources would no longer have been used in the sad, pointless maintenance of Jack's physical existence. Finally, if Jack himself requested to be killed, the act would not have violated his rights. Considering all this, how can active euthanasia in this case be wrong? How can it be wrong to do an action that is merciful, that benefits everyone concerned, and that violates no one's rights?

CHAPTER 18

*A*ssisted Suicide: *Pro-Choice or Anti-Life?*

Richard Doerflinger

In the 1990s, Dr. Jack Kevorkian of Pontiac, Michigan, helped over 100 people commit suicide. These people had a variety of illnesses, and their prognoses were grim, but for many of them, death was not imminent. They came to Kevorkian from around the country, since they felt they could not get what they wanted from their doctors at home. Kevorkian, whose motives seemed sincere, considered himself a crusader for the individual's right to die. His activities got a lot of press. In 1997, Oregon passed a law allowing physician-assisted suicide, but no other states followed suit. Jack Kevorkian was convicted of second-degree murder in Michigan in 1999 and will be eligible for parole in 2007.

Richard Doerflinger is deputy director for pro-life activities for the U.S. Conference of Catholic Bishops. In this essay, he argues against physician-assisted suicide. The act of suicide, he says, robs an individual of his freedom to choose. Moreover, Doerflinger worries that if physician-assisted suicide becomes accepted, then it will come to be used too often.

The intrinsic wrongness of directly killing the innocent, even with the victim's consent, is all but axiomatic in the Jewish and Christian worldviews that have shaped the laws and mores of Western civilization and the self-concept of its medical practitioners. This norm grew out of the conviction that human life is sacred because it is created in the image and likeness of God, and called to fulfillment in love of God and neighbor.

From Richard Doerflinger, "Assisted Suicide: Pro-Choice or Anti-Life?" *Hastings Center Report*, Special Supplement (January/February 1989), pp. 16–19. Reproduced by permission. © The Hastings Center.

With the pervasive secularization of Western culture, norms against euthanasia and suicide have to a great extent been cut loose from their religious roots to fend for themselves. Because these norms seem abstract and unconvincing to many, debate tends to dwell not on the wrongness of the act as such but on what may follow from its acceptance. Such arguments are often described as claims about a "slippery slope," and debate shifts to the validity of slippery slope arguments in general.

Since it is sometimes argued that acceptance of assisted suicide is an outgrowth of respect for personal autonomy, and not lack of respect for the inherent worth of human life, I will outline how autonomy-based arguments in favor of assisting suicide do entail a statement about the value of life. I will also distinguish two kinds of slippery slope argument often confused with each other, and argue that those who favor social and legal acceptance of assisted suicide have not adequately responded to the slippery slope claims of their opponents.

Assisted Suicide versus Respect for Life

Some advocates of socially sanctioned assisted suicide admit (and a few boast) that their proposal is incompatible with the conviction that human life is of intrinsic worth. Attorney Robert Risley has said that he and his allies in the Hemlock Society are "so bold" as to seek to "overturn the sanctity of life principle" in American society. A life of suffering, "racked with pain," is "not the kind of life we cherish."[1]

Others eschew Risley's approach, perhaps recognizing that it creates a slippery slope toward practices almost universally condemned. If society is to help terminally ill patients to commit suicide because it agrees that death is objectively preferable to a life of hardship, it will be difficult to draw the line at the seriously ill or even at circumstances where the victim requests death.

Some advocates of assisted suicide therefore take a different course, arguing that it is precisely respect for the dignity of the human person that demands respect for individual freedom as the noblest feature of that person. On this rationale a decision as to when and how to die deserves the respect and even the assistance of others because it is the ultimate exercise of self-determination—"ultimate" both in the sense that it is the last decision one will ever make and in the sense that through it one takes control of one's entire self. What makes such decisions worthy of respect is not the fact that death is chosen over life but that it is the individual's own free decision about his or her future.

Thus Derek Humphry, director of the Hemlock Society, describes his organization as "pro-choice" on this issue. Such groups favor establishment of a constitutional "right to die" modeled on the right to abortion delineated by the U.S. Supreme Court in 1973. This would be a right to choose *whether or not* to end one's own life, free of outside government interference. In theory, recognition of such a right would betray no bias toward choosing death.

Life versus Freedom

This autonomy-based approach is more appealing than the straightforward claim that some lives are not worth living, especially to Americans accustomed to valuing individual liberty above virtually all else. But the argument departs from American traditions on liberty in one fundamental respect.

When the Declaration of Independence proclaimed the inalienable human rights to be "life, liberty, and the pursuit of happiness," this ordering reflected a long-standing judgment about their relative priorities. Life, a human being's very earthly existence, is the most fundamental right because it is the necessary condition for all other worldly goods including freedom; freedom in turn makes it possible to pursue (without guaranteeing that one will attain) happiness. Safeguards against the deliberate destruction of life are thus seen as necessary to protect freedom and all other human goods. This line of thought is not explicitly religious but is endorsed by some modern religious groups:

> The first right of the human person is his life. He has other goods and some are more precious, but this one is fundamental—the condition of all the others. Hence it must be protected above all others.[2]

On this view suicide is not the ultimate exercise of freedom but its ultimate self-contradiction: A free act that by destroying life, destroys all the individual's future earthly freedom. If life is more basic than freedom, society best serves freedom by discouraging rather than assisting self-destruction. Sometimes one must limit particular choices to safeguard freedom itself, as when American society chose over a century ago to prevent people from selling themselves into slavery even of their own volition.

It may be argued in objection that the person who ends his life has not truly suffered loss of freedom, because unlike the slave he need not continue to exist under the constraints of a loss of freedom. But the slave does have some freedom, including the freedom to seek various means of liberation or at least the freedom to choose what attitude to take regarding his plight. To claim that a slave is worse off than a corpse is to value a situation of limited freedom less than one of no freedom whatsoever, which seems inconsistent with the premise of the "pro-choice" position. Such a claim also seems tantamount to saying that some lives (such as those with less than absolute freedom) are objectively not worth living, a position that "pro-choice" advocates claim not to hold.

It may further be argued in objection that assistance in suicide is only being offered to those who can no longer meaningfully exercise other freedoms due to increased suffering and reduced capabilities and lifespan. To be sure, the suffering of terminally ill patients who can no longer pursue the simplest everyday tasks should call for sympathy and support from everyone in contact with them. But even these hardships do not constitute total loss of freedom of choice. If they did, one could hardly claim that the patient is in a position to make the ultimate free choice about suicide. A dying person capable of making a choice of that kind is also capable of making less monumental free choices about coping with his or her condition. This person generally faces a bewildering array of choices regarding the assessment of his or her past life and the resolution of relationships with family and friends. He or she must finally choose at this time what stance to take regarding the eternal questions about God, personal responsibility, and the prospects of a destiny after death.

In short, those who seek to maximize free choice may with consistency reject the idea of assisted suicide, instead facilitating all choices *except* that one which cuts short all choices.

In fact proponents of assisted suicide do *not* consistently place freedom of choice as their highest priority. They often defend the moderate nature of their project by stating, with Derek Humphry, that "we do not encourage suicide for any reason except to relieve unremitting suffering." It seems their highest priority is the "pursuit of happiness" (or avoidance of suffering) and not "liberty" as such. Liberty or freedom of choice loses its value if one's choices cannot relieve suffering and lead to happiness; life is of instrumental value insofar as it makes possible choices that can bring happiness.

In this value system, choice as such does not warrant unqualified respect. In difficult circumstances, as when care of a suffering and dying patient is a great burden on family and society, the individual who chooses life despite suffering will not easily be seen as rational, thus will not easily receive understanding and assistance for this choice.

In short, an unqualified "pro-choice" defense of assisted suicide lacks coherence because corpses have no choices. A particular choice, that of death, is given priority over all the other choices it makes impossible, so the value of choice as such is not central to the argument.

A restriction of this rationale to cases of terminal illness also lacks logical force. For if ending a brief life of suffering can be good, it would seem that ending a long life of suffering may be better. Surely the approach of the California "Humane and Dignified Death Act"—where consensual killing of a patient expected to die in six months is presumably good medical practice, but killing the same patient a month or two earlier is still punishable as homicide—is completely arbitrary.

Slippery Slopes, Loose Cannons

Many arguments against sanctioning assisted suicide concern a different kind of "slippery slope": Contingent factors in the contemporary situation may make it virtually inevitable in practice, if not compelling at the level of abstract theory, that removal of the taboo against assisted suicide will lead to destructive expansions of the right to kill the innocent. Such factors may not be part of euthanasia advocates' own agenda; but if they exist and are beyond the control of these advocates, they must be taken into account in judging the moral and social wisdom of opening what may be a Pandora's box of social evils.

To distinguish this sociological argument from our dissection of the conceptual *logic* of the rationale for assisted suicide, we might call it a "loose cannon" argument. The basic claim is that socially accepted killing of innocent persons will interact with other social factors to threaten lives that advocates of assisted suicide would agree should be protected. These factors at present include the following:

The psychological vulnerability of elderly and dying patients. Theorists may present voluntary and involuntary euthanasia as polar opposites; in practice there are many steps on the road from dispassionate, autonomous choice to subtle coercion. Elderly and disabled patients are often invited by our achievement-oriented society to see themselves as useless burdens on younger, more vital generations. In this climate, simply offering the *option* of "self-deliverance" shifts a burden of proof, so that helpless patients must ask themselves why they are *not* availing themselves of it. Society's offer of death communicates the message to certain patients that they *may* continue to live if they wish but the rest of us have no strong interest in their survival. Indeed, once the choice of a quick and painless death is officially accepted as rational, resistance to this choice may be seen as eccentric or even selfish.[3]

The crisis in health care costs. The growing incentives for physicians, hospitals, families, and insurance companies to control the cost of health care will bring additional pressures to bear on patients. Curt Garbesi, the Hemlock Society's legal consultant, argues that autonomy-based groups like Hemlock must "control the public debate" so assisted suicide will not be seized upon by public officials as a cost-cutting device. But simply basing one's own defense of assisted suicide on individual autonomy does not solve the problem. For in the economic sphere also, offering the option of suicide would subtly shift burdens of proof.

Adequate health care is now seen by at least some policymakers as a human right, as something a society owes to all its members. Acceptance of assisted suicide as an option for those requiring expensive care would not only offer health care providers an incentive to make that option seem attractive—it would also demote all other options to the status of strictly private choices by the individual. As such they may lose their moral and legal claim to public support—in much the same way that the U.S. Supreme Court, having protected abortion under a constitutional "right of privacy," has quite logically denied any government obligation to provide public funds for this strictly private choice. As life-extending care of the terminally ill is increasingly seen as strictly elective, society may become less willing to appropriate funds for such care, and economic pressures to choose death will grow accordingly.

Legal doctrines on "substituted judgment." American courts recognizing a fundamental right to refuse life-sustaining treatment have concluded that it is unjust to deny this right to the mentally incompetent. In such cases the right is exercised on the patient's behalf by others, who seek either to interpret what the patient's own wishes might have been or to serve his or her best interests. Once assisted suicide is established as a fundamental right, courts will almost certainly find that it is unjust not to extend this right to those unable to express their wishes. Hemlock's political arm, Americans Against Human Suffering, has underscored continuity between "passive" and "active" euthanasia by offering the Humane and Dignified Death Act as an amendment to California's "living will" law, and by including a provision for appointment of a proxy to choose the time and manner of the patient's death.

By such extensions our legal system would accommodate nonvoluntary, if not involuntary, active euthanasia.

Expanded definitions of terminal illness. The Hemlock Society wishes to offer assisted suicide only to those suffering from terminal illnesses. But some Hemlock officials have in mind a rather broad definition of "terminal illness." Derek Humphry says "two and a half million people alone are dying of Alzheimer's disease."[4] At Hemlock's 1986 convention, Dutch physician Pieter Admiraal boasted that he had recently broadened the meaning of terminal illness in his country by giving a lethal injection to a young quadriplegic woman—a Dutch court found that he acted within judicial guidelines allowing euthanasia for the terminally ill, because paralyzed patients have difficulty swallowing and could die from aspirating their food at any time.

The medical and legal meaning of terminal illness has already been expanded in the United States by professional societies, legislatures, and courts in the context of so-called passive euthanasia. A Uniform Rights of the Terminally Ill Act proposed by the National Conference of Commissioners on Uniform State Laws in 1986 defines a terminal illness as one that would cause the patient's death in a relatively short time if life-preserving treatment is *not* provided—prompting critics to ask if all diabetics, for example, are "terminal" by definition. Some courts already see comatose and vegetative states as "terminal" because they involve an inability to swallow that will lead to death unless artificial feeding is instituted. In the *Hilda Peter* case, the New Jersey Supreme Court declared that the traditional state interest in "preserving life" referred only to "cognitive and sapient life" and not to mere "biological" existence, implying that unconscious patients are terminal, or perhaps as good as dead, so far as state interests are concerned. Is there any reason to think that American law would suddenly resurrect the older, narrower meaning of "terminal illness" in the context of *active* euthanasia?

Prejudice against citizens with disabilities. If definitions of terminal illness expand to encompass states of severe physical or mental disability, another social reality will increase the pressure on patients to choose death: long-standing prejudice, sometimes bordering on revulsion, against people with disabilities. While it is seldom baldly claimed that disabled people have "lives not worth living," able-bodied people often say they could not live in a severely disabled state or would prefer death. In granting Elizabeth Bouvia a right to refuse a feeding tube that preserved her life, the California Appeals Court bluntly stated that her physical handicaps led her to "consider her existence meaningless" and that "she cannot be faulted for so concluding." According to disability rights expert Paul Longmore, in a society with such attitudes toward the disabled, "talk of their 'rational' or 'voluntary' suicide is simply Orwellian newspeak."[5]

Character of the medical profession. Advocates of assisted suicide realize that most physicians will resist giving lethal injections because they are trained, in Garbesi's words, to be "enemies of death." The California Medical Association firmly opposed the Humane and Dignified Death Act, seeing it as an attack on the ethical foundation of the medical profession.

Yet California appeals judge Lynn Compton was surely correct in his concurring opinion in the *Bouvia* case, when he said that a sufficient number of willing physicians can be found once legal sanctions against assisted suicide are dropped. Judge Compton said this had clearly been the case with abortion, despite the fact that the Hippocratic Oath condemns abortion as strongly as it condemns euthanasia. Opinion polls of physicians bear out the judgment that a significant number would perform lethal injections if they were legal.

Some might think this division or ambivalence about assisted suicide in the medical profession will restrain broad expansions of the practice. But if anything, Judge Compton's analogy to our experience with abortion suggests the opposite. Most physicians still have qualms about abortion, and those who perform abortions on a full-time basis are not readily accepted by their colleagues as paragons of the healing art. Consequently they tend to form their own professional societies, bolstering each other's positive self-image and developing euphemisms to blunt the moral edge of their work.

Once physicians abandon the traditional medical self-image, which rejects direct killing of patients in all circumstances, their new substitute self-image may require ever more aggressive efforts to make this killing more widely practiced and favorably received. To allow killing by physicians in certain circumstances may create a new lobby of physicians in favor of expanding medical killing.

The human will to power. The most deeply buried yet most powerful driving force toward widespread medical killing is a fact of human nature: Human beings are tempted to enjoy exercising power over others; ending another person's life is the ultimate exercise of that power. Once the taboo against killing has been set aside, it becomes progressively easier to channel one's aggressive instincts into the destruction of life in other contexts. Or as James Burtchaell has said: "There is a sort of virginity about murder; once one has violated it, it is awkward to refuse other invitations by saying, 'But that would be murder!'"[6]

Some will say assisted suicide for the terminally ill is morally distinguishable from murder and does not logically require termination of life in other circumstances. But my point is that the skill and the instinct to kill are more easily turned to other lethal tasks once they have an opportunity to exercise themselves. Thus Robert Jay Lifton has perceived differences between the German "mercy killings" of the 1930s and the later campaign to annihilate the Jews of Europe, yet still says that "at the heart of the Nazi enterprise . . . is the destruction of the boundary between healing and killing."[7] No other boundary separating these two situations was as fundamental as this one, and thus none was effective once it was crossed. As a matter of historical fact, personnel who had conducted the "mercy killing" program were quickly and readily recruited to operate the killing chambers of the death camps.[8] While the contemporary United States fortunately lacks the anti-Semitic and totalitarian attitudes that made the Holocaust possible, it has its own trends and pressures that may combine with acceptance of medical killing to produce a distinctively American catastrophe in the name of individual freedom.

These "loose cannon" arguments are not conclusive. All such arguments by their nature rest upon a reading and extrapolation of certain contingent factors in society. But their combined force provides a serious case against taking the irreversible step of sanctioning assisted suicide for any class of persons, so long as those who advocate this step fail to demonstrate why these predictions are wrong. If the strict philosophical case on behalf of "rational suicide" lacks coherence, the pragmatic claim that its acceptance would be a social benefit lacks grounding in history or common sense.

Notes

1. Presentation at the Hemlock Society's Third National Voluntary Euthanasia Conference, "A Humane and Dignified Death," September 25–27, 1986, Washington, DC. All quotations from Hemlock Society officials are from the proceedings of this conference unless otherwise noted.

2. Vatican Congregation for the Doctrine of the Faith, *Declaration on Procured Abortion* (1974), para. 11.

3. I am indebted for this line of argument to Dr. Eric Chevlen.

4. Denis Herbstein, "Campaigning for the Right to Die," *International Herald Tribune,* September 11, 1986.

5. Paul K. Longmore, "Elizabeth Bouvia, Assisted Suicide, and Social Prejudice," *Issues in Law & Medicine* 3, no. 2 (1987), 168.

6. James T. Burtchaell, *Rachel Weeping and Other Essays on Abortion* (Kansas City: Andrews & McMeel, 1982), 188.

7. Robert Jay Lifton, *The Nazi Doctors: Medical Killing and the Psychology of Genocide* (New York: Basic Books, 1986), 14.

8. Yitzhak Rad, *Belzec, Sobibor, Treblinka* (Bloomington, Ind.: Indiana University Press, 1987), 11, 16–17.

CHAPTER 19

All Animals Are Equal

Peter Singer

Peter Singer's appointment to Princeton in 1999 created a public uproar reminiscent of 1940, when the City College of New York appointed Bertrand Russell, one of the 20th century's greatest philosophers, to a one-year professorship. In Russell's case, the outcry culminated in a judge's ruling that voided the state university's appointment. Commenting on the case, Albert Einstein said, "Great spirits have always found violent opposition from mediocrities." Since Princeton is a private university, Singer's ordeal stayed out of the courts.

The treatment of nonhuman animals has not traditionally been regarded as a serious moral issue. Virtually every thinker and every system of thought have provided some rationale for excluding animals from moral concern. Aristotle said that, in the natural order of things, animals exist to serve human purposes. The Christian tradition added that man alone is made in God's image and that animals do not have souls. Kant said that animals are not self-conscious, so we can have no duties to them.

The utilitarians took a different view, holding that we should consider the interests of all beings, human and nonhuman. When Peter Singer took up this argument in the mid-1970s, many people thought he must be joking. But Singer's work has had a tremendous impact.

For more information on Peter Singer, see Chapter 15.

In recent years a number of oppressed groups have campaigned vigorously for equality. The classic instance is the Black Liberation movement, which demands an end to the prejudice and discrimination that has made blacks second-class citizens. The immediate appeal

---

Reprinted by permission from Peter Singer, "All Animals Are Equal," *Annual Proceedings of the Center for Philosophical Exchange* 1, no. 5 (1974): 103–11, State University of New York College at Brockport, 1974.

of the black liberation movement and its initial, if limited success made it a model for other oppressed groups to follow. We became familiar with liberation movements for Spanish-Americans, gay people, and a variety of other minorities. When a majority group—women—began their campaign, some thought we had come to the end of the road. Discrimination on the basis of sex, it has been said, is the last universally accepted form of discrimination, practiced without secrecy or pretense even in those liberal circles that have long prided themselves on their freedom from prejudice against racial minorities.

One should always be wary of talking of "the last remaining form of discrimination." If we have learnt anything from the liberation movements, we should have learnt how difficult it is to be aware of latent prejudice in our attitudes to particular groups until this prejudice is forcefully pointed out.

A liberation movement demands an expansion of our moral horizons and an extension or reinterpretation of the basic moral principle of equality. Practices that were previously regarded as natural and inevitable come to be seen as the result of an unjustifiable prejudice. Who can say with confidence that all his or her attitudes and practices are beyond criticism? If we wish to avoid being numbered amongst the oppressors, we must be prepared to re-think even our most fundamental attitudes. We need to consider them from the point of view of those most disadvantaged by our attitudes, and the practices that follow from these attitudes. If we can make this unaccustomed mental switch we may discover a pattern in our attitudes and practices that consistently operates so as to benefit one group—usually the one to which we ourselves belong—at the expense of another. In this way we may come to see that there is a case for a new liberation movement. My aim is to advocate that we make this mental switch in respect of our attitudes and practices towards a very large group of beings: members of species other than our own—or, as we popularly though misleadingly call them, animals. In other words, I am urging that we extend to other species the basic principle of equality that most of us recognise should be extended to all members of our own species.

All this may sound a little far-fetched, more like a parody of other liberation movements than a serious objective. In fact, in the past the idea of "The Rights of Animals" really has been used to parody the case for women's rights. When Mary Wollstonecraft, a forerunner of later feminists, published her *Vindication of the Rights of Woman* in 1792, her ideas were widely regarded as absurd, and they were satirized in an anonymous publication entitled *A Vindication of the Rights of Brutes*.

The author of this satire (actually Thomas Taylor, a distinguished Cambridge philosopher) tried to refute Wollstonecraft's reasonings by showing that they could be carried one stage further. If sound when applied to women, why should the arguments not be applied to dogs, cats and horses? They seemed to hold equally well for these "brutes"; yet to hold that brutes had rights was manifestly absurd; therefore the reasoning by which this conclusion had been reached must be unsound, and if unsound when applied to brutes, it must also be unsound when applied to women, since the very same arguments had been used in each case.

One way in which we might reply to this argument is by saying that the case for equality between men and women cannot validly be extended to nonhuman animals. Women have a right to vote, for instance, because they are just as capable of making rational decisions as men are; dogs, on the other hand, are incapable of understanding the significance of voting, so they cannot have the right to vote. There are many other obvious ways in which men and women resemble each other closely, while humans and other animals differ greatly. So, it might be said, men and women are similar beings, and should have equal rights, while humans and nonhumans are different and should not have equal rights.

The thought behind this reply to Taylor's analogy is correct up to a point, but it does not go far enough. There *are* important differences between humans and other animals, and these differences must give rise to *some* differences in the rights that each have. Recognizing this obvious fact, however, is no barrier to the case for extending the basic principle of equality to nonhuman animals. The differences that exist between men and women are equally undeniable, and the supporters of Women's Liberation are aware that these differences may give rise to different rights. Many feminists hold that women have the right to an abortion on request. It does not follow that since these same people are campaigning for equality between men and women they must support the right of men to have abortions too. Since a man cannot have an abortion, it is meaningless to talk of his right to have one. Since a pig can't vote, it is meaningless to talk of its right to vote. There is no reason why either Women's Liberation or Animal Liberation should get involved in such nonsense. The extension of the basic principle of equality from one group to another does not imply that we must treat both groups in exactly the same way, or grant exactly the same rights to both groups. Whether we should do so will depend on the nature of the members of the two groups. The basic principle of equality, I shall argue, is equality of consideration; and equal consideration for different beings may lead to different treatment and different rights.

So there is a different way of replying to Taylor's attempt to parody Wollstonecraft's arguments, a way which does not deny the differences between humans and nonhumans, but goes more deeply into the question of equality, and concludes by finding nothing absurd in the idea that the basic principle of equality applies to so-called "brutes." I believe that we reach this conclusion if we examine the basis on which our opposition to discrimination on grounds of race or sex ultimately rests. We will then see that we would be on shaky ground if we were to demand equality for blacks, women, and other groups of oppressed humans while denying equal consideration to nonhumans.

When we say that all human beings, whatever their race, creed or sex, are equal, what is it that we are asserting? Those who wish to defend a hierarchical, inegalitarian society have often pointed out that by whatever test we choose, it simply is not true that all humans are equal. Like it or not, we must face the fact that humans come in different shapes and sizes; they come with differing moral capacities, differing intellectual abilities, differing amounts of benevolent feeling and sensitivity to the needs of others, differing abilities to communicate effectively, and differing capacities to experience pleasure and pain. In short, if the demand for equality were based on the actual equality of all human beings, we would have to stop demanding equality. It would be an unjustifiable demand.

Still, one might cling to the view that the demand for equality among human beings is based on the actual equality of the different races and sexes. Although humans differ as individuals in various ways, there are no differences between the races and sexes *as such*. From the mere fact that a person is black, or a woman, we cannot infer anything else about that person. This, it may be said, is what is wrong with racism and sexism. The white racist claims that whites are superior to blacks, but this is false—although there are differences between individuals, some blacks are superior to some whites in all of the capacities and abilities that could conceivably be relevant. The opponent of sexism would say the same: a person's sex is no guide to his or her abilities, and this is why it is unjustifiable to discriminate on the basis of sex.

This is a possible line of objection to racial and sexual discrimination. It is not, however, the way that someone really concerned about equality would choose, because taking this line could, in some circumstances, force one to accept a most inegalitarian society. The fact that humans differ as individuals, rather than as races or sexes, is a valid reply to someone who defends a hierarchical society like, say, South Africa, in which all whites are superior in status to all blacks. The existence of individual variations that cut across the lines of race or sex, however, provides us with no defence at all against a more sophisticated opponent of equality, one who proposes, say, the interests of those with ratings above 100. Would a hierarchical society of this sort really be so much better than one based on race or sex? I think not. But if we tie the moral principle of equality to the factual equality of the different races or sexes, taken as a whole, our opposition to racism and sexism does not provide us with any basis for objecting to this kind of inegalitarianism.

There is a second important reason why we ought not to base our opposition to racism and sexism on any kind of factual equality, even the limited kind that asserts that variations in capacities and abilities are spread evenly between the different races and sexes: we can have no absolute guarantee that these abilities and capacities really are distributed evenly, without regard to race or sex, among human beings. So far as actual abilities are concerned, there do seem to be certain measurable differences between both races and sexes. These differences do not, of course, appear in each case, but only when averages are taken. More important still, we do not yet know how much of these differences is really due to the different genetic endowments of the various races and sexes, and how much is due to environmental differences that are the result of past and continuing discrimination. Perhaps all of the important differences will eventually prove to be environmental rather than genetic. Anyone opposed to racism and sexism will certainly hope that this will be so, for it will make the task of ending discrimination a lot easier; nevertheless it would be dangerous to rest the case against racism and sexism on the belief that all significant differences are environmental in origin. The opponent of, say, racism who takes this line will be unable to avoid conceding that if differences in ability did after all prove to have some genetic connection with race, racism would in some way be defensible.

It would be folly for the opponent of racism to stake his whole case on a dogmatic commitment to one particular outcome of a difficult scientific issue which is still a long way from being settled. While attempts to prove that differences in certain selected abilities between races and sexes are primarily genetic in origin have certainly not been conclusive, the same must be said of attempts to prove that these differences are largely the result of environment. At this stage of the investigation we cannot be certain which view is correct, however much we may hope it is the latter.

Fortunately, there is no need to pin the case for equality to one particular outcome of this scientific investigation. The appropriate response to those who claim to have found evidence of genetically-based differences in ability between the races or sexes is not to stick to the belief that the genetic explanation must be wrong, whatever evidence to the contrary may turn up: instead we should make it quite clear that the claim to equality does not depend on intelligence, moral capacity, physical strength, or similar matters of fact. Equality is a moral ideal, not a simple assertion of fact. There is no logically compelling reason for assuming that a factual difference in ability between two people justifies any difference in the amount of consideration we give to satisfying their needs and interests. The principle of the equality of human beings is not a description of an alleged actual equality among humans: it is a prescription of how we should treat humans.

Jeremy Bentham incorporated the essential basis of moral equality into his utilitarian system of ethics in the formula: "Each to count for one and none for more than one." In other words, the interests of every being affected by an action are to be taken into account and given the same weight as the like interests of any other being. A later utilitarian, Henry Sidgwick, put the point in this way: "The good of any one individual is of no more importance, from the point of view (if I may say so) of the Universe, than the good of any other." More recently, the leading figures in contemporary moral philosophy have shown a great deal of agreement in specifying as a fundamental presupposition of their moral theories some similar requirement which operates so as to give everyone's interests equal consideration—although they cannot agree on how this requirement is best formulated.

It is an implication of this principle of equality that our concern for others ought not to depend on what they are like, or what abilities they possess—although precisely what this concern requires us to do may vary according to the characteristics of those affected by what we do. It is on this basis that the case against racism and the case against sexism must both ultimately rest; and it is in accordance with this principle that speciesism is also to be condemned. If possessing a higher degree of intelligence does not entitle one human to use another for his own ends, how can it entitle humans to exploit nonhumans?

Many philosophers have proposed the principle of equal consideration of interests, in some form or other, as a basic moral principle;

but, as we shall see in more detail shortly, not many of them have recognised that this principle applies to members of other species as well as to our own. Bentham was one of the few who did realize this. In a forward-looking passage, written at a time when black slaves in the British dominions were still being treated much as we now treat non-human animals, Bentham wrote:

> The day *may* come when the rest of the animal creation may acquire those rights which never could have been witholden from them but by the hand of tyranny. The French have already discovered that the blackness of the skin is no reason why a human being should be abandoned without redress to the caprice of a tormentor. It may one day come to be recognised that the number of the legs, the villosity of the skin, or the termination of the *os sacrum*, are reasons equally insufficient for abandoning a sensitive being to the same fate. What else is it that should trace the insuperable line? Is it the faculty of reason, or perhaps the faculty of discourse? But a full-grown horse or dog is beyond comparison a more rational, as well as a more conversable animal, than an infant of a day, or a week, or even a month, old. But suppose they were otherwise, what would it avail? The question is not, Can they *reason?* nor Can they *talk?* but, Can they *suffer?*

In this passage Bentham points to the capacity for suffering as the vital characteristic that gives a being the right to equal consideration. The capacity for suffering—or more strictly, for suffering and/or enjoyment or happiness—is not just another characteristic like the capacity for language, or for higher mathematics. Bentham is not saying that those who try to mark "the insuperable line" that determines whether the interests of a being should be considered happen to have selected the wrong characteristic. The capacity for suffering and enjoying things is a pre-requisite for having interests at all, a condition that must be satisfied before we can speak of interests in any meaningful way. It would be nonsense to say that it was not in the interests of a stone to be kicked along the road by a schoolboy. A stone does not have interests because it cannot suffer. Nothing that we can do to it could possibly make any difference to its welfare. A mouse, on the other hand, does have an interest in not being tormented, because it will suffer if it is.

If a being suffers, there can be no moral justification for refusing to take that suffering into consideration. No matter what the nature of the being, the principle of equality requires that its suffering be counted equally with the like suffering—in so far as rough comparisons can be made—of any other being. If a being is not capable of suffering, or of experiencing enjoyment or happiness, there is nothing to be taken into account. This is why the limit of sentience (using the term as a convenient, if not strictly accurate, shorthand for the capacity to suffer or experience enjoyment or happiness) is the only defensible boundary of concern for the interests of others. To mark this boundary by some characteristic like intelligence or rationality would be to mark it in an arbitrary way. Why not choose some other characteristic, like skin color?

The racist violates the principle of equality by giving greater weight to the interests of members of his own race, when there is a clash between their interests and the interests of those of another race. Similarly the speciesist allows the interests of his own species to override the greater interests of members of other species. The pattern is the same in each case. Most human beings are speciesists. I shall now very briefly describe some of the practices that show this.

For the great majority of human beings, especially in urban, industrialized societies, the most direct form of contact with members of other species is at meal-times: we eat them. In doing so we treat them purely as means to our ends. We regard their life and well-being as subordinate to our taste for a particular kind of dish. I say "taste" deliberately—this is purely a matter of pleasing our palate. There can be no defence of eating flesh in terms of satisfying nutritional needs, since it has been established beyond doubt that we could satisfy our need for protein and other essential nutrients far more efficiently with a diet that replaced animal flesh by soy beans, or products derived from soy beans, and other high-protein vegetable products.

It is not merely the act of killing that indicates what we are ready to do to other species in order to gratify our tastes. The suffering we inflict on the animals while they are alive is perhaps an even clearer indication of our speciesism than the fact that we are prepared to kill them. In order to have meat on the table at a price that people can afford, our society tolerates methods of meat production that confine sentient animals in cramped, unsuitable conditions for the entire durations of their lives. Animals are treated like machines that convert fodder into flesh, and any innovation that results in a higher "conversion ratio" is liable to be adopted. As one authority on the subject has said, "cruelty is acknowledged only when profitability ceases." So hens are crowded four or five to a cage with a floor area of twenty inches by eighteen inches, or around the size of a single page of *The New York Times*. The cages have wire floors, since this reduces cleaning costs, though wire is unsuitable for the hens' feet; the floors slope, since this makes the eggs roll down for easy collection, although this makes it difficult for the hens to rest comfortably. In these conditions all the birds' natural instincts are thwarted: they cannot stretch their wings fully, walk freely, dust-bathe, scratch the ground, or build a nest. Although they have never known other conditions, observers have noticed that the birds vainly try to perform these actions. Frustrated at their inability to do so, they often develop what farmers call "vices," and peck each other to death. To prevent this, the beaks of young birds are often cut off.

This kind of treatment is not limited to poultry. Pigs are now also being reared in cages inside sheds. These animals are comparable to dogs in intelligence, and need a varied, stimulating environment if they are not to suffer from stress and boredom. Anyone who kept a dog in the way in which pigs are frequently kept would be liable to prosecution, in England at least, but because our interest in exploiting pigs is greater than our interest in exploiting dogs, we object to cruelty to dogs while consuming the produce of cruelty to pigs. Of the other animals, the condition of veal calves is perhaps worst of all, since these animals are so closely confined that they cannot even turn around or get up and lie down freely. In this way they do not develop unpalatable muscle. They are also made anaemic and kept short of roughage, to keep their flesh pale, since white veal fetches a higher price; as a result they develop a craving for iron and roughage, and have been observed to gnaw wood off the sides of their stalls, and lick greedily at any rusty hinge that is within reach.

Since, as I have said, none of these practices cater for anything more than our pleasures of taste, our practice of rearing and killing other animals in order to eat them is a clear instance of the sacrifice of the most important interests of other beings in order to satisfy trivial interests of our own. To avoid speciesism we must stop this practice, and each of us has a moral obligation to cease supporting the practice. Our custom is all the support that the meat-industry needs. The decision to cease giving it that support may be difficult, but it is no more difficult than it would have been for a white Southerner to go against the traditions of his society and free his slaves; if we do not change our dietary habits, how can we censure those slaveholders who would not change their own way of living?

The same form of discrimination may be observed in the widespread practice of experimenting on other species in order to see if certain substances are safe for human beings, or to test some psychological theory about the effect of severe punishment on learning, or to try out various new compounds just in case something turns up. People sometimes think that all this experimentation is for vital medical purposes, and so will reduce suffering overall. This comfortable belief is very wide of the mark. Drug companies test new shampoos and cosmetics that they are intending to put on the market by dropping them into the eyes of rabbits, held open by metal clips, in order to observe what damage results. Food additives, like artificial colorings and preservatives, are tested by what is known as the "LD_{50}"— a test designed to find the level of consumption at which 50% of a group of animals will die. In the process, nearly all of the animals are made very sick before some finally die, and others pull through. If the substance is relatively harmless, as it often is, huge doses have to be force-fed to the animals, until in some cases sheer volume or concentration of the substance causes death.

Much of this pointless cruelty goes on in the universities. In many areas of science, nonhuman animals are regarded as an item of laboratory equipment, to be used and expended as desired. In psychology laboratories experimenters devise endless variations and repetitions of experiments that were of little value in the first place. To quote just one example, from the experimenter's own account in a psychology journal: at the University of Pennsylvania, Perrin S. Cohen hung six dogs in hammocks with electrodes taped to their hind feet. Electric shock of varying intensity was then administered through the electrodes. If the dog learnt to press its head against a panel on the left, the shock was turned off, but otherwise it remained on indefinitely. Three of the dogs, however, were required to wait periods varying from 2 to 7 seconds while being shocked before making the response that turned off the current. If they failed to wait, they received further shocks. Each dog was given from 26 to 46 "sessions" in the hammock, each session consisting of 80 "trials" or shocks, administered at intervals of one minute. The experimenter reported that the dogs, who were unable to move in the hammock, barked or bobbed their heads when the current was applied. The reported findings of the experiment were that there was a delay in the dogs' responses that increased proportionately to the time the dogs were required to endure the shock, but a gradual increase in the intensity of the shock had no systematic effect in the timing of the response. The experiment was funded by the National Institutes of Health, and the United States Public Health Service.

In this example, and countless cases like it, the possible benefits to mankind are either nonexistent or fantastically remote; while the certain losses to members of other species are very real. This is, again, a clear indication of speciesism.

In the past, argument about vivisection has often missed this point, because it has been put in absolutist terms: would the abolitionist be prepared to let thousands die if they could be saved by experimenting on a single animal? The way to reply to this purely hypothetical question is to pose another: would the experimenter be prepared to perform his experiment on an orphaned human infant, if that were the only way to save many lives? (I say "orphan" to avoid the complication of parental feelings, although in doing so I am being overfair to the experimenter, since the nonhuman subjects of experiments are not orphans.) If the experimenter is not prepared to use an orphaned human infant, then his readiness to use nonhumans is simple discrimination, since adult apes, cats, mice and other mammals are more aware of what is happening to them, more self-directing and, so far as we can tell, at least as sensitive to pain, as any human infant. There seems to be no relevant characteristic that human infants possess that adult mammals do not have to the same or a higher degree. (Someone might try to argue that what makes it wrong to experiment on a human infant is that the infant will, in time and if left alone, develop into more than the nonhuman, but one would then, to be consistent, have to oppose abortion, since the fetus has the same potential as the infant—indeed, even contraception and abstinence might be wrong on this ground, since the egg and sperm, considered jointly, also have the same potential. In any case, this argument still gives us no reason for selecting a nonhuman, rather than a human with severe and irreversible brain damage, as the subject for our experiments.)

The experimenter, then, shows a bias in favor of his own species whenever he carries out an experiment on a nonhuman for a purpose that he would not think justified him in using a human being at an equal or lower level of sentience, awareness, ability to be self-directing, etc. No one familiar with the kind of results yielded by most experiments on animals can have the slightest doubt that if this bias were eliminated the number of experiments performed would be a minute fraction of the number performed today.

CHAPTER 20

Do Animals Have Rights?

Tibor R. Machan

Animals are not moral agents—they are not morally responsible for what they do, nor are they capable of moral goodness. People are more valuable than animals—we are smarter and more complex. You and I *are* moral agents. Tibor R. Machan emphasizes ideas like these. Even though we should treat animals humanely, he says, we should recognize that they have no fundamental rights to life, liberty, or property.

Tibor R. Machan is the author of *Putting Humans First: Why We Are Nature's Favorite* (2004). Machan is a professor at Chapman University and a research fellow at the Hoover Institute.

Although the idea that animals have rights goes back to the 18th century, at least, it has only recently become something of a *cause celebre* among numerous serious and well-placed intellectuals, including moral and political philosophers. Although Jeremy Bentham seems to have suggested legislation requiring humane treatment of animals, he didn't defend animal rights, per se—not surprisingly, since Bentham himself had not been impressed with the more basic (Lockean) doctrine of natural rights—calling them "nonsense upon stilts." John Locke's idea of individual rights has had enormous influence, and even where it is not respected, it is ultimately invoked as some kind of model for what it would take for something to have rights.

In recent years the doctrine of animals rights has found champions in important circles where the general doctrine of rights is itself well respected. For example, Professor Tom Regan, in his important book *The Case for Animal Rights* (UC Press, 1983), finds the idea of natural

Tibor R. Machan, "Do Animals Have Rights?" *Public Affairs Quarterly*, Vol. 5, No. 2, April 1991. Reprinted by permission of Public Affairs Quarterly.

rights intellectually congenial but then extends this idea to cover animals near humans on the evolutionary scale. The tradition from within which Regan works is clearly Lockean, only he does not agree that human nature is distinctive enough, in relevant respects, to restrict the scope of natural rights to human beings alone.

Following a different tradition, namely, utilitarianism, the idea of animal liberation has emerged. And this idea comes to roughly the same thing, practically speaking. Only the argument is different because for utilitarians what is important is not that someone or something must have a specific sphere of dominion but that they be well off in their lives. So long as the bulk of the relevant creatures enjoy a reasonably high living standard, the moral and political objectives for us will have been met. But if this goal is neglected, moral and political steps are required to improve on the situation. Animal liberation is such a step.

This essay will maintain that animals have no rights and need no liberation. I will argue that to think they do is a category mistake— it is, to be blunt, to unjustifiably anthropomorphize animals, to treat them as if they were what they are not, namely, human beings. Rights and liberty are political concepts applicable to human beings because human beings are moral agents, in need of what Harvard philosopher Robert Nozick calls "moral space," that is, a definite sphere of moral jurisdiction where their authority to act is respected and protected so it is they, not intruders, who govern themselves and either succeed or fail in their moral tasks.

Oddly, it is clearly admitted by most animal rights or liberation theorists that only human beings are moral agents—for example, they never urge animals to behave morally (by, e.g., standing up for their rights, by leading a political revolution). No animal rights theorist proposes that animals be tried for crimes and blamed for moral wrongs.

If it is true that the moral nature of human beings gives rise to the conception of basic rights and liberties, then by this alone animal rights and liberation theorists have made an admission fatal to their case.

Before getting under way I want to note that rights and liberty are certainly not the whole of moral concern to us. There are innumerable other moral issues one can raise, including about the way human beings relate to animals. In particular, there is the question how should people treat animals. Should they be hunted even when this does not serve any vital human purpose? Should they be utilized in hurtful—indeed, evidently agonizing—fashion even for trivial human purposes? Should their pain and suffering be ignored in the process of being made use of for admittedly vital human purposes?

It is clear that once one has answered the question of whether animals have rights (or ought to be liberated from human beings) in the negative, one has by no means disposed of these other issues. In this essay I will be dealing mostly with the issue of animal rights and liberation. Yet I will also touch briefly on the other moral issues just raised. I will indicate why they may all be answered in the negative without it being the case that animals have rights or should be liberated—i.e., without raising any serious political issues.

Why Might Animals Have Rights?

To have a right amounts to having those around one who have the choice to abstain from intruding on one within a given sphere of jurisdiction. If I have the right to the use of our community swimming pool, no one may prevent me from making the decision as to whether I do or do not use the pool. Someone's having a right is a kind of freedom from the unavoidable interference of moral agents, beings who are capable of choosing whether they will interfere or not interfere with the rights holder.

When a right is considered natural, the freedom involved in having this right is supposed to be justified by reference to the kind of being one is, one's nature as a certain kind of entity. The idea of natural rights was formulated in connection with the issue of the proper relationship between human beings, especially citizens and governments. The idea goes back many centuries . . .

The major political thinker with an influential doctrine of natural rights was John Locke. In his *Second Treatise on Government* he argued that each human being is responsible to follow the Law of Nature, the source of morality. But to do so, each also requires a sphere of personal authority, which is identified by the principle of the natural right to property—including one's person and estate. In other words, to be a morally responsible being in the company of other persons one needs what Robert Nozick has called "moral space," i.e., a sphere of sovereignty or personal jurisdiction so that one can engage in self-government—for better or for worse.

Locke made it a provision of having such a right that there be sufficient and good enough of whatever one may have a right to left for others—i.e., the Lockean proviso against absolute monopoly. For Locke the reason government is necessary is "that though in the state of Nature [every human being] hath such a right [to absolute freedom], yet the enjoyment of it is very uncertain and constantly exposed to the invasion of others."[1] So we establish government to make us secure in the enjoyment of our rights.

Since Locke's time the doctrine of natural rights has undergone a turbulent intellectual history, falling into disrepute at the hands of empiricism and positivism but gaining a revival at the hands of some influential political philosophers of the second half of the 20th century.

Ironically, at a time in recent intellectual history when natural rights theory had not been enjoying much support, the idea that animals might also have rights came under increasing discussion. Most notable among those who proposed such a notion was Thomas Taylor, whose anonymous work, *Vindication of the Rights of Brutes,* was published in 1792 but discussed animal rights only in the context of demeaning human rights. More positive (though brief) was the contribution of Jeremy Bentham, who in his *An Introduction to the Principles of Morals and Legislation* (1789) argued that those animals that can suffer are owed moral consideration, even if those that molest us or those we may make good use of may be killed—but not "tormented."

In the latter part of the 19th century an entire work was devoted to the idea by Henry S. Salt, entitled *Animals' Rights.*[2] And in our time numerous philosophers and social commentators have made the attempt to demonstrate that if we are able to ascribe basic rights to life, liberty and property to human beings, we can do the same for many of the higher animals. In essentials their arguments can be broken down into two parts. First, they subscribe to Darwin's thesis that no difference of kind, only a difference of degree, can be found between other animals and human beings.[3] Second, even if there were a difference in kind between other animals—especially mammals—and human beings, since they both can be shown to have interests (e.g., the avoidance of pain or suffering), for certain moral and legal purposes the difference does not matter, only the similarity does. In connection with both of these arguments the central conclusion is that if human beings can be said to have certain basic rights—e.g., to life, liberty or consideration for their capacity to suffer—then so do (higher) animals.[4]

Now I do not wish to give the impression that no diversity exists among those who defend animal rights. Some do so from the viewpoint of natural rights, treating animals' rights as basic limiting principles which may not be ignored except when it would also make sense to disregard the rights of human beings. Even on this matter are there serious differences among defenders of animal rights— some do not allow any special regard for human beings,[5] some hold that when it comes to a choice between a person and a dog, it is ordinarily the person who should be given protection.[6] But others choose to defend animal rights on utilitarian grounds—to the extent that it amounts to furthering overall pleasure or happiness in the world, animals must be given equal consideration to what human beings receive. Thus only if there really is demonstrable contribution to the overall pleasure or happiness on earth, may an animal capable of experiencing pleasure or happiness be sacrificed for the sake of some human purpose. Barring such demonstrable contribution, animals and humans enjoy equal rights.[7]

At times the argument for animal rights begins with the rather mild point that "reason requires that other animals are as much within the scope of moral concern as are men" but then moves on to the more radical claim that therefore "we must view our entire history as well as all aspects of our daily lives from a new perspective."[8]

Of course, people have generally invoked some moral considerations as they treated animals—I can recall living on a farm in Hungary when I was 11 and getting all kinds of lectures about how I ought to treat the animals, receiving severe rebuke when I mistreated a cat and lots of praise when I took the favorite cow grazing every day and established a close bond with it over time. Hardly anyone can have escaped one or another moral lecture from parents or neighbors concerning the treatment of pets, household animals, or birds. When a young boy once tried out an air gun by shooting a pigeon sitting on a telephone wire before the apartment house in which he lived, I recall that there was no end of rebuke in response to his wanton callousness. Yet none of those who engaged in the moralizing ever entertained the need to "view our entire history as well as all aspects of our daily lives from a new perspective." Rather they seemed to have understood that reckless disregard for the life or well-being of animals shows a defect of character, lack of sensitivity, callousness—realizing, at the same time, that numerous human purposes justify our killing and using animals in the various ways most of us do use them.

And this really is the crux of the matter. But why? Why is it more reasonable to think of animals as available for our sensible use rather than owed the kind of respect and consideration we ought to extend to other human beings? It is one thing to have this as a commonsense conviction, it is another to know it as a sound viewpoint, in terms of which we may confidently conduct ourselves.

Why We May Use Animals

While I will return to the arguments for animal rights, let me first place on record the case for the use of animals for human purposes. Without this case reasonably well established, it will not be possible to critically assess the case for animal rights. After all, this is a comparative matter—which viewpoint makes better sense, which is, in other words, more likely to be true?

One reason for the propriety of our use of animals is that we are more important or valuable than other animals and some of our projects may require animals for them to be successful. Notice that this is different from saying that human beings are "uniquely important," a position avidly ridiculed by Stephen R. L. Clark, who claims that "there seems no decent ground in reason or revelation to suppose that man is uniquely important or significant."[9] If man were uniquely important, that would mean that one could not assign any value to plants or non-human animals apart from their relationship to human beings. That is not the position I am defending. I argue that there is a scale of importance in nature, and among all the various kinds of being, human beings are the most important—even while it is true that some members of the human species may indeed prove themselves to be the most vile and worthless, as well.

How do we establish that we are more important or valuable? By considering whether the idea of lesser or greater importance or value in the nature of things makes clear sense and applying it to an understanding of whether human beings or other animals are more important. If it turns out that ranking things in nature as more or less important makes sense, and if we qualify as more important than other animals, there is at least the beginning of a reason why we may make use of other animals for our purposes.

That there are things of different degree of value in nature is admitted by animal rights advocates, so there is no great need here to argue about that. When they insist that we treat animals differently from the way we treat, say, rocks or iron ore—so that while we may not use the former as we choose, we may use the latter—they testify, at least by implication, that animals are more important than, say, iron ore. Certainly they invoke some measure of importance or value and place animals higher in line with this measure than they place other aspects of nature. They happen, also, to deny that human beings rank higher than animals, or least they do not admit that human beings' higher ranking warrants their using animals for their purposes. But that is a distinct issue which we can consider later.

Quite independently of the implicit acknowledgment by animal rights advocates of the hierarchy of nature, there simply is evidence through the natural world of the existence of beings of greater complexity and of higher value. For example, while it makes no sense to evaluate as good or bad such things as planets or rocks or pebbles—except as they may relate to human purposes—when it comes to plants and animals the process of evaluation commences very naturally indeed. We can speak of better or worse trees, oaks, redwoods, or zebras, foxes or chimps. While at this point we confine our evaluation to the condition or behavior of such beings without any intimation of their responsibility for being better or worse, when we start discussing human beings our evaluation takes on a moral component. Indeed, none are more ready to testify to this than animal rights advocates who, after all, do not demand any change of behavior on the part of non-human animals and yet insist that human beings conform to certain moral edicts as a matter of their own choice. This means that even animal rights advocates admit outright that to the best of our knowledge it is with human beings that the idea of moral goodness and moral responsibility enters the universe.

Clearly this shows a hierarchical structure in nature: some things do not invite evaluations at all—it is a matter of no significance or of indifference whether they are or are not or what they are or how they behave. Some things invite evaluation but without implying any moral standing with reference to whether they do well or badly. And some things—namely, human beings—invite moral evaluation. The level of importance or value may be noted to move from the inanimate to the animate world, culminating, as far as we now know, with human life. Normal human life involves moral tasks, and that is why we are more important than other beings in nature—we are subject to moral appraisal, it is a matter of our doing whether we succeed or fail in our lives.

Now when it comes to our moral task, namely, to succeed as human beings, we are dependent upon reaching sensible conclusions about what we should do. We can fail to do this and too often do so. But we can also succeed. The process that leads to our success involves learning, among other things, what it is that nature avails us with to achieve our highly varied tasks in life. Clearly among these highly varied tasks could be some that make judicious use of animals—for example, to find out whether some medicine is safe for human use, we might wish to use animals. To do this is the rational thing for us to do, so as to make the best use of nature for our success in living our lives. That does not mean there need be no guidelines involved in how we might make use of animals—any more than there need be no guidelines involved in how we use anything else.

Why Individual Human Rights?

Where do individual *human* rights come into this picture? The rights being talked of in connection with human beings have as their source, as we have noted earlier, the human capacity to make moral choices. We have the right to life, liberty and property—as well as more specialized rights connected with politics, the press, religion—because we have as our central task in life to act morally. And in order to be able to do this throughout the scope of our lives, we require a reasonably clear sphere of personal jurisdiction—a dominion where we are sovereign and can either succeed or fail to live well, to do right, to act properly.

If we did not have rights, we would not have such a sphere of personal jurisdiction and there would be no clear idea as to whether we are acting in our own behalf or those of other persons. No one could be blamed or praised for we would not know clearly enough whether what the person is doing is in his or her authority to do or in someone else's. This is precisely the problem that arises in communal living and, especially, in totalitarian countries where everything is under forced collective governance. The reason moral distinctions are still possible to make under such circumstances is that in fact—as distinct from law—there is always some sphere of personal jurisdiction wherein people may exhibit courage, prudence, justice, honesty, and other virtues. But where collectivism has been successfully enforced, there is no individual responsibility at play and people's morality and immorality are submerged within the group.

Indeed the main reason for governments has for some time been recognized to be nothing other than that our individual human rights should be protected. In the past—and in many places even today—it was thought that government (or the State) has some kind of leadership role in human communities. This belief followed the view that human beings differ amongst themselves radically, some being lower, some higher class, some possessing divine rights, other lacking them, some having a personal communion with God, other lacking this special advantage.

With such views in place, it made clear enough sense to argue that government should have a patriarchal role in human communities—the view against which John Locke forcefully argued his theory of natural individual human rights.[10]

Where Is There Room for Animal Rights?

We have seen that the most sensible and influential doctrine of human rights rests on the fact that human beings are indeed members of a discernibly different species—the members of which have a moral life to aspire to and must have principles upheld for them in communities that make their aspiration possible. Now there is plainly no valid intellectual place for rights in the non-human world, the world in which moral responsibility is for all practical purposes absent. Some would want to argue that some measure of morality can be found within the world of at least higher animals—e.g., dogs. For example, Rollin holds that "In actual fact, some animals even seem to exhibit behavior that bespeaks something like moral agency or moral agreement."[11] His argument for this is rather anecdotal but it is worth considering:

> Canids, including the domesticated dog, do not attack another when the vanquished bares its throat, showing a sign of submission. Animals typically do not prey upon members of their own species. Elephants and porpoises will and do feed injured members of their species. Porpoises will help humans, even at risk to themselves. Some animals will adopt orphaned young of other species. (Such cross-species "morality" would certainly not be explainable by simple appeal to mechanical evolution, since there is no advantage whatever to one's own species.) Dogs will act "guilty" when they break a rule such as one against stealing food from a table and will, for the most part, learn not to take it.[12]

Animal rights advocates such as Rollin maintain that it is impossible to clearly distinguish between human and non-human animals, including on the grounds of the former's characteristic as a moral agent. Yet what they do to defend this point is to invoke borderline cases, imaginary hypotheses and anecdotes.

In contrast, in his book *The Difference of Man and the Difference It Makes*, Mortimer Adler undertakes the painstaking task of showing that even with the full acknowledgment of the merits of Darwinian and, especially, post-Darwinian evolutionary theory, there is ample reason to uphold the doctrine of species-distinction—a distinction, incidentally, that is actually presupposed within Darwin's own work.[13] Adler shows that although the theistic doctrine of radical species differences is incompatible with current evolutionary theory, the more naturalistic view that species are superficially (but nonnegligibly) different is indeed necessary to it. The fact of occasional borderline cases is simply irrelevant—what is crucial is that the generalization is true that human beings are basically different from other animals—by virtue of "a crucial threshold in a continuum of degrees." As Adler explains:

> . . . distinct species are genetically isolated populations between which interbreeding is impossible, arising (except in the case of polyploidy) from varieties between which interbreeding was not impossible, but between which it was prevented. Modern theorists, with more assurance than Darwin could manage, treat distinct species as natural kinds, not as man-made class distinctions.[14]

Adler adds that "Without the critical insight provided by the distinction between superficial and radical differences in kind, biologists [as well as animal rights advocates, one should add] might be tempted to follow Darwin in thinking that all differences in kind must be apparent, not real."[15]

Since Locke's admittedly incomplete—sometimes even confusing— theory had gained respect and, especially, practical import (e.g., in British and American political history), it became clear enough that the only justification for the exercise of state power—namely the force of the law—is that the rights of individuals are being or have been violated. But as with all successful doctrines, Locke's idea became corrupted by innumerable efforts to concoct rights that government must protect, rights that were actually disguised special interest objectives— values that some people, perhaps quite legitimately, wanted very badly to have secured for them.

While it is no doubt true that many animal rights advocates sincerely believe that they have found a justification for the actual existence of animal rights, it is equally likely that if the Lockean doctrine of rights had not become so influential, they would now be putting their point differently—in a way, namely, that would secure for them what they, as a special interest group, want: the protection of animals they have such love and sympathy for.

Closing Reflections

As with most issues on the minds of many intelligent people as well as innumerable crackpots, a discussion of whether there are animal rights and how we ought to treat animals cannot be concluded with dogmatic certainty one way or the other. Even though those who defend animal rights are certain almost beyond a shadow of doubt, all I can claim is to being certain beyond a reasonable doubt. Animals are not the sort of beings with basic rights to life, liberty and property, whereas human beings, in the main, are just such beings. Yet we know that animals can feel pain and can enjoy themselves and this must give us pause when we consider using them for our legitimate purposes. We ought to be humane, we ought to kill them and rear them and train them and hunt them in a fashion consistent with such care about them as sentient beings.

In a review of Tom Regan's provocative book already mentioned, *The Case for Animal Rights*, John Hospers makes the following observations that I believe put the matter into the best light we can shed on our topic:

> As one reads page after page of Regan's book, one has the growing impression that his thesis is in an important way "going against nature." It is a fact of nature that living things have to live on other living things in order to stay alive themselves. It is a fact of nature that carnivores must consume, not plants (which they can't digest), but other sentient beings capable of intense pain and suffering, and that they can survive in no other way. It is a fact of nature that animal reproduction is such that far more creatures are born or hatched than can possibly survive. It is a fact of nature that most creatures die slow lingering tortuous deaths, and that few animals in the wild ever reach old age. It is a fact of nature that we cannot take one step in the woods without killing thousands of tiny organisms whose lives we thereby extinguish. This has been the order of nature for millions of years before man came on the scene, and has indeed been the means by which any animal species has survived to the present day; to fight it is like trying to fight an atomic bomb with a dartgun. . . . This is the world as it is, nature in the raw, unlike the animals in Disney cartoons.[16]

Of course, one might then ask, why should human beings make any attempt to behave differently among themselves, why bother with morality at all?

The fact is that with human nature a problem arose in nature that had not been there before—basic choices had to be confronted, which other animals do not have to confront. The question "How should I live?" faces each human being. And that is what makes it unavoidable for human beings to dwell on moral issues as well as to see other human beings as having the same problem to solve, the same question to dwell on. For this reason we are very different from other animals—we also do terrible, horrible, awful things to each other as well as to nature, but we can also do much, much better and achieve incredible feats nothing else in nature can come close to.

Indeed, then, the moral life is the exclusive province of human beings, so far as we can tell for now. Other—lower(!)—animals simply cannot be accorded the kind of treatment that such a moral life demands, namely, respect for and protection of basic rights.

Notes

1. John Locke, *Two Treatises on Government*, Par. 123.

2. Henry S. Salt, *Animals' Rights* (London: George Bell & Sons, Ltd., 1892; Clark Summit, PA: Society for Animals Rights, Inc., 1980). This is perhaps *the* major philosophical effort to defend animals rights prior to Tom Regan's treatises on the same topic.

3. Charles Darwin, *The Descent of Man*, Chpts. 3 and 4. Reprinted in Tom Regan and Peter Singer, eds., *Animal Rights and Human Obligations* (Englewood Cliffs, NJ: Prentice-Hall, 1976), pp. 72–81.

4. On these points both the deontologically oriented Tom Regan and the utilitarian Peter Singer tend to agree, although they differ considerably in their arguments.

5. Peter Singer holds that "we would be on shaky grounds if we were to demand equality for blacks, women, and other groups of oppressed humans while denying equal consideration to nonhumans." "All Animals Are Equal," op. cit., Regan & Singer, *Animal Rights*, p. 150.

6. Tom Regan contends that "[it] is not to say that practices that involve taking the lives of animals cannot possibly be justified . . . in order to seriously consider approving such a practice [it] would [have to] prevent, reduce, or eliminate a much greater amount of evil . . . there is no other way to bring about these consequences . . . and . . . we have very good reason to believe that these consequences will obtain." "Do Animals Have a Right to Life?" Op. cit., Regan & Singer, *Animal Rights*, pp. 205–6.

7. This is the gist of Singer's thesis.

8. Bernard E. Rollin, *Animal Rights and Human Morality* (Buffalo, NY: Prometheus Books, 1981), p. 4.

9. Stephen R. L. Clark, *The Moral Status of Animals* (Oxford, England: Clarendon Press, 1977), p. 13.

10. John Locke, *Two Treatises.*

11. Rollin, *Animal Rights,* p. 14.

12. Ibid.

13. See a discussion of this in Mortimer Adler, *The Difference of Man and the Difference It Makes* (New York: World Publishing Co., 1968), pp. 73ff.

14. Ibid.

15. Ibid., p. 75.

16. John Hospers, "Review of the Case for Animal Rights," *Reason Papers,* No. 10, p. 123.

CHAPTER 21

The Immorality of SUVs and Trucks

Douglas Husak

Scientists tell us that the world is not what it appears to be: Solid objects like tables and desks are made up of mostly empty space; disease is often caused by living things too small for us to see; and the universe as we know it began with a mighty explosion some 12 to 15 billion years ago.

Ethicists, too, often say that the world is not what it seems; our beliefs about right and wrong are often mistaken. Unfortunately, these ethicists almost never say that something we do is morally better than we think. Rather, they often conclude that we should stop doing something that is normally regarded as unobjectionable. In previous selections, Peter Singer argued that eating meat and spending money on luxuries are wrong in the current state of things. Here, Douglas Husak of Rutgers University argues that about 500 billion miles of the driving done annually on American roads is morally wrong.

Philosophers should begin to think more seriously about the many moral issues that arise from our frequent use of personal motor vehicles (automobiles, vans, SUVs, motorcycles, trucks, and the like). I will argue that greater attention is warranted for two simple reasons. First and most obviously, personal vehicles cause tremendous amounts of harm. Second and more controversially, much of this harm is caused culpably. When culpable conduct causes serious harm, the state often responds by imposing criminal or civil liability. Yet the specific problems I will discuss have never led anyone to recommend the enactment of criminal

Excerpted from Douglas Husak, "Vehicles and Crashes: Why Is This Moral Issue Overlooked?" *Social Theory and Practice*, Vol. 30, No. 3 (July 2004).

legislation. A few commentators have proposed the imposition of tort liability, but no courts have yet complied. Even more surprising, however, is the fact that moral philosophers have not been vocal in condemning the culpable, harmful conduct I will describe. . . .

Personal motor vehicles give rise to a host of important and difficult moral questions I will ignore. I will simply mention five such issues, but the list could go on and on.[1] We spend far too much time in our vehicles—on average, nearly an hour per day—and become sedentary, obese, and unhealthy as a result. Our environment is degraded by concrete and contaminated by pollution. Personal vehicles facilitate white flight to suburbia and beyond, contributing to the racial segregation and decay of our inner cities. Our international policy is distorted by our thirst for foreign oil. Erratic and discriminatory enforcement of our traffic regulations compromises our status as a government of laws, not of men.[2] But these are not the topics I will examine. I cite them only to indicate that the following discussion merely scratches the surface in describing one of the many moral issues that arise from our use of personal motor vehicles.

I will argue that a surprising amount of driving in the United States today is morally problematic. To support this conclusion, I must establish that the types of driving I will identify cause serious harms culpably. I will not make the trivial observation that many motor vehicle accidents result from speeding, alcohol impairment, or some other kind of unlawful mode of operation. The wrongfulness of this conduct is widely appreciated.[3] I will defend the much less obvious claim that a great deal of driving is morally suspect even when persons drive carefully, conforming to all of the rules and regulations in the Code of Motor Vehicles. The objectionable but lawful kinds of driving on which I will focus involve trips taken for *frivolous purposes* in *crash-incompatible* vehicles.

My contention that many of the risks created by lawful driving are culpable is controversial partly because of disagreement about the nature of culpability itself. I believe that a significant number of these risks are imposed *negligently*—a low but familiar type of culpability. Although I hope to raise *moral* questions about the use of personal motor vehicles, I will borrow a conception of negligence from the law. Legal accounts vary a bit from one jurisdiction to another, but the most widely cited definition is that conduct is negligent when a person creates a substantial and unjustifiable risk of harm that deviates from a standard of care to which a reasonable person in his situation would have conformed.[4] When a person is conscious of these unreasonable risks, his conduct is *reckless* rather than negligent—a higher degree of culpability.[5] But drivers need not be aware of the risks I will describe to be culpable.

In order to establish that many of the risks of driving are imposed negligently, we must identify the conditions under which driving subjects others to a substantial and unjustifiable risk that deviates from the standard of care we should expect from reasonable persons. This question requires a determination of whether and under what circumstances the risks of driving are (1) substantial and (2) unjustifiable. Each of these topics will be discussed in turn. If I am correct that the kinds of driving I will describe subject others to a substantial and unjustifiable risk, I assume that I will have shown that these acts are negligent and therefore objectionable from a moral point of view.[6] I will suppose, in other words, that reasonable (non-negligent) persons would not engage in conduct that creates substantial and unjustifiable risks.

Virtually any activity involves *some* risk of harm; risks become negligent only when they are substantial. Everyone is aware that personal motor vehicles cause tremendous amounts of harm. Still, a few of the statistics are worth rehearsing. The love affair between Americans and the automobile shows no signs of abating, as households around the country possess more motor vehicles than ever—even more than the number of licensed drivers. About 204 million personal vehicles are available for regular use. Daily travel in the United States totals about 4 trillion miles annually, an average of about 14,500 miles per person per year. Americans took 411 billion daily trips in 2001, or about 1,500 trips per individual. Long-distance travel added another 760 billion miles to this total. Approximately 87% of all daily trips and 90% of all long-distance trips took place in a personal motor vehicle.[7]

Although the safety of vehicles has improved,[8] driving in the United States remains an extraordinarily dangerous activity. The number of fatalities has remained fairly stable throughout the last decade, although it rose in 2003 to 43,200—a fourteen-year high. To put this figure in perspective, we might note that more Americans were killed in car accidents in the month of September 2001 than died in the terrorist attacks of September 11. Motor vehicle crashes are the leading cause of death for persons of *every* age from 4 through 33 years old. But the number of fatalities offers a very limited perspective on the real hazards of personal motor vehicles. In 2001, an estimated 6,323,000 crashes injured 3,033,000 people; 4,282,000 of these crashes involved property damage alone. The economic cost of these accidents in 2000 was a staggering $230.6 billion.[9]

We might have somewhat less reason to be alarmed about these grim statistics if the dangers of motor vehicles fell almost exclusively on drivers.[10] It is plausible to suppose that our moral and legal theories should distinguish the risks imposed on oneself from those imposed on others.[11] The use of tobacco products and the consumption of high-calorie foods compete as the leading causes of preventable death in the United States today, but (in the vast majority of cases) the victims of these behaviors are the same persons who engage in and benefit from them.[12] Vehicles are different in this crucial respect. Admittedly, the driver himself is the individual most likely to be killed or injured in a motor vehicle accident. Nonetheless, controversies about paternalism need not detain us, since drivers subject other persons to enormous risks of harm. Passengers account for about 30% of all fatalities in motor vehicle accidents; many other victims of crashes were not occupants in motor vehicles at all. In 2002, pedestrians suffered 4,808 deaths in accidents involving motor vehicles; 662 cyclists were killed as well.[13] Clearly, personal motor vehicles pose a *public* health problem fundamentally different from the hazards of smoking or excessive eating.

Do these statistics show that driving subjects others to a *substantial* risk? The answer is unclear—and not simply because of the lack of consensus about how great a given risk must be in order to qualify as substantial. More fundamentally, theorists disagree about what statistic is most relevant in assessing the magnitude of a risk. The degree of risk appears very different when we focus on driving as a type of activity rather than on tokens of driving. In the aggregate, no one doubts that the forgoing data suffice to show that driving creates a substantial risk of harm to others. No other type of activity comes close to injuring millions of other people each year. But the dangers of driving become far less apparent when expressed by the *probability* of harm on a particular occasion. The likelihood that a serious injury will result from a given incident of driving is very small. On average, Americans travel 68 million miles before causing a fatality. Still, it is not unusual for a person to drive a million miles in the course of his life, and most of us are involved in at least one fairly serious accident at some time or another. More significantly, driving is the riskiest activity in which the vast majority of Americans routinely engage. It is safe to predict that if the typical reader of these pages (directly) kills or seriously injures another person, his weapon is likely to be a motor vehicle.

So which statistic is more significant? No single answer will suffice for all normative purposes.[14] In my judgment, both the total amount of harm and the probability of its occurrence on a particular occasion are relevant to deciding whether the risk of driving is substantial. For purposes of moral evaluation, aggregate figures must be taken into account in cases in which individuals tend to perform tens of thousands of tokens of the same type of activity. The same is true of prudential assessment. For example, no one should believe that the risks of smoking are trivial by examining data about the probability of contracting cancer from a single cigarette. It is fair to describe the risks of smoking as substantial because the vast majority of smokers consume several thousand cigarettes in their lifetimes. The same point applies to operating a motor vehicle. I conclude that driving *per se* should probably be thought to create substantial risks of harm to others.

But I do not claim that driving per se is wrongful; I reserve this judgment for a particular *type* of driving that satisfies two conditions. Operating a vehicle with an unacceptable degree of *crash incompatibility* is the first of these conditions. When one vehicle collides with another, the vehicle that hits may be described as the *encroaching* vehicle, and the vehicle being hit may be described as the *crash partner* vehicle.[15] Consumers who purchase vehicles often are interested in data about how their own vehicle is likely to fare in an impact. Questions about crash compatibility—about how their vehicle will affect their crash partner—are seldom asked. Moral issues arise when persons drive vehicles with too high a degree of crash incompatibility.[16]

Pickup trucks and SUVs (sport utility vehicles) are two common categories of vehicles that tend to exhibit alarmingly high rates of crash incompatibility.[17] In other words, occupants of cars involved in accidents have good reason to prefer to be hit by other cars rather than by SUVs or trucks.[18] Although precise data change each year, there is no question that these vehicles, as a class, pose enhanced risks for crash partner cars—even when the weight of the encroaching vehicle is held constant.[19] For every million registered encroaching cars weighing two tons (a very heavy car), 45 deaths occur in crash partner cars each year. But in collisions between cars and SUVs of the same weight, the fatality rate in crash partner cars soars to 76, and rises still further to 87 in the case of pickup trucks.[20] The net consequences of crash incompatibility are lethal. Keith Bradsher estimates that "the replacement of cars with SUVs is currently causing close to 3,000 needless deaths a year in the United States."[21]

Weight, height, and stiffness of construction are the three most important characteristics of vehicles that contribute to their crash incompatibility.[22] On average, SUVs and pickup trucks are 900 pounds heavier than cars, and the gap between them is widening as very large SUVs account for a higher and higher percentage of sales. The conservation of momentum in a collision places smaller vehicles at an enormous disadvantage when the encroaching vehicle is heavier.[23] In addition, SUVs and pickup trucks, as a class, are much more rigid than passenger cars. These types of vehicles frequently use a stiff frame-rail design rather than the softer unibody structure employed in cars. Finally, SUVs and pickup trucks tend to ride much higher than cars. Although this differential creates a mismatch during frontal impacts, side collisions pose a far greater concern. Side impacts are a growing problem in highway safety; in 2001, they caused about half of all car driver deaths in collisions involving two vehicles.[24] Most cars are equipped with beams designed to reduce cabin deformation during side impacts. But the higher bumpers of SUVs and trucks miss these side beams, striking unreinforced doors and increasing the probability of intrusion into the cabin of the crash partner car.[25] In combination, these three factors give SUVs and pickup trucks their high degree of crash incompatibility. When side impacts cause a fatality, occupants of the crash partner car are six times more likely to be killed than occupants of the encroaching vehicle; this differential rises to 25 when the encroaching vehicle is an SUV or pickup truck.[26]

Of course, incompatibility creates a problem only in the event of a crash, so one might be tempted to respond that the solution is to drive more carefully so that fewer crashes occur.[27] It is far easier, however, to manufacture safer vehicles than to produce better drivers. In any event, it is important to notice that the problem of crash incompatibility is posed regardless of how fault is distributed in an accident. Suppose a vehicle with a high degree of crash incompatibility collides with a car that negligently goes through a red light or stop sign. The driver of the encroaching vehicle may have been as careful as anyone could have demanded. Nonetheless, by operating a vehicle with a high degree of crash incompatibility, he imposes elevated levels of risk on those drivers who are negligent. Even reckless drivers have a right to expect that others not subject them to unreasonable risks of harm in the event of a crash.

My claim thus far is that moral issues are raised when drivers subject others to substantial risks by operating vehicles with an unacceptable degree of crash incompatibility. But the supposition that one person imposes a substantial risk on another does not suffice to establish that his conduct is culpable. To be negligent, his risky behavior must also be *unjustifiable*. I believe that most of the controversy about the morality of personal motor vehicles centers around the issue of whether and under what circumstances the risks of driving are imposed justifiably. The textbook illustration of conduct that justifiably subjects others to a substantial risk is speeding by an ambulance to rush a seriously injured patient to a hospital. Some commentators argue that *all* justified actions share this feature; each prevents a more imminent or serious harm than it causes.[28]

Are the risks of driving imposed unjustifiably? Whether a risk is justifiable depends partly on its magnitude; I have already argued that these are substantial. But an equally important factor is the reason(s) to create the risk. What are these reasons? Why are vehicles with a high degree of crash incompatibility manufactured, and why do so many consumers choose to buy them? Might the answers to these questions justify the substantial risks that these vehicles impose upon others? Many consumers suppose that the structural features that contribute to crash incompatibility cannot be eliminated without negating the advantages of operating the vehicles in question. Buses and heavy trucks, for example, have extraordinarily high rates of crash incompatibility, but few commentators believe it is wrongful to operate them for the simple reason that these vehicles are indispensable and could not be made significantly safer without detracting from their valuable purpose. Is the same true of the categories of vehicles on which I have focused—SUVs and pickup trucks? In addressing this question, I will concentrate on SUVs—even though they have a better record of crash compatibility than small trucks. I focus on SUVs for three simple reasons. First, they are more popular than trucks. SUVs account for 37% of the registered vehicles in the United States, and represent 49.3% of the 5.9 million vehicles sold in the first eight months of 2003.[29] Second, data about SUVs are more widely available. Third, the geometrical features that contribute to the high degree of crash incompatibility in pickup trucks allow these vehicles to haul heavy loads—a purpose that is more likely to justify the heightening levels of risk they impose. Still, it is important to remain aware that most of my subsequent remarks about SUVs apply even more forcefully to pickup trucks.

The three structural features of SUVs that contribute to their crash incompatibility—weight, bumper height, and rigidity—are included in the design of these vehicles mainly in order to allow them to be driven off-road. If altering these structural features precluded off-road driving, the substantial risks caused by these vehicles might be justified on grounds of necessity, and persons would not be negligent for operating them. But this supposition provides a dubious ground to believe that the risks of crash-incompatible vehicles can be justified. In the first place, as Howard Latin and Bobby Kasolas have shown in their pioneering study, there is good reason to suspect that SUVs could have been designed with greater crash compatibility without detracting from their off-road function.[30] Of course, this matter raises empirical questions in engineering about which philosophers should remain cautious. Still, consider the recent announcements from representatives of the auto industry in December of 2003.[31] Manufacturers promised to improve crash compatibility by making the rail frames and front-end structures of their SUVs and pickups overlap with at least half of the corresponding areas on cars by 2009. These innovations will not impair off-road performance, and are estimated to add only $300 to the cost of new vehicles.[32] Perhaps more importantly for present purposes, these improvements do not require new innovations in engineering. I conclude that *if* existing vehicles could have been designed to be safer to crash partners at a reasonable cost, their substantial risks to others could hardly be justifiable.

The more fundamental problem, however, is that few of these drivers really have sufficient reasons to leave the road. Admittedly, *some* owners of crash-incompatible vehicles may have a legitimate need for off-road performance that would justify subjecting others to heightened levels of risk. But SUVs in particular are rarely driven for this purpose. Depending on how the question is asked, between 99% and 87% of SUV drivers *never* take their vehicles off-road; many of the remaining minority do so very infrequently.[33] J.C. Collins, Ford's top marketing manager for SUVs, admits that "the only time those SUVs are going to be off-road is when they miss the driveway at 3 A.M."[34] No plausible moral analysis of crash-incompatible vehicles would permit persons to impose substantial risks on others because corrective measures to reduce these risks would prevent an extremely rare activity of dubious value.

To be sure, many purchasers are attracted to SUVs not because of their off-road capabilities, but because they believe them to be safer.[35] Although data on this topic are controversial,[36] one matter is clear. Perceptions about the safety of these vehicles are typically exaggerated; SUVs fare better only in crashes involving other cars, not in single-vehicle crashes.[37] In accidents not involving other vehicles— which account for almost half of all traffic deaths—the very features that make SUVs unsafe to others tend to make them unsafe to their occupants. In particular, SUVs as a class are notoriously susceptible to rollovers.[38] Although less than 1% of crashes involve rollovers, these accidents cause one-quarter of all traffic deaths—more than side and rear impacts combined.[39] More importantly, however, this attempt to defend crash-incompatible vehicles is completely unresponsive to the moral problem I have raised. As Nicholas Dixon observes, measures to protect my family and me are laudable unless they subject other equally innocent persons to substantial risks of harm.[40] Only an ethical egoist could think that the pursuit of one's rational self-interest provides a justification for negligent conduct.

Thus far, my case for condemning some types of driving as wrongful has focused on the issue of crash incompatibility. But a second factor is just as important in supporting my conclusion. Why do people drive at all—even vehicles with an acceptable degree of crash compatibility? Recent studies yield surprising answers. All too often, our reasons for driving and subjecting others to risks are frivolous. Only 14.8% of all daily trips taken by Americans are to and from work (although an additional 2.9% are "work-related").[41] Even if we concede that trips back and forth to work are sufficiently important to the prosperity of our country to justify the risks they create, we should question whether the time and distance these trips involve is really necessary. Many persons elect to live great distances from their place of employment; the average time required to commute to work is longer than at any point in our history. On some occasions, the choice to locate one's home so far from work probably represents the lesser of several evils. On other occasions, however, this preference is based on no reason that would justify the elevated level of risk it creates.

More significantly, however, over 82% of all trips are *not* work-related. Travel to and from school and church consumes an additional 10%. Nearly half of all trips (44.6%) are for "family or personal reasons"; more than one-quarter (27.1%) are for "social and recreational" purposes.[42] Reliable data that further subdivide the latter purposes into finer categories are hard to find. But everyone has ample experience with frivolous reasons for driving that would raise no moral qualms in any part of the country. Shoppers drive from one outlet to another to pay lower taxes on luxury goods like cosmetics and fashion accessories. People think nothing (apart from the prospects of being caught in traffic) of traveling across town to patronize a new bar or restaurant. Some simply sightsee or have no tangible objective other than to "go for a ride." No one would have any difficulty adding even more extreme examples of frivolous journeys to this list. Lots of driving in America today—perhaps more than a trillion miles per year—is

purely recreational and cannot be justified under any plausible interpretation of a necessity requirement. Unless we pretend to be wholly
agnostic about what activities have value, we must conclude that these
reasons to subject others to risks of harm are unjustifiable. When the
objective of a trip is truly frivolous, no one can pretend that it is necessary. Obviously, there are no precise criteria to decide whether the
purpose for taking a given trip is truly frivolous. But if *these* reasons justify the most dangerous activity in which we routinely engage, what
reasons could possibly *fail* to do so? . . .

I have argued that many instances of driving in the United States
today cause harm culpably: when people operate vehicles with unacceptable levels of crash incompatibility, or subject others to risks of
harm for wholly frivolous reasons. A plausible case can be made that
driving is wrongful when *either* of these two conditions obtain. This
position might be described as the *stronger* version of my thesis. It may
be *too* strong, and I prefer to be cautious and to minimize controversy.
In light of the structure of our society and our nearly irreversible
dependence on motor vehicles, I need not conclude that we act
wrongfully by engaging in purely recreational activities like golf when
we have no realistic alternative than to drive to our country clubs.

Therefore, I explicitly endorse only the *weaker* thesis—that driving
is wrongful when *both* conditions obtain. Clearly, the risks of driving are
most likely to be substantial and unjustifiable when these two considerations combine in a single case: a driver takes a frivolous journey in
a crash-incompatible vehicle. According to the weaker thesis, we are
permitted to drive to a prime location just to view a sunset, as long as
we take a vehicle with an acceptable degree of crash compatibility.
Even this conclusion is a bit too sweeping, since I have conceded that
some people have a legitimate need for crash-incompatible vehicles
that justifies the heightened levels of risk they impose. Such a person
may only own one vehicle, and it is hard to see why he acts wrongfully
when he drives it across town to his favorite fast food restaurant. My
conclusions apply to those individuals—certainly the vast majority of
SUV owners—who have no justificatory need to own a vehicle with a
high degree of crash incompatibility. These persons, I claim, act
wrongfully when they subject others to substantial risks for frivolous
purposes. I believe it is likely that far more driving is objectionable
than my weaker thesis suggests. Still, my argument has its most powerful application to cases that satisfy each of my two conditions.

An extraordinary amount of driving turns out to be morally
impermissible, even if only the weaker thesis is correct. If Americans

drive more than 4.75 trillion miles each year, and about one third of all driving takes place in a vehicle with an unacceptable degree of crash incompatibility, and roughly one-quarter of all trips are taken for frivolous purposes—all fairly conservative estimates—nearly half of a trillion miles of driving per year is objectionable. Even the weaker thesis suffices to show that an astounding amount of personal motor vehicle use in the United States today is morally wrongful.

Notes

1. For a readable survey of many of these issues, see Jane Holtz Kay, *Asphalt Nation* (New York: Crown Publishing Co., 1997).

2. See Illya Lichtenberg, "Police Discretion and Traffic Enforcement: A Government of Men?" *Cleveland State Law Review* 50 (2002–2003): 425–53.

3. Moral norms are evolving about other potentially dangerous modes of operation—like the use of cell phones while driving. At this time, it is hard to know what conclusion should be reached. According to one survey, "data tying cell phone use to crashes are scarce, and studies have yielded conflicting risk estimates." See Insurance Institute for Highway Safety (IIHS), *Status Report* 38:8 (26 August 2003), "One Year after New York's Cell Phone Law, Drivers Resume Previous Calling Habits," p. 6.

4. American Law Institute, *Model Penal Code*, §2.02(2)(d). To differentiate criminal from civil negligence, this definition also requires that the former involve a *gross* deviation from a standard of care. I do not know whether the degree of negligence I subsequently describe qualifies as gross. Since I do not conclude that *criminal* liability is appropriate for this conduct, however, the question need not be resolved.

5. Ibid., §2.02(2)(c).

6. A few commentators believe that subjecting others to risks is not wrong unless these risks materialize in actual harm. See Heidi Hurd, "What in the World Is Wrong?" *Journal of Contemporary Legal Issues* 5 (1994): 157–216.

7. The statistics in this paragraph are drawn from the U.S. Department of Transportation, Bureau of Transportation Statistics, *Highlights of the 2001 National Household Travel Survey* (2002). The 2001 National Household Travel Survey (NHTS) is the most recent update of the information gathered in the Nationwide Personal Transportation Survey (NPTS) conducted in 1969, 1977, 1983, 1990, and 1995, and the American Travel Survey (ATS) conducted in 1977 and 1995. Telephone interviews are the primary source of data for these surveys.

8. By most measures, driving in the United States is safer than ever. The rate of fatalities per mile driven continues its steady decline. As Americans

drive more and more, a constant number of fatalities indicate that driving has become safer. See Insurance Institute for Highway Safety, *Status Report* 38:7 (28 June 2003), "Side Impact Crashworthiness," p. 5.

9. The statistics in this paragraph are drawn from the U.S. Department of Transportation, National Center for Statistics & Analysis (http://www-fars.nhtsa.dot.gov).

10. Surprisingly, nearly all of the litigation involving the risks of driving has been brought by owners who allege that their vehicles contain defective designs that failed to protect them from harm. Passengers in cars that are hit have rarely sued on the ground that design defects make other vehicles dangerous to them. In *de Veer v. Morris*, No. GC 020209 (Cal. Sup. Ct. Mar. 28, 2000), one such suit was dismissed on the ground that the driver of the hitting vehicle owned no duty of care to occupants of the car hit.

11. See Douglas N. Husak, "Legal Paternalism," in Hugh LaFollette (ed.), *Oxford Handbook of Practical Ethics* (Oxford: Oxford University Press, 2003), pp. 387–412.

12. The same is true of the risks of illicit drugs—widely but dubiously condemned as unjustifiable. See Douglas Husak, *Drugs and Rights* (Cambridge: Cambridge University Press, 1992).

13. See http://www-fars.nhtsa.dot.gov.

14. Since *criminal* liability is imposed for act-tokens, we have less reason to consider aggregate risks. Typically, the fact that the defendant has engaged in a series of comparable acts—or that others behave similarly—is irrelevant to his guilt. I do not propose, however, that criminal liability be used for the kinds of objectionable conduct I describe here.

15. This distinction is useful in order to assess the impact of one's conduct on others. From a third-person perspective, however, there may be no fact of the matter about whether the vehicle in question is the encroaching or the crash partner car.

16. I make no attempt to "draw the line" by identifying the precise point at which a given degree of crash incompatibility becomes *too* high. I simply assert that this point exists. Everyone would agree that a tank, for example, has too high a degree of crash incompatibility.

17. The problem on which I propose to focus is that of vehicles with an unacceptable degree of crash incompatibility. All too often, SUVs and pickup trucks manifest this problem. But I do not mean to suggest that *all* SUVs have too high a degree of crash incompatibility, or that crash incompatibility is unvarying across the entire class of SUVs and pickup trucks.

18. Commentators have noted the oddity of the fact that crash partner cars are generally made by the very same manufacturers as vehicles with a high degree of crash incompatibility: "The manufacturers were improving the safety of their passenger cars through the adoption of crush zones while the same manufacturers designed their SUVs to miss the cars' crush zones and to smash into the cars' passenger compartments during multivehicle collisions." See Howard Latin and Bobby Kasolas, "Bad Designs, Lethal Profits:

The Duty to Protect Other Motorists against SUV Collision Risks," *Boston University Law Review* 82 (2002): 1161–213, p. 1170.

19. Perhaps the foremost difficulty in attempts to generalize about the entire class of SUVs is that no standard definition of an SUV is available. For a rough approximation, see Keith Bradsher, *High and Mighty: SUVs— The World's Most Dangerous Vehicles and How They Got That Way* (Cambridge, Mass.: Perseus Books, 2002), p. 4.

20. Insurance Institute for Highway Safety, *Status Report* 34:9 (30 October 1999), "Putting the Crash Compatibility Issue in Perspective," pp. 3–4.

21. Bradsher, *High and Mighty*, p. xvii.

22. Other geometrical characteristics are also relevant, but to a lesser degree. See the discussion in IIHS, "Putting the Crash Compatibility Issue in Perspective."

23. Weight is the most important factor affecting crash incompatibility. Obviously, weight differentials make crash incompatibility a problem even in collisions between two cars.

24. Insurance Institute for Highway Safety, *Status Report* 39:5 (24 April 2004), "Side Impact Crashworthiness," p. 7.

25. Unlike cars, SUVs are not required to conform to regulations that limit bumper height. See U.S. National Highway Traffic Safety Administration, "The Aggressivity of Light Trucks and Vans in Traffic Crashes" (1998), pp. 10, 15.

26. Insurance Institute for Highway Safety, *Status Report* 38:4 (26 April 2003), "Incompatibility of Vehicles in Crashes," p. 10.

27. Although my case against SUVs and trucks emphasizes their high degree of crash incompatibility, these vehicles contribute to accidents and jeopardize the safety of others even when no issue of crash incompatibility is involved. SUVs and trucks obstruct the vision of other drivers, increasing the risk of crashes between vehicles other than the truck or SUV. This difficulty may pose an even greater safety hazard to drivers of cars than crash incompatibility.

28. See Paul Robinson, *Structure and Function in Criminal Law* (Oxford: Clarendon Press, 1997), p. 95.

29. See AdAge, "Study Finds More Americans Than Ever Buying Sport Utility Vehicles" (29 September 2003) (http://www.adage.com/news.cms?newsId=38829).

30. When this issue is litigated, courts typically perform a risk-utility balancing process (RUB). In practice, RUB simply requires a balancing of the risks, costs, and benefits of the product as it existed against those of the product if the safer design had been implemented. See Latin and Kasolas, "Bad Designs, Lethal Profits," pp. 1185–86.

31. Insurance Institute for Highway Safety, *Status Report* 39:1 (3 January 2004). "Automakers Pledge Series of Steps to Improve Crash Compatibility," p. 4.

32. "S.U.V.'s to Be Redesigned to Reduce Risks to Cars," *The New York Times* (4 December 2003), C:7.

33. Bradsher, *High and Mighty*, p. 113.

34. Ibid.

35. Other buyers cite the need for space. But vehicles like minivans can be equally spacious without incorporating the geometrical features that contribute to the crash incompatibility of most SUVs.

36. "The risk to drivers of average midsize and large cars is about the same as for the average SUV." Tom Wenzel and Marc Ross, "Are SUVs Really Safer Than Cars?" *Access* 21 (Fall 2002): 2–7, p. 3. Bradsher's claims are somewhat stronger. He claims "SUVs are no safer than cars for their occupants . . . SUV occupants die slightly more often than car occupants in crashes" (*High and Mighty*, p. 427). He also points out that "the safety hazards of SUVs have been mitigated until now because they have mainly attracted the safest drivers in America. The principal buyers of SUVs . . . have been baby boomers in their 40s. . . . These affluent first owners of SUVs tend to be the most cautious drivers on the road, because they are mostly middle-aged people who have plenty of driving experience and still have acute vision, hearing and mental faculties. Half of them also have families, so they are much less likely to be out driving in the wee hours of the morning, when crash rates soar" (p. xvi).

37. See IIHS, "Putting the Crash Compatibility Issue in Perspective," pp. 3–4.

38. IIHS calls this fact "undeniable" (ibid., p. 6). Many courts have held SUV designs to be defective because they are prone to rollovers. See Latin and Kasolas, "Bad Designs, Lethal Profits," p. 1195.

39. Bradsher, *High and Mighty*, p. 150.

40. Nicholas Dixon, "Light Trucks, Road Safety, and the Environment," *Philosophy in the Contemporary World* 9 (2002), p. 60.

41. See U.S. Department of Transportation, *Highlights of the 2001 National Household Travel Survey* (see n. 7), p. 10.

42. Ibid.

CHAPTER 22

Preserving the Environment

Thomas E. Hill, Jr.

Philosophical discussions of environmental ethics generally take one of two forms: Either the argument is that the environment must be protected in order to serve the needs of human beings, or it is argued that the environment itself has "intrinsic value" that must be respected. Thomas E. Hill, Jr., takes a different approach. He asks, *What kind of people would we be if we destroyed the natural environment?*

A professor of philosophy at the University of North Carolina at Chapel Hill, Thomas Hill's most recent book is *Human Welfare and Moral Worth: Kantian Perspectives* (2002).

I

A wealthy eccentric bought a house in a neighborhood I know.[1] The house was surrounded by a beautiful display of grass, plants, and flowers, and it was shaded by a huge old avocado tree. But the grass required cutting, the flowers needed tending, and the man wanted more sun. So he cut the whole lot down and covered the yard with asphalt. After all it was his property and he was not fond of plants.

It was a small operation, but it reminded me of the strip mining of large sections of the Appalachians. In both cases, of course, there were reasons for the destruction, and property rights could be cited as justification. But I could not help but wonder, "What sort of person would do a thing like that?"

Many Californians had a similar reaction when a recent governor defended the leveling of ancient redwood groves, reportedly saying, "If you have seen one redwood, you have seen them all."

From Thomas E. Hill, Jr., "Ideals of Human Excellence and Preserving Natural Environments," *Environmental Ethics* 5 (1983): 211–24. Reprinted by permission.

Incidents like these arouse the indignation of ardent environmentalists and leave even apolitical observers with some degree of moral discomfort. The reasons for these reactions are mostly obvious. Uprooting the natural environment robs both present and future generations of much potential use and enjoyment. Animals too depend on the environment; and even if one does not value animals for their own sakes, their potential utility for us is incalculable. Plants are needed, of course, to replenish the atmosphere quite aside from their aesthetic value. These reasons for hesitating to destroy forests and gardens are not only the most obvious ones, but also the most persuasive for practical purposes. But, one wonders, is there nothing more behind our discomfort? Are we concerned solely about the potential use and enjoyment of the forests, etc., for ourselves, later generations, and perhaps animals? Is there not something else which disturbs us when we witness the destruction or even listen to those who would defend it in terms of cost/benefit analysis?

Imagine that in each of our examples those who would destroy the environment argue elaborately that, even considering future generations of human beings and animals, there are benefits in "replacing" the natural environment which outweigh the negative utilities which environmentalists cite.[2] No doubt we could press the argument on the facts, trying to show that the destruction is short-sighted and that its defenders have underestimated its potential harm or ignored some pertinent rights or interests. But is this all we could say? Suppose we grant, for a moment, that the utility of destroying the redwoods, forests, and gardens is equal to their potential for use and enjoyment by nature lovers and animals. Suppose, further, that we even grant that the pertinent human rights and animal rights, if any, are evenly divided for and against destruction. Imagine that we also concede, for argument's sake, that the forests contain no potentially useful endangered species of animals and plants. Must we then conclude that there is no further cause for moral concern? Should we then feel morally indifferent when we see the natural environment uprooted?

II

Suppose we feel that the answer to these questions should be negative. Suppose, in other words, we feel that our moral discomfort when we confront the destroyers of nature is not fully explained by our belief that they have miscalculated the best use of natural resources or violated rights in exploiting them. Suppose, in particular, we sense that part of the problem is that the natural environment is being viewed exclusively as a natural *resource*. What could be the ground of such a feeling? That is, what is there in our system of normative principles and values that could account for our remaining moral dissatisfaction?[3]

Some may be tempted to seek an explanation by appeal to the interests, or even the rights, of plants. After all, they may argue, we only gradually came to acknowledge the moral importance of all human beings, and it is even more recently that consciences have been aroused to give full weight to the welfare (and rights?) of animals. The next logical step, it may be argued, is to acknowledge a moral requirement to take into account the interests (and rights?) of plants. The problem with the strip miners, redwood cutters, and the like, on this view, is not just that they ignore the welfare and rights of people and animals; they also fail to give due weight to the survival and health of the plants themselves.

The temptation to make such a reply is understandable if one assumes that all moral questions are exclusively concerned with whether *acts* are right or wrong, and that this, in turn, is determined entirely by how the acts impinge on the rights and interests of those directly affected. On this assumption, if there is cause for moral concern, some right or interest has been neglected; and if the rights and interests of human beings and animals have already been taken into account, then there must be some other pertinent interests, for example, those of plants. A little reflection will show that the assumption is mistaken; but, in any case, the conclusion that plants have rights or morally relevant interests is surely untenable. We do speak of what is "good for" plants, and they can "thrive" and also be "killed." But this does not imply that they have "interests" in any morally relevant sense. Some people apparently believe that plants grow better if we talk to them, but the idea that the plants suffer and enjoy, desire and dislike, etc., is clearly outside the range of both common sense and scientific belief. The notion that the forests should be preserved to avoid *hurting* the trees or because they have a *right* to life is not part of a widely shared moral consciousness, and for good reason.[4]

Another way of trying to explain our moral discomfort is to appeal to certain religious beliefs. If one believes that all living things were created by a God who cares for them and entrusted us with the use of plants and animals only for limited purposes, then one has a reason to avoid careless destruction of the forests, etc., quite aside from their future utility. Again, if one believes that a divine force is immanent in all nature, then too one might have reason to care for more than sentient things. But such arguments require strong and controversial premises, and, I suspect, they will always have a restricted audience.

Early in this century, due largely to the influence of G. E. Moore, another point of view developed which some may find promising.[5] Moore introduced, or at least made popular, the idea that certain states of affairs are intrinsically valuable—not just valued, but valuable, and not necessarily because of their effects on sentient beings. Admittedly Moore came to believe that in fact the only intrinsically valuable things were conscious experiences of various sorts, but this restriction was not inherent in the idea of intrinsic value.[6] The intrinsic goodness of something, he thought, was an objective, nonrelational property of the thing, like its texture or color, but not a property perceivable by sense perception or detectable by scientific instruments. In theory at least, a single tree thriving alone in a universe without sentient beings, and even without God, could be intrinsically valuable. Since, according to Moore, our duty is to maximize intrinsic value, his theory could obviously be used to argue that we have reason not to destroy natural environments independently of how they affect human beings and animals. The survival of a forest might have worth beyond its worth *to* sentient beings.

This approach, like the religious one, may appeal to some but is infested with problems. There are, first, the familiar objections to intuitionism, on which the theory depends. Metaphysical and epistemological doubts about nonnatural, intuited properties are hard to suppress, and many have argued that the theory rests on a misunderstanding of the words *good, valuable,* and the like.[7] Second, even if we try to set aside these objections and think in Moore's terms, it is far from obvious that everyone would agree that the existence of forests, etc., is intrinsically valuable. The test, says Moore, is what we would say when we imagine a universe with just the thing in question, without any effects or accompaniments, and then we ask, "Would its existence be better than its nonexistence?" Be careful, Moore would remind us, not to construe this question as, "Would you *prefer* the existence of that universe to its nonexistence?" The question is, "Would its existence have the objective, nonrelational property, intrinsic goodness?"

Now even among those who have no worries about whether this really makes sense, we might well get a diversity of answers. Those prone to destroy natural environments will doubtless give one answer, and nature lovers will likely give another. When an issue is as controversial as the one at hand, intuition is a poor arbiter.

The problem, then, is this. We want to understand what underlies our moral uneasiness at the destruction of the redwoods, forests, etc., even apart from the loss of these as resources for human beings and animals. But I find no adequate answer by pursuing the questions, "Are rights or interests of plants neglected?" "What is God's will on the matter?" and "What is the intrinsic value of the existence of a tree or forest?" My suggestion, which is in fact the main point of this paper, is that we look at the problem from a different perspective. That is, let us turn for a while from the effort to find reasons why certain *acts* destructive of natural environments are morally wrong to the ancient task of articulating our ideals of human excellence. Rather than argue directly with destroyers of the environment who say, "Show me why what I am doing is *immoral*," I want to ask, "What sort of person would want to do what they propose?" The point is not to skirt the issue with an *ad hominem*, but to raise a different moral question, for even if there is no convincing way to show that the destructive acts are wrong (independently of human and animal use and enjoyment), we may find that the willingness to indulge in them reflects the absence of human traits that we admire and regard morally important.

This strategy of shifting questions may seem more promising if one reflects on certain analogous situations. Consider, for example, the Nazi who asks, in all seriousness, "Why is it wrong for me to make lampshades out of human skin—provided, of course, I did not myself kill the victims to get the skins?" We would react more with shock and disgust than with indignation, I suspect, because it is even more evident that the question reveals a defect in the questioner than that the proposed act is itself immoral. Sometimes we may not regard an act wrong at all though we see it as reflecting something objectionable about the person who does it. Imagine, for example, one who laughs spontaneously to himself when he reads a newspaper account of a plane crash that kills hundreds. Or, again, consider an obsequious grandson who, having waited for his grandmother's inheritance with mock devotion, then secretly spits on her grave when at last she dies. Spitting on the grave may have no adverse consequences and perhaps it violates no rights. The moral uneasiness which it arouses is explained more by our view of the agent than by any conviction that what he did was immoral. Had he hesitated and asked, "Why shouldn't I spit on her grave?" it seems more fitting to ask him to reflect on the sort of person he is than to try to offer reasons why he should refrain from spitting.

III

What sort of person, then, would cover his garden with asphalt, strip-mine a wooded mountain, or level an irreplaceable redwood grove? Two sorts of answers, though initially appealing, must be ruled out. The first is that persons who would destroy the environment in these ways are either shortsighted, underestimating the harm they do, or else are too little concerned for the well-being of other people. Perhaps too they have insufficient regard for animal life. But these considerations have been set aside in order to refine the controversy. Another tempting response might be that we count it a moral virtue, or at least a human ideal, to love nature. Those who value the environment only for its utility must not really love nature and so in this way fall short of an ideal. But such an answer is hardly satisfying in the present context, for what is at issue is *why* we feel moral discomfort at the activities of those who admittedly value nature only for its utility. That it is ideal to care for nonsentient nature beyond its possible use is really just another way of expressing the general point which is under controversy.

What is needed is some way of showing that this ideal is connected with other virtues, or human excellences, not in question. To do so is difficult and my suggestions, accordingly, will be tentative and subject to qualification. The main idea is that, though indifference to nonsentient nature does not *necessarily* reflect the absence of virtues, it often signals the absence of certain traits which we want to encourage because they are, in most cases, a natural basis for the development of certain virtues. It is often thought, for example, that those who would destroy the natural environment must lack a proper appreciation of their place in the natural order, and so must either be ignorant or have too little humility. Though I would argue that this is not necessarily so, I suggest that, given certain plausible empirical assumptions, their attitude may well be rooted in ignorance, a narrow perspective, inability to see things as important apart from themselves and the limited groups they associate with, or reluctance to accept themselves as natural beings. Overcoming these deficiencies will not guarantee a proper moral humility, but for most of us it is probably an important psychological preliminary. Later I suggest, more briefly, that indifference to nonsentient nature typically reveals absence of either aesthetic sensibility or a disposition to cherish what has enriched one's life and that these, though not themselves moral virtues, are a natural basis for appreciation of the good in others and gratitude.[8]

Consider first the suggestion that destroyers of the environment lack an appreciation of their place in the universe.[9] Their attention, it seems, must be focused on parochial matters, on what is, relatively speaking, close in space and time. They seem not to understand that we are a speck on the cosmic scene, a brief stage in the evolutionary process, only one among millions of species on Earth, and an episode in the course of human history. Of course, they know that there are stars, fossils, insects, and ancient ruins; but do they have any idea of the complexity of the processes that led to the natural world as we find it? Are they aware how much the forces at work within their own bodies are like those which govern all living things and even how much they have in common with inanimate bodies? Admittedly scientific knowledge is limited and no one can master it all; but could one who had a broad and deep understanding of his place in nature really be indifferent to the destruction of the natural environment?

This first suggestion, however, may well provoke a protest from a sophisticated anti-environmentalist.[10] "Perhaps *some* may be indifferent to nature from ignorance," the critic may object, "but *I* have studied astronomy, geology, biology, and biochemistry, and I still unashamedly regard the nonsentient environment as simply a resource for our use. It should not be wasted, of course, but what should be preserved is decidable by weighing long-term costs and benefits." "Besides," our critic may continue, "as philosophers you should know the old Humean formula, 'You cannot derive an *ought* from an *is*.' All the facts of biology, biochemistry, etc., do not entail that I ought to love nature or want to preserve it. What one understands is one thing; what one values is something else. Just as nature lovers are not necessarily scientists, those indifferent to nature are not necessarily ignorant."

Although the environmentalist may concede the critic's logical point, he may well argue that, as a matter of fact, increased understanding of nature tends to heighten people's concern for its preservation. If so, despite the objection, the suspicion that the destroyers of the environment lack deep understanding of nature is not, in most cases, unwarranted, but the argument need not rest here.

The environmentalist might amplify his original idea as follows: "When I said that the destroyers of nature do not appreciate their place in the universe, I was not speaking of intellectual understanding alone, for, after all, a person can *know* a catalog of facts without ever putting them together and seeing vividly the whole picture which they form. To see oneself as just one part of nature is to look at oneself and the world from a certain perspective which is quite different from being able to recite detailed information from the natural sciences. What the destroyers of nature lack is this perspective, not particular information."

Again our critic may object, though only after making some concessions: "All right," he may say, "*some* who are indifferent to nature may lack the cosmic perspective of which you speak, but again there is no *necessary* connection between this failing, if it is one, and any particular evaluative attitude toward nature. In fact, different people respond quite differently when they move to a wider perspective. When *I* try to picture myself vividly as a brief, transitory episode in the course of nature, I simply get depressed. Far from inspiring me with a love of nature, the exercise makes me sad and hostile. You romantics think only of poets like Wordsworth and artists like Turner, but you should consider how differently Omar Khayyám responded when he took your wider perspective. His reaction, when looking at his life from a cosmic viewpoint, was 'Drink up, for tomorrow we die.' Others respond in an almost opposite manner with a joyless Stoic resignation, exemplified by the poet who pictures the wise man, at the height of personal triumph, being served a magnificent banquet, and then consummating his marriage to his beloved, all the while reminding himself, 'Even this shall pass away.'"[11] In sum, the critic may object, "Even if one should try to see oneself as one small transitory part of nature, doing so does not dictate any particular normative attitude. Some may come to love nature, but others are moved to live for the moment; some sink into sad resignation; others get depressed or angry. So indifference to nature is not necessarily a sign that a person fails to look at himself from the larger perspective."

The environmentalist might respond to this objection in several ways. He might, for example, argue that even though some people who see themselves as part of the natural order remain indifferent to nonsentient nature, this is not a common reaction. Typically, it may be argued, as we become more and more aware that we are parts of the larger whole we come to value the whole independently of its effect on ourselves. Thus, despite the possibilities the critic raises, indifference to nonsentient nature is still in most cases a sign that a person fails to see himself as part of the natural order.

If someone challenges the empirical assumption here, the environmentalist might develop the argument along a quite different line. The initial idea, he may remind us, was that those who would destroy the natural environment fail to *appreciate* their place in the natural order. "Appreciating one's place" is not simply an intellectual appreciation. It is also an attitude, reflecting what one values as well as what one knows. When we say, for example, that both the servile and the arrogant person fail to *appreciate* their place in a society of equals, we do not mean simply that they are ignorant of certain empirical facts, but rather that they have certain objectionable attitudes about their importance relative to other people. Similarly, to fail to appreciate one's place in nature is not merely to lack knowledge or breadth of perspective, but to take a certain attitude about what matters. A person who *understands* his place in nature but still views nonsentient nature merely as a resource takes the attitude that nothing is *important* but human beings and animals. Despite first appearances, he is not so much like the pre-Copernican astronomers who made the intellectual error of treating the Earth as the "center of the universe" when they made their calculations. He is more like the racist who, though well aware of other races, treats all races but his own as insignificant.

So construed, the argument appeals to the common idea that awareness of nature typically has, and should have, a humbling effect. The Alps, a storm at sea, the Grand Canyon, towering redwoods, and "the starry heavens above" move many a person to remark on the comparative insignificance of our daily concerns and even of our species, and this is generally taken to be a quite fitting response.[12] What seems to be missing, then, in those who understand nature but remain unmoved is a proper humility.[13] Absence of proper humility is not the same as selfishness or egoism, for one can be devoted to self-interest while still viewing one's own pleasures and projects as trivial and unimportant.[14] And one can have an exaggerated view of one's own importance while grandly sacrificing for those one views as inferior. Nor is the lack of humility identical with the belief that one has power and influence, for a person can be quite puffed up about himself while believing that the foolish world will never acknowledge him. The humility we miss seems not so much a belief about one's relative effectiveness and recognition as an attitude which measures the importance of things independently of their relation to oneself or to some narrow group with which one identifies. A paradigm of a person who lacks humility is the self-important emperor who grants status to his family because it is *his,* to his subordinates because *he* appointed them, and to his country because *he* chooses to glorify it. Less extreme but still lacking proper humility is the elitist who counts events significant solely in proportion to how they affect his class. The suspicion about those who would destroy the environment, then, is that what they count important is too narrowly confined insofar as it encompasses only what affects beings who, like us, are capable of feeling.

This idea that proper humility requires recognition of the importance of nonsentient nature is similar to the thought of those who charge meat eaters with "species-ism." In both cases it is felt that people too narrowly confine their concerns to the sorts of beings that are most like them. But, however intuitively appealing, the idea will surely arouse objections from our anti-environmentalist critic. "Why," he will ask, "do you suppose that the sort of humility I *should* have requires me to acknowledge the importance of nonsentient nature aside from its utility? You cannot, by your own admission, argue that nonsentient nature *is* important, appealing to religious or intuitionist grounds. And simply to assert, without further argument, that an ideal humility requires us to view nonsentient nature as important for its own sake begs the question at issue. If proper humility is acknowledging the relative importance of things as one should, then to show that I must lack this you must first establish that one *should* acknowledge the importance of nonsentient nature."

Though some may wish to accept this challenge, there are other ways to pursue the connection between humility and response to nonsentient nature. For example, suppose we grant that proper humility requires only acknowledging a due status to sentient beings. We must admit, then, that it is logically possible for a person to be properly humble even though he viewed all nonsentient nature simply as a resource. But this logical possibility may be a psychological rarity. It may be that, given the sort of beings we are, we would never learn humility before persons without developing the general capacity to cherish, and regard important, many things for their own sakes. The major obstacle to humility before persons is self-importance, a tendency to measure the significance of everything by its relation to oneself and those with whom one identifies. The processes by which we overcome self-importance are doubtless many and complex, but it seems unlikely that they are exclusively concerned with how we relate to other people and animals. Learning humility requires learning to feel that something matters besides what will affect oneself and one's circle of associates. What leads a child to care about what happens to a lost hamster or a stray dog he will not see again is likely also to generate concern for a lost toy or a favorite tree where he used to live.[15] Learning to value things for their own sake, and to count what affects them important aside from their utility, is not the same as judging them to have some intuited objective property, but it is necessary to the development of humility and it seems likely to take place in experiences with nonsentient nature as well as with people and animals. If a person views all nonsentient nature merely as a resource, then it seems unlikely that he has developed the capacity needed to overcome self-importance.

IV

This last argument, unfortunately, has its limits. It presupposes an empirical connection between experiencing nature and overcoming self-importance, and this may be challenged. Even if experiencing nature promotes humility before others, there may be other ways people can develop such humility in a world of concrete, glass, and plastic. If not, perhaps all that is needed is limited experience of nature in one's early, developing years; mature adults, having overcome youthful self-importance, may live well enough in artificial surroundings. More importantly, the argument does not fully capture the spirit of the intuition that an ideal person stands humbly before nature. That idea is not simply that experiencing nature tends to foster proper humility before other people; it is, in part, that natural surroundings encourage and are appropriate to an ideal sense of oneself as part of the natural world. Standing alone in the forest, after months in the city, is not merely good as a means of curbing one's arrogance before others; it reinforces and fittingly expresses one's acceptance of oneself as a natural being.

Previously we considered only one aspect of proper humility, namely, a sense of one's relative importance with respect to other human beings. Another aspect, I think, is a kind of *self-acceptance*. This involves acknowledging, in more than a merely intellectual way, that we are the sort of creatures that we are. Whether one is self-accepting is not so much a matter of how one attributes *importance* comparatively to oneself, other people, animals, plants, and other things as it is a matter of understanding, facing squarely, and responding appropriately to who and what one is, e.g., one's powers and limits, one's affinities with other beings and differences from them, one's unalterable nature and one's freedom to change. Self-acceptance is not merely intellectual awareness, for one can be intellectually aware that one is growing old and will eventually die while nevertheless behaving in a thousand foolish ways that reflect a refusal to acknowledge these facts. On the other hand, self-acceptance is not passive resignation, for refusal to pursue what one truly wants within one's limits is a failure to accept the freedom and power one has. Particular behaviors, like dyeing one's gray hair and dressing like those twenty years younger, do not *necessarily* imply lack of self-acceptance, for there could be reasons for acting in these ways other than the wish to hide from oneself what one really is. One fails to accept oneself when the patterns of behavior and emotion are rooted in a desire to disown and deny features of oneself, to pretend to oneself that they are not there. This is not to say that a self-accepting person makes no value judgments about himself, that he likes all facts about himself, wants equally to develop and display them; he can, and should feel remorse for his past misdeeds and strive to change his current vices. The point is that he does not disown them, pretend that they do not exist or are facts about something other than himself. Such pretense is incompatible with proper humility because it is seeing oneself as better than one is.

Self-acceptance of this sort has long been considered a human excellence, under various names, but what has it to do with preserving nature? There is, I think, the following connection. As human beings we are part of nature, living, growing, declining, and dying by natural laws similar to those governing other living beings; despite our awesomely distinctive human powers, we share many of the needs, limits, and liabilities of animals and plants. These facts are neither good nor bad in themselves, aside from personal preference and varying conventional values. To say this is to utter a truism which few will deny, but to accept these facts, as facts about oneself, is not so easy—or so common. Much of what naturalists deplore about our increasingly artificial world reflects, and encourages, a denial of these facts, an unwillingness to avow them with equanimity.

Like the Victorian lady who refuses to look at her own nude body, some would like to create a world of less transitory stuff, reminding us only of our intellectual and social nature, never calling to mind our affinities with "lower" living creatures. The "denial of death," to which psychiatrists call attention, reveals an attitude incompatible with the sort of self-acceptance which philosophers, from the ancients to Spinoza and on, have admired as a human excellence.[16] My suggestion is not merely that experiencing nature causally promotes such self-acceptance, but also that those who fully accept themselves as part of the natural world lack the common drive to disassociate themselves from nature by replacing natural environments with artificial ones. A storm in the wilds helps us to appreciate our animal vulnerability, but, equally important, the reluctance to experience it may *reflect* an unwillingness to accept this aspect of ourselves. The person who is too ready to destroy the ancient redwoods may lack humility, not so much in the sense that he exaggerates his importance relative to others, but rather in the sense that he tries to avoid seeing himself as one among many natural creatures.

V

My suggestion so far has been that, though indifference to nonsentient nature is not itself a moral vice, it is likely to reflect either ignorance, a self-importance, or a lack of self-acceptance which we must overcome to have proper humility. A similar idea might be developed connecting attitudes toward nonsentient nature with other human excellences. For example, one might argue that indifference to nature reveals a lack of either an aesthetic sense or some of the natural roots of gratitude.

When we see a hillside that has been gutted by strip miners or the garden replaced by asphalt, our first reaction is probably, "How ugly!" The scenes assault our aesthetic sensibilities. We suspect that no one with a keen sense of beauty could have left such a sight. Admittedly not everything in nature strikes us as beautiful, or even aesthetically interesting, and sometimes a natural scene is replaced with a more impressive architectural masterpiece. But this is not usually the situation in the problem cases which environmentalists are most concerned about. More often beauty is replaced with ugliness.

At this point our critic may well object that, even if he does lack a sense of beauty, this is no moral vice. His cost/benefit calculations take into account the pleasure others may derive from seeing the forests, etc., and so why should he be faulted?

Some might reply that, despite contrary philosophical traditions, aesthetics and morality are not so distinct as commonly supposed. Appreciation of beauty, they may argue, is a human excellence which morally ideal persons should try to develop. But, setting aside this controversial position, there still may be cause for moral concern about those who have no aesthetic response to nature. Even if aesthetic sensibility is not itself a moral virtue, many of the capacities of mind and heart which it presupposes may be ones which are also needed for an appreciation of other people. Consider, for example, curiosity, a mind open to novelty, the ability to look at things from unfamiliar perspectives, empathetic imagination, interest in details, variety, and order, and emotional freedom from the immediate and the practical. All these, and more, seem necessary to aesthetic sensibility, but they are also traits which a person needs to be fully sensitive to people of all sorts. The point is not that a moral person must be able to distinguish beautiful from ugly people; the point is rather that unresponsiveness to what is beautiful, awesome, dainty, dumpy, and otherwise aesthetically interesting in nature probably reflects a lack of the openness of mind and spirit necessary to appreciate the best in human beings.

The anti-environmentalist, however, may refuse to accept the charge that he lacks aesthetic sensibility. If he claims to appreciate seventeenth-century miniature portraits, but to abhor natural wildernesses, he will hardly be convincing. Tastes vary, but aesthetic sense is not *that* selective. He may, instead, insist that he *does* appreciate natural beauty. He spends his vacations, let us suppose, hiking in the Sierras, photographing wildflowers, and so on. He might press his argument as follows: "I enjoy natural beauty as much as anyone, but I fail to see what this has to do with preserving the environment independently of human enjoyment and use. Nonsentient nature is a resource, but one of its best uses is to give us pleasure. I take this into account when I calculate the costs and benefits of preserving a park, planting a garden, and so on. But the problem you raised explicitly set aside the desire to preserve nature as a means to enjoyment. I say, let us enjoy nature fully while we can, but if all sentient beings were to die tomorrow, we might as well blow up all plant life as well. A redwood grove that no one can use or enjoy is utterly worthless."

The attitude expressed here, I suspect, is not a common one, but it represents a philosophical challenge. The beginnings of a reply may be found in the following. When a person takes joy in something, it is a common (and perhaps natural) response to come to cherish it. To cherish something is not simply to be happy with it at the moment, but to care for it for its own sake. This is not to say that one necessarily sees it as having feelings and so wants it to feel good; nor does it imply that one judges the thing to have Moore's intrinsic value. One simply wants the thing to survive and (when appropriate) to thrive, and not simply for its utility. We see this attitude repeatedly regarding mementos. They are not simply valued as a means to remind us of happy occasions; they come to be valued for their own sake. Thus, if someone really took joy in the natural environment, but was prepared to blow it up as soon as sentient life ended, he would lack this common human tendency to cherish what enriches our lives. While this response is not itself a moral virtue, it may be a natural basis of the virtue we call "gratitude." People who have no tendency to cherish things that give them pleasure may be poorly disposed to respond gratefully to persons who are good to them. Again the connection is not one of logical necessity, but it may nevertheless be important. A nonreligious person unable to "thank" anyone for the beauties of nature may nevertheless feel "grateful" in a sense; and I suspect that the person who feels no such "gratitude" toward nature is unlikely to show proper gratitude toward people.

Suppose these conjectures prove to be true. One may wonder what is the point of considering them. Is it to disparage all those who view nature merely as a resource? To do so, it seems, would be unfair, for, even if this attitude typically stems from deficiencies which affect one's attitudes toward sentient beings, there may be exceptions and we have not shown that their view of nonsentient nature is itself blameworthy. But when we set aside questions of blame and inquire what sorts of human traits we want to encourage, our reflections become relevant in a more positive way. The point is not to insinuate that all anti-environmentalists are defective, but to see that those who value such traits as humility, gratitude, and sensitivity to others have reason to promote the love of nature.

Notes

1. The author thanks Gregory Kavka, Catherine Harlow, the participants at a colloquium at the University of Utah, and the referees for *Environmental Ethics*, Dale Jamieson and Donald Scherer, for helpful comments on earlier drafts of this paper.

2. When I use the expression "the natural environment," I have in mind the sort of examples with which I began. For some purposes it is important to distinguish cultivated gardens from forests, virgin forests from replenished ones, irreplaceable natural phenomena from the replaceable, and so on; but these distinctions, I think, do not affect my main points here. There is also a broad sense, as Hume and Mill noted, in which all that occurs, miracles aside, is "natural." In this sense, of course, strip mining is as natural as a beaver cutting trees for his dam, and, as parts of nature, we cannot destroy the "natural" environment but only alter it. As will be evident, I shall use *natural* in a narrower, more familiar sense.

3. This paper is intended as a preliminary discussion in *normative* ethical theory (as opposed to *metaethics*). The task, accordingly, is the limited, though still difficult, one of articulating the possible basis in our beliefs and values for certain particular moral judgments. Questions of ultimate justification are set aside. What makes the task difficult and challenging is not that conclusive proofs from the foundation of morality are attempted; it is rather that the particular judgments to be explained seem at first not to fall under the most familiar moral principles (e.g., utilitarianism, respect for rights).

4. I assume here that having a right presupposes having interests in a sense which in turn presupposes a capacity to desire, suffer, etc. Since my main concern lies in another direction, I do not argue the point, but merely note that some regard it as debatable. See, for example, W. Murray Hunt, "Are *Mere Things* Morally Considerable?" *Environmental Ethics* 2 (1980), 59–65; Kenneth E. Goodpaster, "On Stopping at Everything," *Environmental Ethics* 2 (1980), 288–94; Joel Feinberg, "The Rights of Animals and Unborn Generations," in William Blackstone, ed., *Philosophy and Environmental Crisis* (Athens: University of Georgia Press, 1974), 43–68; Tom Regan, "Feinberg on What Sorts of Beings Can Have Rights," *Southern Journal of Philosophy* (1976), 485–98; Robert Elliot, "Regan on the Sort of Beings That Can Have Rights," *Southern Journal of Philosophy* (1978), 701–5; Scott Lehmann, "Do Wildernesses Have Rights?" *Environmental Ethics* 2 (1981), 129–46.

5. G. E. Moore, *Principia Ethica* (Cambridge: Cambridge University Press, 1903); *Ethics* (London: H. Holt, 1912).

6. G. E. Moore, "Is Goodness a Quality?" *Philosophical Papers* (London: George Allen and Unwin, 1959), 95–97.

7. See, for example, P. H. Nowell-Smith, *Ethics* (New York: Penguin Books, 1954).

8. The issues I raise here, though perhaps not the details of my remarks, are in line with Aristotle's view of moral philosophy, a view revitalized recently by Philippa Foot's *Virtue and Vice* (Berkeley: University of California Press, 1979), Alasdair McIntyre's *After Virtue* (Notre Dame: Notre Dame Press, 1981), and James Wallace's *Virtues and Vices* (Ithaca and London: Cornell University Press, 1978), and other works. For other reflections on relationships between character and natural environments, see John Rodman, "The Liberation of Nature," *Inquiry* (1976), 83–131, and L. Reinhardt, "Some Gaps in Moral Space: Reflections on Forests and Feelings," in Mannison, McRobbie, and Routley, eds., *Environmental Philosophy* (Canberra: Australian National University Research School of Social Sciences, 1980).

9. Though for simplicity I focus upon those who do strip mining, etc., the argument is also applicable to those whose utilitarian calculations lead them to preserve the redwoods, mountains, etc., but who care for only sentient nature for its own sake. Similarly the phrase "indifferent to nature" is meant to encompass those who are indifferent *except* when considering its benefits to people and animals.

10. For convenience I use the labels *environmentalist* and *anti-environmentalist* (or *critic*) for the opposing sides in the rather special controversy I have raised. Thus, for example, my "environmentalist" not only favors conserving the forests, etc., but finds something objectionable in wanting to destroy them even aside from the costs to human beings and animals. My "anti-environmentalist" is not simply one who wants to destroy the environment; he is a person who has no qualms about doing so independent of the adverse effects on human beings and animals.

11. "Even This Shall Pass Away," by Theodore Tildon, in *The Best Loved Poems of the American People,* ed. Hazel Felleman (Garden City, N.Y.: Doubleday & Co., 1936).

12. An exception, apparently, was Kant, who thought "the starry heavens" sublime and compared them with "the moral law within," but did not for all that see our species as comparatively insignificant.

13. By "*proper* humility" I mean that sort and degree of humility that is a morally admirable character trait. How precisely to define this is, of course, a controversial matter; but the point for present purposes is just to set aside obsequiousness, false modesty, underestimation of one's abilities, and the like.

14. I take this point from some of Philippa Foot's remarks.

15. The causal history of this concern may well depend upon the object (tree, toy) having given the child pleasure, but this does not mean that the object is then valued only for further pleasure it may bring.

16. See, for example, Ernest Becker, *The Denial of Death* (New York: Free Press, 1973).

CHAPTER 23

*T*he Ethics of War and Peace

Douglas P. Lackey

Is it ever right to wage war? According to Saint Matthew, Jesus taught his disciples that it is never justified:

> You have heard it said, "An eye for an eye and a tooth for a tooth." But I say to you, Do not resist one who is evil. But if any one strikes you on the right cheek, turn to him the other also; and if any one would sue you and take your coat, let him have your cloak as well; and if anyone forces you to go one mile, go with him two miles . . .
>
> You have heard that it was said, "You shall love your neighbor and hate your enemy." But I say to you, Love your enemies and pray for those who persecute you, so that you may be sons of your Father who is in heaven . . .

Since this teaching is so clear, we might expect that Christians would be pacifists; and since Christianity is the dominant religion of our culture, this would mean that pacifism would be very widespread indeed. Surprisingly, however, most Christians support their countries' wars just as enthusiastically as any other citizens.

This was not always so. The early Christians, living when the New Testament was being written and shortly afterward, thought that Jesus's teaching was perfectly unambiguous: He did not permit meeting violence with violence. (This was Saint Paul's understanding, as he emphasizes in the 12th chapter of Romans.) Tertullian, quoting another of Jesus's sayings, wrote: "Can it be lawful to handle the sword, when the Lord himself has declared that he who uses the sword shall perish by it?"

But as Christianity grew larger and more influential, an accommodation had to be reached with the state. Christianity could not become the state's religion if it persisted in banning war—waging war was, after all, something that all states did. So the church's doctrine changed.

Excerpted from Douglas P. Lackey, *The Ethics of War and Peace*, pp. 28–37, 39–40, 43–44, 58–61, © 1989. Reprinted by permission of Prentice-Hall, Inc., Upper Saddle River, N.J.

Rather than following the pacifist teachings, church thinkers adopted the Greek notion that some wars are just and some are not. Thus, theologians from Saint Augustine on have concentrated on defining the conditions that must be satisfied for a war to be just. Saint Thomas Aquinas, for example, said that a war is just if three conditions are met: First, it must be declared by a legitimate authority; second, there must be a "just cause" for which the war is waged; and third, the war must be fought using "just means."

In the modern era, the Doctrine of the Just War has provided both religious and secular thinkers with a framework for thinking about the ethics of warfare. In the following selection, Douglas P. Lackey, a professor of philosophy at Baruch College of the City University of New York, outlines the essential points of the doctrine.

When to Fight

1. Introduction. Rightly or wrongly, pacifism has always been a minority view. Most people believe that *some* wars are morally justifiable; the majority of Americans believe that World War II was a moral war. But though most people have clear-cut intuitions about the moral acceptability of World War II, the Vietnam War, and so forth, few people have a theory that justifies and organizes their intuitive judgments. If morally concerned nonpacifists are to defeat the pacifists to their moral left and the cynics to their moral right, they must develop a theory that will distinguish justifiable wars from unjustifiable wars, using a set of consistent and consistently applied rules.

The work of specifying these rules, which dates at least from Aristotle's *Politics*, traditionally goes under the heading of "just war theory." The name is slightly misleading, since justice is only one of several primary moral concepts, all of which must be consulted in a complete moral evaluation of war. A just war—a morally good war—is not merely a war dictated by principles of justice. A just war is a morally justifiable war after justice, human rights, the common good, and all other relevant moral concepts have been consulted and weighed against the facts and against each other. . . .

2. Competent Authority. From the time of Augustine, theorists have maintained that a just war can be prosecuted only by a "competent authority." Augustine . . . considered the use of force by private persons to be immoral; consequently the only permissible uses of force were those sanctioned by public authorities. Medieval authors, with a watchful eye for peasant revolts, followed Augustine in confining the just use of force to princes, whose authority and patronage were divinely sanctioned. Given these scholastic roots, considerations of competent authority might appear archaic, but it is still helpful for purposes of moral judgment to distinguish wars from spontaneous uprisings, and soldiers and officers from pirates and brigands. Just war must, first of all, be war.

To begin, most scholars agree that war is a controlled use of force, undertaken by persons organized in a functioning chain of command. An isolated assassin cannot wage war; New York City's Mad Bomber in the 1950s only metaphorically waged war against Con Edison. In some sense, then, war is the contrary of violence. Second, the use of force in war must be directed to an identifiable political result, a requirement forever associated with the Prussian theorist Karl von Clauswitz. An "identifiable political result" is some change in a government's policy, some alteration in a form of government, or some extension or limitation of the scope of its authority. Since the extermination of a people is not an identifiable political result, most acts of genocide are not acts of war: the Turks did not wage war against the Armenians, nor did Hitler wage war on the Jews. (The American frontier cliché, "the only good Indian is a dead Indian," expresses the hopes of murderers, not soldiers.) And since the religious conversion of people is, in most cases, not a political result, many holy wars, by this definition, have not been wars. . . .

3. Right Intention. One can imagine cases in which a use of military force might satisfy all the external standards of just war while those who order this use of force have no concern for justice. Unpopular political leaders, for example, might choose to make war in order to stifle domestic dissent and win the next election. The traditional theory of just war insists that a just war be a war for the right, fought for the sake of the right.

In the modern climate of political realism, many authors are inclined to treat the standard of right intention as a quaint relic of a more idealistic age, either on the grounds that moral motives produce disastrous results in international politics or on the grounds that motives are subjective and unobservable. ("I will not speculate on the motives of the North Vietnamese," Henry Kissinger once remarked, "I have too much difficulty understanding our own.") But it is unfair to dismiss idealistic motives on the grounds that they produce disaster in international politics, since realistic motives have produced their own fair share of disasters. It is a mistake to dismiss motives as unobservable, when they are so often clearly exhibited in behavior. . . .

4. Just Cause. The most important of the *jus ad bellum* rules is the rule that the moral use of military force requires a just cause. From the earliest writings, just war theorists rejected love of war and love of conquest as morally acceptable causes for war: "We [should] wage war," Aristotle wrote, "for the sake of peace" (*Politics*, 1333A). Likewise, the seizure of plunder was always rejected as an acceptable cause for war. Beyond these elementary restrictions, however, a wide variety of "just causes" were recognized. The history of the subject is the history of how this repertoire of just causes was progressively cut down to the modern standard, which accepts only the single cause of self-defense.

As early as Cicero in the first century B.C., analysts of just war recognized that the only proper occasion for the use of force was a "wrong received." It follows from this that the condition or characteristics of potential enemies, apart from their actions, cannot supply a just cause for war. Aristotle's suggestion that a war is justified to enslave those who naturally deserve to be slaves, John Stuart Mill's claim that military intervention is justified in order to bestow the benefits of Western civilization on less advanced peoples, and the historically common view that forcible conversion to some true faith is justified as obedience to divine command are all invalidated by the absence of a "wrong received."

Obviously, the concept of a "wrong received" stands in need of considerable analysis. In the eighteenth century, the notion of wrong included the notion of insult, and sovereigns considered it legitimate to initiate war in response to verbal disrespect, desecrations of national symbols, and so forth. The nineteenth century, which saw the abolition of private duels, likewise saw national honor reduced to a secondary role in the moral justification of war. For most nineteenth-century theorists, the primary wrongs were not insults, but acts or policies of a government resulting in violations of the rights of the nation waging just war.

By twentieth-century standards, this definition of international wrongs providing conditions of just war was both too restrictive and too loose. It was too restrictive in that it failed to recognize any rights of *peoples,* as opposed to *states:* rights to cultural integrity, national self-determination, and so forth. It was too loose in that it sanctioned the use of military force in response to wrongs the commission of which may not have involved military force, thus condoning, on occasion, the first use of arms.

These two excesses were abolished in twentieth-century international law. The right to national self-determination was a prevailing theme at the Versailles conference in 1919 and was repeatedly invoked in the period of decolonization following World War II. Prohibition of first use of force was attempted in drafting of the U.N. Charter in 1945:

> Article 2(4): All Members shall refrain in their international relations from the threat or use of force against the territorial integrity or political independence of any state or in any other manner inconsistent with the Purposes of the United Nations.
>
> Article 51: Nothing in the present Charter shall impair the inherent right of individual or collective self-defense if an armed attack occurs against a member of the United Nations, until the Security Council has taken the measures necessary to maintain international peace and security.

Strictly speaking, Article 51 does not prohibit first use of military force: to say that explicitly, the phrase "if an armed attack occurs" would have to be replaced by "if and only if an armed attack occurs." Nevertheless, Article 51, coupled with Article 2(4), rules out anticipatory self-defense. Legitimate self-defense must be self-defense against an actual attack. . . .

5. Anticipation and Just Cause. One of the most radical features of the United Nations analysis of just cause is its rejection of anticipatory self-defense. The decision of those who framed the Charter was informed by history: the argument of anticipatory self-defense had been repeatedly and cynically invoked by political leaders set on military adventures, and the framers were determined to prevent a repetition of August 1914, when nations declared war in response to mobilizations, that is, to anticipated attacks rather than actual attacks. The U.N. view stands on good logical ground: if the use of force by nation A is justified on the grounds that its rights have been violated by nation B, then nation B must have already done something that has violated A's rights. To argue that force is necessary in order to *prevent* a future rights violation by nation B is not to make an argument based on rights at all: it is a call to use force in order to make a better world—a very different sort of moral argument than the argument that a right has been violated, and one rejected by the mainstream tradition that defines just war as a response to a "wrong received."

Nevertheless, many scholars are uncomfortable with an absolute ban on anticipatory self-defense. It might be wise, as a point of international law, to reject anticipatory self-defense in order to deprive nations of a convenient legal pretext for war, but from the point of view of moral principles, it is implausible that *every* case of anticipatory self-defense should be morally wicked. After all, people accept the morality of ordinary self-defense on the grounds that cases arise in which survival requires force directed against the attacker, and the use of force is morally proper in such cases. But exactly the same argument, "the use of force when necessary for survival," could be made in some cases of anticipatory self-defense. . . .

6. Intervention and Just Cause. At first sight it would appear that the U.N. Charter rules out the use of force by all nations except the victims of aggression. But there is an escape clause in Article 51, which grants nations the right of *collective* self-defense. In cases of legitimate collective self-defense, a nation can permissibly use force against an aggressor without itself being the victim of aggression.

So far as international law and custom are concerned, most scholars are agreed that legitimate use of force by A on behalf of B against aggressor C requires some prior mutual defense agreement between A and B. The legal logic of this interpretation of collective self-defense is straightforward: the main intent of the U.N. Charter is to prevent nations from having recourse to force, and to achieve this end it would not be a good idea to let any nation rush to the aid of any other nation that seems to be the victim of aggression. But international law here may be too strict for our moral sensibilities. We do not, at the personal level, require that Good Samaritans have prior contracts with those they seek to aid, even if the Good Samaritan, unlike his biblical predecessor, must use force to rescue the victim of attack. By analogy it seems unreasonable to require prior collective defense agreements between international Good Samaritans and nations that are the victims of aggression. . . .

7. The Rule of Proportionality. It is a superficially paradoxical feature of just war theory that a just cause need not make for a just war. If the just cause can be achieved by some means other than war, then war for that just cause is not morally justified. If the just cause *might* be achieved by other means that have not been attempted, then war for that just cause is not just war. If the cause is just but cannot be achieved by war, then war for that cause is not just war. These rules, sometimes called the rule of necessity, the rule of last resort, or the "chance of victory" requirement, are part of that section of just war theory which acknowledges that some just causes are not sufficiently weighty, on the moral scales, to justify the evils that war for those just causes might produce. The rule of proportionality states that a war cannot be just unless the evil that can reasonably be expected to ensue from the war is less than the evil that can reasonably be expected to ensue if the war is not fought. . . .

8. The Rule of Just Peace. The preceding sections considered all the traditional rules of *jus ad bellum*. Since the rules are addressed to decision makers contemplating war, they take into consideration only such facts as are available to decision makers before war begins. There is room for one further rule, a rule that takes into consideration facts available to moral judges after the war ends. For war to be just, the winning side must not only have obtained justice for itself; it must not have achieved it at the price of violating the rights of others. A just war must lead to a just peace.

The rule of just outcome provides a solution to an ancient controversy concerning just cause. In the modern analysis, for nation A to have just cause, its rights must have been violated by nation B. Pursuit of this just cause permits nation A to use force to restore its rights. But do the rules of morality restrict A to just the restoration of its rights? In civil law, if party B has wrongfully injured party A, A is often entitled not just to compensation for the loss sustained through the injury but also to damages. By analogy, a nation acting in self-defense is entitled not merely to a restoration of the status quo ante but also to further rewards. In considering the scope of these rewards, authors have looked charitably on such rewards as might provide nation A with improved security in the future and teach the lesson that international crime does not pay.

The analogy, however, between civil law and international affairs is weak. The party that pays damages in civil law deserves to be forced to pay, but changes in international arrangements resulting from successful wars fought in self-defense may involve thousands of persons who were not parties to the conflict. It is in the interest of these victims of international upheaval that the rule of just outcome be applied. Such acts as go beyond the restoration of the status quo ante, acts that provide the victor with improved security or assess damages against the loser, must not violate the rights of the citizens in the losing nation or the rights of third parties. . . .

How to Fight

1. Introduction. People who believe that there are moral limits defining *when* wars should be fought naturally believe that there are moral limits defining *how* they should be fought. The idea that there are right and wrong ways to conduct war is an ancient one. In the Hebrew Bible, God states that though it may be necessary to kill one's enemy, it is never permissible to cut down his fruit trees (Deut. 20:19). In the sixth century B.C. the Hindu Laws of Manu specified, "When the King fights with his foes in battle, let him not strike with weapons concealed in wood, nor with barbed, poisoned, or flaming arrows."

Over the centuries, a vast array of rules and customs constituting *jus in bello* have been elaborated. There are rules that specify proper behavior toward neutral countries, toward the citizens of neutral countries, and toward neutral ships. There are rules governing what can and cannot be done to enemy civilians, to enemy soldiers on the battlefield, and to enemy soldiers when they are wounded and when they have surrendered. There are rules concerning proper and improper weapons of war, and proper and improper tactics on the battlefield. . . .

2. Necessity, Proportionality, and Discrimination. For the student approaching the laws of war for the first time, the profusion of convenants, treaties, customs, and precedents can be bewildering. But fortunately there are a few leading ideas that have governed the development of the laws of war. The first is that the destruction of life and property, even enemy life and property, is inherently bad. It follows that military forces should cause no more destruction than is strictly necessary to achieve their objectives. (Notice that the principle does not say that whatever is necessary is permissible, but that everything permissible must be necessary.) This is the principle of necessity: that *wanton* destruction is forbidden. More precisely, the principle of necessity specifies that a military operation is forbidden if there is some alternative operation that causes less destruction but has the same probability of producing a successful military result.

The second leading idea is that the amount of destruction permitted in pursuit of a military objective must be proportionate to the importance of the objective. This is the *military* principle of proportionality (which must be distinguished from the *political* principle of proportionality in the *jus ad bellum*). It follows from the military principle of proportionality that certain objectives should be ruled out of consideration on the grounds that too much destruction would be caused in obtaining them.

The third leading idea, the principle of noncombatant immunity, is that civilian life and property should not be subjected to military force: military force must be directed only at military objectives. Obviously, the principle of noncombatant immunity is useful only if there is a consensus about what counts as "civilian" and what counts as "military." In the older Hague Conventions, a list of explicit nonmilitary targets is developed: "buildings dedicated to religion, art, science, or charitable purposes, historic monuments, hospitals . . . undefended towns, buildings, or dwellings." Anything that is not explicitly mentioned qualifies as a military target. But this list is overly restrictive, and the consensus of modern thought takes "military" targets to include servicemen, weapons, and supplies; the ships and vehicles that transport them; and the factories and workers that produce them. Anything that is not "military" is "civilian." Since, on either definition, the principle of noncombatant immunity distinguishes acceptable military objectives from unacceptable civilian objectives, it is often referred to as the principle of discrimination. (In the morality of war, discrimination is good, not evil.)

There is an objective and subjective version of the principle of noncombatant immunity. The objective version holds that if civilians are killed as a result of military operations, the principle is violated. The subjective version holds that if civilians are *intentionally* killed as a result of military operations, the principle is violated. The interpretation of "intentional" in the subjective version is disputed, but the general idea is that the killing of civilians is intentional if, and only if, they are the chosen *targets* of military force. It follows, on the subjective version, that if civilians are killed in the course of a military operation directed at a military target, the principle of discrimination has *not* been violated. Obviously, the objective version of the principle of discrimination is far more restrictive than the subjective. . . .

The principles of necessity, proportionality, and discrimination apply with equal force to all sides in war. Violation of the rules cannot be justified or excused on the grounds that one is fighting on the side of justice. Those who developed the laws of war learned through experience that just causes must have moral limits.

CHAPTER 24

In Defense of the Death Penalty

Ernest van den Haag

Most countries no longer perform executions. In 2004, the United States was fourth in its use of this punishment, behind China, Iran, and Vietnam. China was first by an uncomfortably large margin—in China, there were at least 3400 executions. In 2005, the United States executed its 1000th prisoner since the Supreme Court confirmed the constitutionality of the death penalty in 1976. The United States, it seems, does a lot of executing.

But by other standards, the United States does not kill many of its criminals. In 2004, there were 59 executions but over 16,000 murders. Recently, the trend has been toward fewer executions. Today there are about 3450 inmates on death row, but most of them will die of natural causes.

The death penalty is allowed in 38 states, of which 32 use it regularly. Texas uses it most, conducting almost one-quarter of America's executions. In 2004, every execution in the United States but one was carried out by lethal injection, which is the most humane way to kill prisoners.

The most significant legal development regarding capital punishment, in recent years, is that the U.S. Supreme Court has ruled it unconstitutional to execute juveniles—those under the age of 18—and the mentally retarded. The high court ruled that executing members of either group would be "cruel and unusual."

Ernest van den Haag, who died in 2002, was a professor of jurisprudence and public policy at Fordham University. In this selection, he argues in favor of the death penalty.

From Ernest van den Haag, "The Ultimate Punishment: A Defense," *Harvard Law Review*, Vol. 99 (May 1986, pp. 1662–69 (whole article, footnotes omitted)). Copyright © 1986 by the Harvard Law Review Association.

In an average year about 20,000 homicides occur in the United States. Fewer than 300 convicted murderers are sentenced to death. But because no more than 30 murderers have been executed in any recent year, most convicts sentenced to death are likely to die of old age. Nonetheless, the death penalty looms large in discussions: it raises important moral questions independent of the number of executions.

The death penalty is our harshest punishment. It is irrevocable: it ends the existence of those punished, instead of temporarily imprisoning them. Further, although not intended to cause physical pain, execution is the only corporal punishment still applied to adults. These singular characteristics contribute to the perennial, impassioned controversy about capital punishment.

Distribution

Consideration of the justice, morality, or usefulness, of capital punishment is often conflated with objections to its alleged discriminatory or capricious distribution among the guilty. Wrongly so. If capital punishment is immoral *in se,* no distribution among the guilty could make it moral. If capital punishment is moral, no distribution would make it immoral. Improper distribution cannot affect the quality of what is distributed, be it punishments or rewards. Discriminatory or capricious distribution thus could not justify abolition of the death penalty. Further, maldistribution inheres no more in capital punishment than in any other punishment.

Maldistribution between the guilty and the innocent is, by definition, unjust. But the injustice does not lie in the nature of the punishment. Because of the finality of the death penalty, the most grievous maldistribution occurs when it is imposed upon the innocent. However, the frequent allegations of discrimination and capriciousness refer to maldistribution among the guilty and not to the punishment of the innocent.

Maldistribution of any punishment among those who deserve it is irrelevant to its justice or morality. Even if poor or black convicts guilty of capital offenses suffer capital punishment, and other convicts equally guilty of the same crimes do not, a more equal distribution, however desirable, would merely be more equal. It would not be more just to the convicts under sentence of death.

Punishments are imposed on persons, not on racial or economic groups. Guilt is personal. The only relevant question is: does the person to be executed deserve the punishment? Whether or not others who deserved the same punishment, whatever their economic or racial group, have avoided execution is irrelevant. If they have, the guilt of the executed convicts would not be diminished, nor would their punishment be less deserved. To put the issue starkly, if the death penalty were imposed on guilty blacks, but not on guilty whites, or, if it were imposed by a lottery among the guilty, this irrationally discriminatory or capricious distribution would neither make the penalty unjust, nor cause anyone to be unjustly punished, despite the undue impunity bestowed on others.

Equality, in short, seems morally less important than justice. And justice is independent of distributional inequalities. The ideal of equal justice demands that justice be equally distributed, not that it be replaced by equality. Justice requires that as many of the guilty as possible be punished, regardless of whether others have avoided punishment. To let these others escape the deserved punishment does not do justice to them, or to society. But it is not unjust to those who could not escape.

These moral considerations are not meant to deny that irrational discrimination, or capriciousness, would be inconsistent with constitutional requirements. But I am satisfied that the Supreme Court has in fact provided for adherence to the constitutional requirement of equality as much as is possible. Some inequality is indeed unavoidable as a practical matter in any system. But, *ultra posse nemo obligatur.* (Nobody is bound beyond ability.)

Recent data reveal little direct racial discrimination in the sentencing of those arrested and convicted of murder. The abrogation of the death penalty for rape has eliminated a major source of racial discrimination. Concededly, some discrimination based on the race of murder victims may exist; yet, this discrimination affects criminal victimizers in an unexpected way. Murderers of whites are thought more likely to be executed than murderers of blacks. Black victims, then, are less fully vindicated than white ones. However, because most black murderers kill blacks, black murderers are spared the death penalty more often than are white murderers. They fare better than most white murderers. The motivation behind unequal distribution of the death penalty may well have been to discriminate against blacks, but the result has favored them. Maldistribution is thus a straw man for empirical as well as analytical reasons.

Miscarriages of Justice

In a recent survey Professors Hugo Adam Bedau and Michael Radelet found that 7,000 persons were executed in the United States between 1900 and 1985 and that 25 were innocent of capital crimes. Among the innocents they list Sacco and Vanzetti as well as Ethel and Julius Rosenberg. Although their data may be questionable, I do not doubt that, over a long enough period, miscarriages of justice will occur even in capital cases.

Despite precautions, nearly all human activities, such as trucking, lighting, or construction, cost the lives of some innocent bystanders. We do not give up these activities, because the advantages, moral or material, outweigh the unintended losses. Analogously, for those who think the death penalty just, miscarriages of justice are offset by the moral benefits and the usefulness of doing justice. For those who think the death penalty unjust even when it does not miscarry, miscarriages can hardly be decisive.

Deterrence

Despite much recent work, there has been no conclusive statistical demonstration that the death penalty is a better deterrent than are alternative punishments. However, deterrence is less than decisive for either side. Most abolitionists acknowledge that they would continue to favor abolition even if the death penalty were shown to deter more murders than alternatives could deter. Abolitionists appear to value the life of a convicted murderer or, at least, his non-execution, more highly than they value the lives of the innocent victims who might be spared by deterring prospective murderers.

Deterrence is not altogether decisive for me either. I would favor retention of the death penalty as retribution even if it were shown that the threat of execution could not deter prospective murderers not already deterred by the threat of imprisonment. Still, I believe the death penalty, because of its finality, is more feared than imprisonment, and deters some prospective murderers not deterred by the threat of imprisonment. Sparing the lives of even a few prospective victims by deterring their murderers is more important than preserving the lives of convicted murderers because of the possibility, or even the probability, that executing them would not deter others. Whereas the lives of the victims who might be saved are valuable, that of the murderer has only negative value, because of his crime. Surely the criminal law is meant to protect the lives of potential victims in preference to those of actual murderers.

Murder rates are determined by many factors; neither the severity nor the probability of the threatened sanction is always decisive. However, for the long run, I share the view of Sir James Fitzjames Stephen: "Some men, probably, abstain from murder because they fear that if they committed murder they would be hanged. Hundreds of thousands abstain from it because they regard it with horror. One great reason why they regard it with horror is that murderers are hanged." Penal sanctions are useful in the long run for the formation of the internal restraints so necessary to control crime. The severity and finality of the death penalty is appropriate to the seriousness and the finality of murder.

Incidental Issues: Cost, Relative Suffering, Brutalization

Many nondecisive issues are associated with capital punishment. Some believe that the monetary cost of appealing a capital sentence is excessive. Yet most comparisons of the cost of life imprisonment with the cost of execution, apart from their dubious relevance, are flawed at least by the implied assumption that life prisoners will generate no judicial costs during their imprisonment. At any rate, the actual monetary costs are trumped by the importance of doing justice.

Others insist that a person sentenced to death suffers more than his victim suffered, and that this (excess) suffering is undue according to the *lex talionis* (rule of retaliation). We cannot know whether the murderer on death row suffers more than his victim suffered; however, unlike the murderer, the victim deserved none of the suffering inflicted. Further, the limitations of the *lex talionis* were meant to restrain private vengeance, not the social retribution that has taken its place. Punishment—regardless of the motivation—is not intended to revenge, offset, or compensate for the victim's suffering, or to be measured by it. Punishment is to vindicate the law and the social order undermined by the crime. This is why a kidnapper's penal confinement is not limited to the period for which he imprisoned his victim; nor is a burglar's confinement meant merely to offset the suffering or the harm he caused his victim; nor is it meant only to offset the advantage he gained.

Another argument heard at least since Beccaria is that, by killing a murderer, we encourage, endorse, or legitimize unlawful killing. Yet, although all punishments are meant to be unpleasant, it is seldom argued that they legitimize the unlawful imposition of identical unpleasantness. Imprisonment is not thought to legitimize kidnapping; neither are fines thought to legitimize robbery. The difference between murder and execution, or between kidnapping and imprisonment, is that the first is unlawful and undeserved, the second a lawful and deserved punishment for an unlawful act. The physical similarities of the punishment to the crime are irrelevant. The relevant difference is not physical, but social.

Justice, Excess, Degradation

We threaten punishments in order to deter crime. We impose them not only to make the threats credible but also as retribution (justice) for the crimes that were not deterred. Threats and punishments are necessary to deter and deterrence is a sufficient practical justification for them. Retribution is an independent moral justification. Although penalties can be unwise, repulsive, or inappropriate, and those punished can be pitiable, in a sense the infliction of legal punishment on a guilty person cannot be unjust. By committing the crime, the criminal volunteered to assume the risk of receiving a legal punishment that he could have avoided by not committing the crime. The punishment he suffers is the punishment he voluntarily risked suffering and, therefore, it is no more unjust to him than any other event for which one knowingly volunteers to assume the risk. Thus, the death penalty cannot be unjust to the guilty criminal.

There remain, however, two moral objections. The penalty may be regarded as always excessive as retribution and always morally degrading. To regard the death penalty as always excessive, one must believe that no crime—no matter how heinous—could possibly justify capital punishment. Such a belief can be neither corroborated nor refuted; it is an article of faith.

Alternatively, or concurrently, one may believe that everybody, the murderer no less than the victim, has an imprescriptible (natural?) right to life. The law therefore should not deprive anyone of life. I share Jeremy Bentham's view that any such "natural and imprescriptible rights" are "nonsense upon stilts."

Justice Brennan has insisted that the death penalty is "uncivilized," "inhuman," inconsistent with "human dignity" and with "the sanctity of life," that it "treats members of the human race as nonhumans, as objects to be toyed with and discarded," that it is "uniquely degrading to human dignity" and "by its very nature, [involves] a denial of the executed person's humanity." Justice Brennan does not say why he thinks execution "uncivilized." Hitherto most civilizations have had the death penalty, although it has been discarded in Western Europe, where it is currently unfashionable probably because of its abuse by totalitarian regimes.

By "degrading," Justice Brennan seems to mean that execution degrades the executed convicts. Yet philosophers, such as Immanuel Kant and G. F. W. Hegel, have insisted that, when deserved, execution, far from degrading the executed convict, affirms his humanity by affirming his rationality and his responsibility for his actions. They thought that execution, when deserved, is required for the sake of the convict's dignity. (Does not life imprisonment violate human dignity more than execution, by keeping alive a prisoner deprived of all autonomy?)

Common sense indicates that it cannot be death—our common fate—that is inhuman. Therefore, Justice Brennan must mean that death degrades when it comes not as a natural or accidental event, but as a deliberate social imposition. The murderer learns through his punishment that his fellow men have found him unworthy of living; that because he has murdered, he is being expelled from the community of the living. This degradation is self-inflicted. By murdering, the murderer has so dehumanized himself that he cannot remain among the living. The social recognition of his self-degradation is the punitive essence of execution. To believe, as Justice Brennan appears to, that the degradation is inflicted by the execution reverses the direction of causality.

Execution of those who have committed heinous murders may deter only one murder per year. If it does, it seems quite warranted. It is also the only fitting retribution for murder I can think of.

CHAPTER 25

*T*he Case against the Death Penalty

Hugo A. Bedau

In 1991, four days after Christmas, Kim Ancona was found murdered on the men's room floor of a bar in Phoenix, Arizona. She worked as a bartender there and had closed up the previous night. Kim's friends said that she had been planning to meet up that night with barfly Ray Krone. Kim's friends did not think much of Ray. At Krone's trial, an expert testified that the bite marks found on Ancona matched Krone's teeth, and so Krone became known as "the snaggletooth killer." He was sentenced to death in 1992. Three years later, he got a new trial but was convicted again.

The case against Krone was, in fact, pitifully weak. In 2002, saliva found on the victim's tank top was tested for DNA. Not only did the results exonerate Krone, but they pointed to another man, Kenneth Phillips. The odds that the saliva did *not* come from Phillips were estimated at 1.3 quadrillion to 1. And in 1991, Phillips had lived only a few hundred yards from where the murder took place. The police did not have to look hard for Phillips, since he was already incarcerated for child molestation. Ray Krone was released from prison in 2002, having spent 10 years in a tiny cell for a crime he had nothing to do with.

Since 1973, 122 death row inmates have been exonerated and released from prison. Ray Krone was number 100. "They would have executed me," he said. "Could I have any faith in the death penalty anymore? Absolutely not. I can't be the only one. . . . People need to address this issue."

Hugo Adam Bedau agrees with Krone. For many years, Bedau has been the leading philosophical critic of capital punishment. Today he is Emeritus Professor of Philosophy at Tufts University.

Hugo Adam Bedau, American Civil Liberties Union. Reprinted with permission.

In 1972, the Supreme Court declared that under then-existing laws "the imposition and carrying out of the death penalty . . . constitutes cruel and unusual punishment in violation of the Eighth and Fourteenth Amendments" (*Furman v. Georgia,* 408 U.S. 238). The Court, concentrating its objections on the manner in which death penalty laws had been applied, found the result so "harsh, freakish, and arbitrary" as to be constitutionally unacceptable. Making the nationwide impact of its decision unmistakable, the Court summarily reversed death sentences in the many cases then before it, which involved a wide range of state statutes, crimes and factual situations.

But within four years after the *Furman* decision, several hundred persons had been sentenced to death under new capital punishment statutes written to provide guidance to juries in sentencing. These statutes typically require a two-stage trial procedure, in which the jury first determines guilt or innocence and then chooses imprisonment or death in the light of aggravating or mitigating circumstances.

In 1976, the Supreme Court moved away from abolition, holding that "the punishment of death does not invariably violate the Constitution." The Court ruled that the new death penalty statutes contained "objective standards to guide, regularize, and make rationally reviewable the process for imposing the sentence of death" (*Gregg v. Georgia,* 428 U.S. 153). Subsequently 38 state legislatures and the Federal government have enacted death penalty statutes patterned after those the Court upheld in *Gregg.* In recent years, Congress has enacted death penalty statutes for peacetime espionage by military personnel and for drug-related murders.

Executions resumed in 1977, and as of May 1997, over 3,200 men and women were under a death sentence and more than 360 had been executed.

Capital Punishment Is Not a Deterrent to Capital Crimes

Deterrence is a function not only of a punishment's severity, but also of its certainty and frequency. The argument most often cited in support of capital punishment is that the threat of execution influences criminal behavior more effectively than imprisonment does. As plausible as this claim may sound, in actuality the death penalty fails as a deterrent for several reasons.

(1) A punishment can be an effective deterrent only if it is consistently and promptly employed. Capital punishment cannot be administered to meet these conditions.

The proportion of first-degree murderers who are sentenced to death is small, and of this group, an even smaller proportion of people are executed. Although death sentences in the mid-1990s have increased to about 300 per year, this is still only about 1 percent of all homicides known to the police. Of all those convicted on a charge of criminal homicide, only 3 percent—about 1 in 33—are eventually sentenced to death.

Mandatory death row sentencing is unconstitutional. The possibility of increasing the number of convicted murderers sentenced to death and executed by enacting mandatory death penalty laws was ruled unconstitutional in 1976 (*Woodson v. North Carolina,* 428 U.S. 280).

A considerable time between the imposition of the death sentence and the actual execution is unavoidable, given the procedural safeguards required by the courts in capital cases. Starting with selecting the trial jury, murder trials take far longer when the ultimate penalty is involved. Furthermore, postconviction appeals in death penalty cases are far more frequent than in other cases. These factors increase the time and cost of administering criminal justice.

We can reduce delay and costs only by abandoning the procedural safeguards and constitutional rights of suspects, defendants, and convicts—with the attendant high risk of convicting the wrong person and executing the innocent.

(2) Persons who commit murder and other crimes of personal violence either may or may not premeditate their crimes.

When crime is planned, the criminal ordinarily concentrates on escaping detection, arrest, and conviction. The threat of even the severest punishment will not discourage those who expect to escape detection and arrest. It is impossible to imagine how the threat of any punishment could prevent a crime that is not premeditated. Gangland killings, air piracy, drive-by shootings, and kidnapping for ransom are among the graver felonies that continue to be committed because some individuals think they are too clever to get caught.

Most capital crimes are committed in the heat of the moment. Most capital crimes are committed during moments of great emotional stress or under the influence of drugs or alcohol, when logical thinking has been suspended. In such cases, violence is inflicted by persons heedless of the consequences to themselves as well as to others. Furthermore, the death penalty is a futile threat for political terrorists because they usually act in the name of an ideology that honors its martyrs.

Capital Punishment Is Unfair

Constitutional due process and elementary justice both require that the judicial functions of trial and sentencing be conducted with fundamental fairness, especially where the irreversible sanction of the death penalty is involved. In murder cases (since 1930, 88 percent of all executions have been for this crime), there has been substantial evidence to show that courts have sentenced some persons to prison while putting others to death in a manner that has been arbitrary, racially biased, and unfair.

Racial discrimination was one of the grounds on which the Supreme Court ruled the death penalty unconstitutional in *Furman*. Half a century ago, in his classic *American Dilemma* (1944), Gunnar Myrdal reported that "the South makes the widest application of the death penalty, and Negro criminals come in for much more than their share of the executions." A recent study of the death penalty in Texas shows that the current capital punishment system is an outgrowth of the racist "legacy of slavery." Between 1930 and the end of 1996, 4,220 prisoners were executed in the United States; more than half (53 percent) were black.

Our nation's death rows have always held a disproportionately large population of African Americans, relative to their percentage of the total population. Comparing black and white offenders over the past century, the former were often executed for what were considered less-than-capital offenses for whites, such as rape and burglary. (Between 1930 and 1976, 455 men were executed for rape, of whom 405—90 percent—were black.) A higher percentage of the blacks who were executed were juveniles; and the rate of execution without having one's conviction reviewed by any higher court was higher for blacks.

In recent years, it has been widely believed that such flagrant racial discrimination is a thing of the past. However, since the revival of the death penalty in the mid-1970s, about half of those on death row at any given time have been black. Of the 3,200 prisoners on death row in 1996, 40 percent were black. This rate is not so obviously unfair if one considers that roughly 50 percent of all those arrested for murder were also black. Nevertheless, when those under death sentence are examined more closely, it turns out that race is a decisive factor after all.

An exhaustive statistical study of racial discrimination in capital cases in Georgia, for example, showed that "the average odds of receiving a death sentence among all indicted cases were 4.3 times higher in cases with white victims." In 1987 these data were placed before the Supreme Court in *McCleskey v. Kemp* and while the Court did not dispute the statistical evidence, it held that evidence of an overall pattern of racial bias was not sufficient. Mr. McCleskey would have to prove racial bias in his own case—an impossible task. The Court also held that the evidence failed to show that there was "a constitutionally significant risk of racial bias . . ." (481 U.S. 279). Although the Supreme Court declared that the remedy sought by the plaintiff was "best presented to the legislative bodies," subsequent efforts to persuade Congress to remedy the problem by enacting the Racial Justice Act were not successful.

In 1990, the U.S. General Accounting Office reported to the Congress the results of its review of empirical studies on racism and the death penalty. The GAO concluded: "Our synthesis of the 28 studies shows a pattern of evidence indicating racial disparities in the charging, sentencing, and imposition of the death penalty after the *Furman* decision" and that "race of victim influence was found at all stages of the criminal justice system process. . . ."

These results cannot be explained away by relevant non-racial factors, such as prior criminal record or type of crime. Furthermore, they lead to a very unsavory conclusion: In the trial courts of this nation, even at the present time, the killing of a white person is treated much more severely than the killing of a black person. Of the 313 persons executed between January 1977 and the end of 1995, 36 had been convicted of killing a black person while 249 (80%) had killed a white person. Of the 178 white defendants executed, only three had been convicted of murdering people of color. Our criminal justice system essentially reserves the death penalty for murderers (regardless of their race) who kill white victims.

Both gender and socio-economic class also determine who receives a death sentence and who is executed. During the 1980s and early 1990s, only about 1 percent of all those on death row were women even though women commit about 15 percent of all criminal homicides. A third or more of the women under death sentence were guilty of killing men who had victimized them with years of violent abuse. Since 1930, only 33 women (12 of them black) have been executed in the United States.

Discrimination against the poor (and in our society, racial minorities are disproportionately poor) is also well established.

Fairness in capital cases requires, above all, competent counsel for the defendant. Yet "approximately 90 percent of those on death row could not afford to hire a lawyer when they were tried." Common characteristics of death-row defendants are poverty, the lack of firm social roots in the community, and inadequate legal representation at trial or on appeal. As Justice William O. Douglas noted in *Furman,* "One searches our chronicles in vain for the execution of any member of the affluent strata in this society" (408 U.S. 238).

The demonstrated inequities in the actual administration of capital punishment should tip the balance against it in the judgment of fair-minded and impartial observers. "Whatever else might be said for the use of death as a punishment, one lesson is clear from experience: this is a power that we cannot exercise fairly and without discrimination."

Capital Punishment Is Irreversible

Unlike all other criminal punishments, the death penalty is irrevocable. Speaking to the French Chamber of Deputies in 1830, years after having witnessed the excesses of the French Revolution, the Marquis de Lafayette said, "I shall ask for the abolition of the punishment of death until I have the infallibility of human judgment demonstrated to me." Although some proponents of capital punishment would argue that its merits are worth the occasional execution of innocent people, most would hasten to insist that there is little likelihood of the innocent being executed. However, a large body of evidence from the 1980s and 1990s shows that innocent people are often convicted of crimes—including capital crimes—and that some have been executed.

Since 1900, in this country, there have been on the average more than four cases each year in which an entirely innocent person was convicted of murder. Scores of these individuals were sentenced to death. In many cases, a reprieve or commutation arrived just hours, or even minutes, before the scheduled execution. These erroneous convictions have occurred in virtually every jurisdiction from one end of the nation to the other. Nor have they declined in recent years, despite the new death penalty statutes approved by the Supreme Court.

Consider this handful of representative cases:

In 1985, in Maryland, Kirk Bloodsworth was sentenced to death for rape and murder, despite the testimony of alibi witnesses. In 1986 his conviction was reversed on grounds of withheld evidence pointing to another suspect; he was retried, reconvicted, and sentenced to life in prison.

In 1993, newly available DNA evidence proved he was not the rapist-killer, and he was released after the prosecution dismissed the case. A year later he was awarded $300,000 for wrongful punishment.

In Mississippi, in 1990, Sabrina Butler was sentenced to death for killing her baby boy. She claimed the child died after attempts at resuscitation failed. On technical grounds her conviction was reversed in 1992. At retrial, she was acquitted when a neighbor corroborated Butler's explanation of the child's cause of death and the physician who performed the autopsy admitted his work had not been thorough.

In 1985, in Illinois, Rolando Cruz and Alejandro Hernandez were convicted of abduction, rape, and murder of a young girl and were sentenced to death. Shortly after, another man serving a life term in prison for similar crimes confessed that he alone was guilty; but his confession was inadmissible because he refused to repeat it in court unless the state waived the death penalty. Awarded a new trial in 1988, Cruz was again convicted and sentenced to death; Hernandez was also re-convicted, and sentenced to 80 years in prison. In 1992 the assistant attorney general assigned to prosecute the case on appeal resigned after becoming convinced of the defendants' innocence. The convictions were again overturned on appeal after DNA tests exonerated Cruz and implicated the prisoner who had earlier confessed. In 1995 the court ordered a directed verdict of acquittal, and sharply criticized the police for their unprofessional handling of the case. Hernandez was released on bail and the prosecution dropped all charges.

In Alabama, Walter McMillian was convicted of murdering a white woman in 1988. Despite the jury's recommendation of a life sentence, the judge sentenced him to death. The sole evidence leading the police to arrest McMillian was testimony of an ex-convict seeking favor with the prosecution. A dozen alibi witnesses (all African Americans, like McMillian) testified on McMillian's behalf, to no avail. On appeal, after tireless efforts by his attorney Bryan Stevenson, McMillian's conviction was reversed by the Alabama Court of Appeals. Stevenson uncovered prosecutorial suppression of exculpatory evidence and perjury by prosecution witnesses, and the new district attorney joined the defense in seeking dismissal of the charges.

Another 1980s Texas case tells an even more sordid story. In 1980 a black high school janitor, Clarence Brandley, and his white co-worker found the body of a missing 16-year-old white schoolgirl. Interrogated by the police, they were told, "One of you two is going to hang for this." Looking at Brandley, the officer said, "Since you're the nigger, you're elected." In a classic case of rush to judgment, Brandley was tried, convicted, and sentenced to death. The circumstantial evidence against him was thin, other leads were ignored by the police, and the courtroom atmosphere reeked of racism. In 1986, Centurion Ministries—a volunteer group devoted to freeing wrongly convicted prisoners—came to Brandley's aid. Evidence had meanwhile emerged that another man had committed the murder for which Brandley was awaiting execution. Brandley was not released until 1990.

Each of these cases has a reassuring ending: The innocent prisoner is saved from execution and released. But other cases are more troubling.

In 1992, Roger Keith Coleman was executed in Virginia despite widely publicized doubts surrounding his guilt and evidence that pointed to another person as the murderer—evidence that was never submitted at his trial. Not until late in the appeal process did anyone take seriously the possibility that the state was about to kill an innocent man, and then efforts to delay or nullify his execution failed. Coleman's case was marked with many of the circumstances found in other cases where the defendant was eventually cleared. Were Coleman still incarcerated, his friends and attorneys would have a strong incentive to resolve these questions. But because Coleman is dead, further inquiry into the crime for which he was convicted is extremely unlikely.

In 1990, Jesse Tafero was executed in Florida. He had been convicted in 1976 along with his wife, Sonia Jacobs, for murdering a state trooper. In 1981 Jacobs' death sentence was reduced on appeal to life imprisonment, and 11 years later her conviction was vacated by a federal court. The evidence on which Tafero and Jacobs had been convicted and sentenced was identical; it consisted mainly of the perjured testimony of an ex-convict who turned state's witness in order to avoid a death sentence. Had Tafero been alive in 1992, he no doubt would have been released along with Jacobs. Tafero's death is probably the clearest case in recent years of the execution of an innocent person.

Several factors help explain why the judicial system cannot guarantee that justice will never miscarry: overzealous prosecution, mistaken or perjured testimony, faulty police work, coerced confessions, the defendant's previous criminal record, inept defense counsel, seemingly conclusive circumstantial evidence, and community pressure for a conviction, among others. And when the system does go wrong, it is volunteers outside the criminal justice system—journalists, for example—who rectify the errors, not the police or prosecutors. To retain the death penalty in the face of the demonstrable failures of the system is unacceptable, especially since there are no strong over-riding reasons to favor the death penalty.

Capital Punishment Is Unjustified Retribution

Justice, it is often insisted, requires the death penalty as the only suit-able retribution for heinous crimes. This claim does not bear scrutiny, however. By its nature, all punishment is retributive. Therefore, what-ever legitimacy is to be found in punishment as just retribution can, in principle, be satisfied without recourse to executions.

Moreover, the death penalty could be defended on narrowly retributive grounds only for the crime of murder, and not for any of the many other crimes that have frequently been made subject to this mode of punishment (rape, kidnapping, espionage, treason, drug trafficking). Few defenders of the death penalty are willing to confine themselves consistently to the narrow scope afforded by retribution. In any case, execution is more than a punishment exacted in retribu-tion for the taking of a life. As Nobel Laureate Albert Camus wrote, "For there to be equivalence, the death penalty would have to punish a criminal who had warned his victim of the date at which he would inflict a horrible death on him and who, from that moment onward, had confined him at his mercy for months. Such a monster is not encountered in private life."

It is also often argued that death is what murderers deserve, and that those who oppose the death penalty violate the fundamental prin-ciple that criminals should be punished according to their just deserts—"making the punishment fit the crime." If this rule means punishments are unjust unless they are like the crime itself, then the principle is unacceptable: It would require us to rape rapists, torture torturers, and inflict other horrible and degrading punishments on offenders. It would require us to betray traitors and kill multiple mur-derers again and again—punishments that are, of course, impossible to inflict. Since we cannot reasonably aim to punish all crimes accord-ing to this principle, it is arbitrary to invoke it as a requirement of justice in the punishment of murder.

If, however, the principle of just deserts means the severity of pun-ishments must be proportional to the gravity of the crime—and since murder is the gravest crime, it deserves the severest punishment—then the principle is no doubt sound. Nevertheless, this premise does not compel support for the death penalty; what it does require is that other crimes be punished with terms of imprisonment or other deprivations less severe than those used in the punishment of murder.

Criminals no doubt deserve to be punished, and the severity of the punishment should be appropriate to their culpability and the harm they have caused the innocent. But severity of punishment has its limits—imposed by both justice and our common human dignity. Governments that respect these limits do not use premeditated, violent homicide as an instrument of social policy.

Some people who have lost a loved one to murder believe that they cannot rest until the murderer is executed. But this sentiment is by no means universal. Coretta Scott King has observed, "As one whose husband and mother-in-law have died the victims of murder and assassination, I stand firmly and unequivocally opposed to the death penalty for those convicted of capital offenses. An evil deed is not redeemed by an evil deed of retaliation. Justice is never advanced in the taking of a human life. Morality is never upheld by a legalized murder."

Internationally, Capital Punishment Is Widely Viewed as Inhumane and Anachronistic

An international perspective on the death penalty helps us understand the peculiarity of its use in the United States. As long ago as 1962, it was reported to the Council of Europe that "the facts clearly show that the death penalty is regarded in Europe as something of an anachronism. . . ."

Today, either by law or in practice, all of Western Europe has abolished the death penalty. In Great Britain, it was abolished (except for cases of treason) in 1971; France abolished it in 1981. Canada abolished it in 1976. The United Nations General Assembly affirmed in a formal resolution that throughout the world, it is desirable to "progressively restrict the number of offenses for which the death penalty might be imposed, with a view to the desirability of abolishing this punishment." By mid-1995, eighteen countries had ratified the Sixth Protocol to the European Convention on Human Rights, outlawing the death penalty in peacetime.

Underscoring worldwide support for abolition was the action of the South African constitutional court in 1995, barring the death penalty as an "inhumane" punishment. Between 1989 and 1995, two dozen other countries abolished the death penalty for all crimes. More than half of all nations have abolished it either by law or in practice.

Once in use everywhere and for a wide variety of crimes, the death penalty today is generally forbidden by law and widely abandoned in practice, in most countries outside the United States. Indeed, the unmistakable worldwide trend is toward the complete abolition of capital punishment. In the United States, opposition to the death penalty is widespread and diverse. Catholic, Jewish, and Protestant religious groups are among the more than fifty national organizations that constitute the National Coalition to Abolish the Death Penalty.

CHAPTER 26

America's Unjust Drug War

Michael Huemer

Over 2 million Americans are imprisoned; 5 million more are on probation or parole. The United States has the highest rate of incarceration of any country in the world. If current trends continue, 1 in every 20 Americans will be locked up, sooner or later.

There were not always so many people behind bars. For the past 35 years, the federal government has waged a "war on drugs," and the ballooning prison population is a result. In 2005, more than half of the inmates in federal prisons had been convicted of drug possession or trafficking. In the larger state prison system, around 20% of the inmates are drug offenders.

Such criminals are disproportionately black and Hispanic. In 2005, the federal prison population was 40% black, 32% Hispanic, and 24.5% Caucasian; the noninstitutionalized population was around 14% black, 14% Hispanic, and 68% Caucasian. Thirty-two percent of African-American males can expect to be incarcerated at some point in their lives. The comparable figure for Hispanics is 17%, while for whites it is 6%.

The war on drugs is well financed. In 2003, the federal government spent nearly $11.4 billion fighting drug use, while state governments spent billions more. Nevertheless, drug use has not declined over the past five years, but has remained stable.

Michael Huemer, who teaches philosophy at the University of Colorado at Boulder, thinks we should call off the war on drugs. Drug use, he says, is less harmful than smoking or obesity, but no one wants to outlaw french fries or cigarettes. Huemer thinks drug laws are seriously unjust because they violate one's right to control one's own body.

Michael Huemer, "America's Unjust Drug War" from Bill Masters, *The New Prohibition*, Accurate Press, 2004. Reprinted by permission of the author and Accurate Press.

Should the recreational use of drugs such as marijuana, cocaine, heroin, and LSD be prohibited by law? *Prohibitionists* answer yes. They usually argue that drug use is extremely harmful both to drug users and to society in general, and possibly even immoral, and they believe that these facts provide sufficient reasons for prohibition. *Legalizers* answer no. They usually give one or more of three arguments. First, some argue that drug use is not as harmful as prohibitionists believe, and even that it is sometimes beneficial. Second, some argue that drug prohibition "does not work," i.e., is not very successful in preventing drug use and/or has a number of very bad consequences. Lastly, some argue that drug prohibition is unjust or violates rights.

I won't attempt to discuss all these arguments here. Instead, I will focus on what seem to me the three most prominent arguments in the drug legalization debate: first, the argument that drugs should be outlawed because of the harm they cause to drug users; second, the argument that they should be outlawed because they harm people other than the user; and third, the argument that drugs should be legalized because drug prohibition violates rights. I shall focus on the moral/philosophical issues that these arguments raise, rather than medical or sociological issues. I shall show that the two arguments for prohibition fail, while the third argument, for legalization, succeeds.

I. Drugs and Harm to Users

The first major argument for prohibition holds that drugs should be prohibited because drug use is extremely harmful to the users themselves, and prohibition decreases the rate of drug abuse. This argument assumes that the proper function of government includes preventing people from harming themselves. Thus, the argument is something like this:

(1) Drug use is very harmful to users.

(2) The government should prohibit people from doing things that harm themselves.

(3) Therefore, the government should prohibit drug use.

Obviously, the second premise is essential to the argument; if I believed that drug use was very harmful, but I did *not* think that the government should prohibit people from harming themselves, then I would not take this as a reason for prohibiting drug use. Furthermore, premise (2), if taken without qualification, is extremely implausible.

Consider some examples of things people do that are harmful (or entail a risk of harm) to themselves: smoking tobacco, drinking alcohol, eating too much, riding motorcycles, having unprotected or promiscuous sex, maintaining relationships with inconsiderate or abusive boyfriends and girlfriends, maxing out their credit cards, working in dead-end jobs, dropping out of college, moving to New Jersey, and being rude to their bosses. Should the government prohibit all of these things?[1] Most of us would agree that the government should not prohibit *any* of these things, let alone all of them. And this is not merely for logistical or practical reasons; rather, we think that controlling those activities is not the business of government.

Perhaps the prohibitionist will argue, not that the government should prohibit *all* activities that are harmful to oneself, but that it should prohibit activities that harm oneself in a certain way, or to a certain degree, or that also have some other characteristic. It would then be up to the prohibitionist to explain how the harm of drug use (to users) differs from the harms (to those who engage in them) of the other activities mentioned above. Let's consider three possibilities.

(1) One suggestion would be that drug use also harms people other than the user; we will discuss this harm to others in Section II below. If, as I will contend, neither the harm to drug users nor the harm to others justifies prohibition, then there will be little plausibility in the suggestion that the combination of harms justifies prohibition. Of course, one could hold that a certain threshold level of total harm must be reached before prohibition of an activity is justified, and that the combination of the harm of drugs to users and their harm to others passes that threshold even though neither kind of harm does so by itself. But if, as I will contend, the "harm to users" and "harm to others" arguments both fail for the reason that it is not the government's business to apply criminal sanctions to prevent the kinds of harms in question, *then* the combination of the two harms will not make a convincing case for prohibition.

(2) A second suggestion is that drug use is generally *more* harmful than the other activities listed above. But there seems to be no reason to believe this. As one (admittedly limited) measure of harmfulness, consider the mortality statistics. The Office of National Drug Control Policy claims that drugs kill 18,000 Americans per year.[2] By contrast, tobacco causes an estimated 440,000 deaths per year.[3] Of course, more people use tobacco than use illegal drugs,[4] so let us divide by the number of users: tobacco kills 15 people per 1,000 users per year; drugs kill 2.6 people per 1,000 users per year.[5] Yet almost no one favors outlawing

tobacco and putting smokers in prison. On a similar note, obesity may cause 420,000 deaths per year (due to increased incidence of heart disease, strokes, and so on), or 11 per 1,000 at-risk persons.[6] Health professionals have warned about the pandemic of obesity, but no one has yet called for imprisoning overweight people.

There are less tangible harms of drug use—harms to one's general quality of life. These are difficult to quantify. But compare the magnitude of the harm to one's quality of life that one can bring about by, say, dropping out of high school, working in a dead-end job for several years, or marrying a jerk—these things can cause extreme and lasting detriment to one's well-being. And yet no one proposes jailing those who drop out, work in bad jobs, or make poor marriage decisions. The idea of doing so would seem ridiculous, clearly beyond the state's prerogatives.

(3) Another suggestion is that drug use harms users in a *different way* than the other listed activities. Well, what sorts of harms do drugs cause? First, illicit drugs may worsen users' health and, in some cases, entail a risk of death. But many other activities—including the consumption of alcohol, tobacco, and fatty foods; sex; and (on a broad construal of "health") driving automobiles—entail health risks, and yet almost no one believes those activities should be criminalized.

Second, drugs may damage users' relationships with others—particularly family, friends, and lovers—and prevent one from developing more satisfying personal relationships.[7] Being rude to others can also have this effect, yet no one believes you should be put in jail for being rude. Moreover, it is very implausible to suppose that people should be subject to criminal sanctions for ruining their personal relationships. I don't have a general theory of what sort of things people should be punished for, but consider the following example: suppose that I decide to break up with my girlfriend, stop calling my family, and push away all my friends. I do this for no good reason—I just feel like it. This would damage my personal relationships as much as anything could. Should the police now come and arrest me, and put me in jail? If not, then why should they arrest me for doing something that has only a *chance* of indirectly bringing about a similar result? The following seems like a reasonable political principle: if it would be wrong (because not part of the government's legitimate functions) to punish people for *directly bringing about* some result, then it would also be wrong to punish people for doing some other action on the grounds that the action has a *chance* of bringing about that result indirectly. If the state may not prohibit me from directly cutting off my relationships with others, then the fact that my drug use might have the result of damaging those relationships does not provide a good reason to prohibit me from using drugs.

Third, drugs may harm users' financial lives, costing them money, causing them to lose their jobs or not find jobs, and preventing them from getting promotions. The same principle applies here: if it would be an abuse of government power to prohibit me from directly bringing about those sorts of negative financial consequences, then surely the fact that drug use might indirectly bring them about is not a good reason to prohibit drug use. Suppose that I decide to quit my job and throw all my money out the window, for no reason. Should the police come and arrest me, and put me in prison?

Fourth and finally, drugs may damage users' moral character, as James Q. Wilson believes:

> [I]f we believe—as I do—that dependency on certain mind-altering drugs *is* a moral issue and that their illegality rests in part on their immorality, then legalizing them undercuts, if it does not eliminate altogether, the moral message. That message is at the root of the distinction between nicotine and cocaine. Both are highly addictive; both have harmful physical effects. But we treat the two drugs differently not simply because nicotine is so widely used as to be beyond the reach of effective prohibition, but because its use does not destroy the user's essential humanity. Tobacco shortens one's life, cocaine debases it. Nicotine alters one's habits, cocaine alters one's soul. The heavy use of crack, unlike the heavy use of tobacco, corrodes those natural sentiments of sympathy and duty that constitute our human nature and make possible our social life.[8]

In this passage, Wilson claims that the use of cocaine (a) is immoral, (b) destroys one's humanity, (c) alters one's soul, and (d) corrodes one's sense of sympathy and duty. One problem with Wilson's argument is the lack of evidence supporting claims (a)–(d). Before we put people in prison for corrupting their souls, we should require some objective evidence that their souls are in fact being corrupted. Before we put people in prison for being immoral, we should require some argument showing that their actions are in fact immoral. Perhaps Wilson's charges of immorality and corruption all come down to the charge that drug users lose their sense of sympathy and duty—that is, claims (a)–(c) all rest upon claim (d). It is plausible that *heavy* drug users experience a decreased sense of sympathy with others and a decreased sense of duty and responsibility.[9] Does this provide a good reason to prohibit drug use?

Again, it seems that one should not prohibit an activity on the grounds that it may indirectly cause some result, unless it would be appropriate to prohibit the direct bringing about of that result. Would it be appropriate, and within the legitimate functions of the state, to punish people for being unsympathetic and undutiful, or for behaving in an unsympathetic and undutiful way? Suppose that Howard—though not a drug user—doesn't sympathize with others. When people try to tell Howard their problems, he just tells them to quit whining. Friends and co-workers who ask Howard for favors are rudely rebuffed. Furthermore—though he does not harm others in ways that would be against our current laws—Howard has a poor sense of duty. He doesn't bother to show up for work on time, nor does he take any pride in his work; he doesn't donate to charity; he doesn't try to improve his community. All around, Howard is an ignoble individual. Should he be put in jail?

If not, then why should someone be put in jail merely for doing something that would have a *chance* of causing them to become like Howard? If it would be an abuse of governmental power to punish people for being jerks, then the fact that drug use may cause one to become a jerk is not a good reason to prohibit drug use.

II. Drugs and Harm to Others

Some argue that drug use must be outlawed because drug use harms the user's family, friends and co-workers, and/or society in general. A report produced by the Office of National Drug Control Policy (ONDCP) states:

> Democracies can flourish only when their citizens value their freedom and embrace personal responsibility. Drug use erodes the individual's capacity to pursue both ideals. It diminishes the individual's capacity to operate effectively in many of life's spheres—as a student, a parent, a spouse, an employee—even as a coworker or fellow motorist. And, while some claim it represents an expression of individual autonomy, drug use is in fact inimical to personal freedom, producing a reduced capacity to participate in the life of the community and the promise of America.[10]

At least one of these alleged harms—dangerous driving—*is* clearly the business of the state. For this reason, I entirely agree that people should be prohibited from driving while under the influence of drugs. But what about the rest of the alleged harms?

Return to our hypothetical citizen Howard. Imagine that Howard—again, for reasons having nothing to do with drugs—does not value freedom, nor does he embrace personal responsibility. It is unclear exactly what this means, but, for good measure, let us suppose that Howard embraces a totalitarian political ideology and denies the existence of free will. He constantly blames other people for his problems and tries to avoid making decisions. Howard is a college student with a part-time job. However, he is a terrible student and worker. He hardly ever studies and frequently misses assignments, and, as a result, he gets poor grades. As we mentioned earlier, Howard comes to work late and takes no pride in his work. Though he does nothing against our current laws, he is an inattentive and inconsiderate spouse and parent. Nor does he make any effort to participate in the life of his community, or the promise of America. He would rather lie around the house, watching television and cursing the rest of the world for his problems. In short, Howard does all the bad things to his family, friends, co-workers, and society that the ONDCP says *may* result from drug use. And most of this is voluntary.

Should Congress pass laws against what Howard is doing? Should the police then arrest him, and the district attorney prosecute him, for being a loser?

Once again, it seems absurd to suppose that we would arrest and jail someone for behaving in these ways, undesirable as they may be. Since drug use has only a *chance* of causing one to behave in each of these ways, it is even more absurd to suppose that we should arrest and jail people for drug use on the grounds that drug use has these potential effects.

III. The Injustice of Drug Prohibition

Philosopher Douglas Husak has characterized drug prohibition as the greatest injustice perpetrated in the United States since slavery.[11] This is no hyperbole. If the drug laws are unjust, then we have 450,000 people unjustly imprisoned at any given time.[12]

Why think the drug laws are *unjust*? Husak's argument invokes a principle with which few could disagree: it is unjust for the state to punish people without having a good reason for doing so.[13] We have seen the failure of the most common proposed rationales for drug prohibition. If nothing better is forthcoming, then we must conclude that prohibitionists have no rational justification for punishing drug users. We have deprived hundreds of thousands of people of basic liberties and subjected them to severe hardship conditions, for no good reason.

This is bad enough. But I want to say something stronger. It is not just that we are punishing people for no good reason; we are punishing people for exercising their natural rights. Individuals have a right to use drugs. This right is neither absolute nor exceptionless. Suppose, for example, that there existed a drug which, once ingested, caused a significant proportion of users, without any further free choices on their part, to attack other people without provocation. I would think that stopping the use of this drug would be the business of the government. But no existing drug satisfies this description. Indeed, though I cannot take time to delve into the matter here, I think it is clear that the drug *laws* cause far more crime than drugs themselves do.

The idea of a right to use drugs derives from the idea that individuals own their own bodies. That is, a person has the right to exercise control over his own body—including the right to decide how it should be used, and to exclude others from using it—in a manner similar to the way one may exercise control over one's (other) property. This statement is somewhat vague; nevertheless, we can see the general idea embodied in commonsense morality. Indeed, it seems that if there is *anything* one would have rights to, it would be one's own body. This explains why we think others may not physically attack you or kidnap you. It explains why we do not accept the use of unwilling human subjects for medical experiments, even if the experiments are beneficial to society—the rest of society may not decide to use your body for its own purposes without your permission. It explains why some believe that women have a right to an abortion—and why some others do not. The former believe that a woman has the right to do what she wants with her own body; the latter believe that the fetus is a distinct person, and a woman does not have the right to harm *its* body. Virtually no one disputes that, *if* a fetus is merely a part of the woman's body, *then* a woman has a right to choose whether to have an abortion; just as virtually no one disputes that, *if* a fetus is a distinct person, *then* a woman lacks the right to destroy it. Almost no one disputes that persons have rights over their own bodies but not over other people's bodies.

The right to control one's body cannot be interpreted as implying a right to use one's body in *every* conceivable way, any more than we have the right to use our property in every conceivable way. Most importantly, we may not use our bodies to harm others in certain ways, just as we may not use our property to harm others. But drug use seems to be a paradigm case of a legitimate exercise of the right to control one's own body. Drug consumption takes place in and immediately around the user's own body; the salient effects occur *inside* the user's body. If we consider drug use merely as altering the user's own body and mind, it is hard to see how anyone who believes in rights at all could deny that it is protected by a right, for (a) it is hard to see how anyone who believes in rights could deny that individuals have rights over their own bodies and minds, and (b) it is hard to see how anyone who believes in such rights could deny that drug use, considered merely as altering the user's body and mind, is an example of the exercise of one's rights over one's own body and mind.

Consider two ways a prohibitionist might object to this argument. First, a prohibitionist might argue that drug use does not *merely* alter the user's own body and mind, but also harms the user's family, friends, co-workers, and society. I responded to this sort of argument in Section II. Not just *any* way in which an action might be said to "harm" other people makes the action worthy of criminal sanctions. Here we need not try to state a general criterion for what sorts of harms make an action worthy of criminalization; it is enough to note that there are some kinds of "harms" that virtually no one would take to warrant criminal sanctions, and that these include the "harms" I cause to others by being a poor student, an incompetent worker, or an apathetic citizen.[14] That said, I agree with the prohibitionists at least this far: no one should be permitted to drive or operate heavy machinery while under the influence of drugs that impair their ability to do those things; nor should pregnant mothers be permitted to ingest drugs, if it can be proven that those drugs cause substantial risks to their babies (I leave aside the issue of what the threshold level of risk should be, as well as the empirical questions concerning the actual level of risk created by illegal drugs—I don't know those things). But, in the great majority of cases, drug use does not harm anyone in any *relevant* ways—that is, ways that we normally take to merit criminal penalties—and should not be outlawed.

Second, a prohibitionist might argue that drug use fails to qualify as an exercise of the user's rights over his own body, because the individual is not truly acting freely in deciding to use drugs. Perhaps individuals use drugs only because they have fallen prey to some sort of psychological compulsion, because drugs exercise a siren-like allure that distorts users' perceptions, because users don't realize how bad drugs are, or something of that sort. The exact form of this objection doesn't matter; in any case, the prohibitionist faces a dilemma. If users do not freely choose to use drugs, then it is unjust to *punish* them for using drugs. For if users do not choose freely, then they are not morally responsible for their decision, and it is unjust to punish a person for something he is not responsible for. But if users *do* choose freely in deciding to use drugs, then this choice is an exercise of their rights over their own bodies.

I have tried to think of the best arguments prohibitionists could give, but in fact prohibitionists have remained puzzlingly silent on this issue. When a country goes to war, it tends to focus on its national interests, sparing little thought for the rights of the victims in the enemy country. Similarly, one effect of America's declaring "war" on drug users seems to have been that prohibitionists have given almost no thought to the rights of drug users. Most either ignore the issue or mention it briefly, only to dismiss it without argument.[15] In an effort to discredit legalizers, the Office of National Drug Control Policy produced the following caricature:

> The easy cynicism that has grown up around the drug issue is no accident. Sowing it has been the deliberate aim of a decades-long campaign by proponents of legalization, critics whose mantra is "nothing works," and whose central insight appears to be that they can avoid having to propose the unmentionable—a world where drugs are ubiquitous and where use and addiction would skyrocket—if they can hide behind the bland management critique that drug control efforts are "unworkable."[16]

This apparently denies the existence of the central issues I have discussed in this essay. It seems reasonable to assume that an account of the state's right to forcibly interfere with individuals' decisions regarding their own bodies is not forthcoming from these prohibitionists.

IV. Conclusion

Undoubtedly, the drug war has been disastrous in many ways that others can more ably describe—in terms of its effects on crime, on police corruption, and on other civil liberties, to name a few. But more than that, the drug war is morally outrageous in its very conception. If we are to retain some sort of respect for human rights, we cannot deploy force to deprive people of their liberty and property for whimsical reasons. The exercise of such coercion requires a powerful and clearly stated rationale. Most of the reasons that have actually been proposed in the case of drug prohibition would be considered feeble if advanced in other contexts. Few would take seriously the suggestion that people should be imprisoned for harming their own health, being poor students, or failing to share in the American dream. It is still less credible that we should imprison people for an activity that only *may* lead to those consequences. Yet these and other, similarly weak arguments form the core of prohibition's defense.

Prohibitionists are likewise unable to answer the argument that individuals have a right to use drugs. Any such answer would have to deny either that persons have rights of control over their own bodies, or that consuming drugs constitutes an exercise of those rights. We have seen that the sort of harms drug use allegedly causes to society does not make a case against its being an exercise of the user's rights over his own body. And the claim that drug users can't control their behavior or don't know what they are doing renders it even more mysterious why one would believe drug users deserve to be punished for what they are doing.

I will close by responding to a query posed by prohibition-advocate James Inciardi:

> The government of the United States is not going to legalize drugs anytime soon, if ever, and certainly not in this [the 20th] century. So why spend so much time, expense, and intellectual and emotional effort on a quixotic undertaking? . . . [W]e should know by now that neither politicians nor the polity respond positively to abrupt and drastic strategy alterations.[17]

The United States presently has 450,000 people unjustly imprisoned. Inciardi may—tragically—be correct that our government has no intention of stopping its massive violations of the rights of its people any time soon. Nevertheless, it remains the duty of citizens and of political and social theorists to identify the injustice, and not to tacitly assent to it. Imagine a slavery advocate, decades before the Civil War, arguing that abolitionists were wasting their breath and should move on to more productive activities—such as arguing for incremental changes in the way slaves are treated—since the southern states had no intention of ending slavery any time soon. The institution of slavery is a black mark on our nation's history, but it would be even more shameful if no one at the time had spoken against it.

Is this comparison overdrawn? I don't think so. The harm of being unjustly imprisoned is qualitatively comparable (though it usually ends sooner) to the harm of being enslaved. The increasingly popular scapegoating and stereotyping of drug users and sellers on the part of our nation's leaders is comparable to the racial prejudices of previous generations. Yet very few seem willing to speak on behalf of drug users. Perhaps the unwillingness of those in public life to defend drug users' rights stems from the negative image we have of drug users and the fear of being associated with them. Yet these attitudes remain baffling. I have used illegal drugs myself. I know many decent and successful individuals, both in and out of my profession, who have used illegal drugs. We have had one United States President, one Vice-President, a Speaker of the House, and a Supreme Court Justice who have admitted to having used illegal drugs.[18] More than a third of all Americans over the age of 11 have used illegal drugs.[19] But now leave aside the absurdity of recommending criminal sanctions for all these people. My point is this: if we are convinced of the injustice of drug prohibition, then—even if our protests should fall on deaf ears—we should not remain silent in the face of such a large-scale injustice in our own country. And, fortunately, radical social reforms *have* occurred, more than once in our history, in response to moral arguments.

Notes

1. Douglas Husak (*Legalize This! The Case for Decriminalizing Drugs*, London: Verso, 2002, pages 7 and 101–3) makes this sort of argument (I have added my own examples of harmful activities to his list).

2. Office of National Drug Control Policy (ONDCP), "Drug Use Consequences," www.whitehousedrugpolicy.gov/publications/policy/03ndcs/table19 .html. The statistic includes both prescription and illegal drugs.

3. Centers for Disease Control and Prevention (CDC), "Annual Smoking-Attributable Mortality, Years of Potential Life Lost, and Economic Costs—United States, 1995–1999," *Morbidity and Mortality Weekly Report* 51, 2002, www.cdc.gov/mmwr/PDF/wk/mm5114.pdf, page 300.

4. James A. Inciardi ("Against Legalization of Drugs" in Arnold Trebach and James Inciardi, *Legalize It? Debating American Drug Policy*, Washington, D.C.: American University Press, 1993, pages 161 and 165) makes this point, accusing drug legalizers of "sophism." He does not go on to calculate the number of deaths per user, however.

5. Based on the assumption of 29.7 million smokers in 1999 and 7.0 million users of illicit drugs (U.S. Census Bureau, *Statistical Abstract of the United States* 2001, Washington, D.C.: Government Printing Office, page 122). However,

these figures may be off by quite a bit. CDC ("Annual Smoking-Attributable Mortality, Years of Potential Life Lost, and Economic Costs—United States, 1995–1999," *Morbidity and Mortality Weekly Report* 51, 2002, www.cdc.gov/mmwr/ PDF/wk/ mm5114.pdf, page 303) reports 46.5 million smokers in the same year, based on a different survey. The Substance Abuse and Mental Health Services Administration reports, "An estimated 14.8 million Americans were current users of illicit drugs in 1999, meaning they used an illicit drug at least once during the 30 days prior to the interview" for the *National Household Survey* (www.samhsa.gov/news/ newsreleases/000831nrhousehold.htm).

6. Based on the assumptions of 240,000 premature deaths caused by obesity in 1991 (David B. Allison, et al., "Annual Deaths Attributable to Obesity in the United States," *Journal of the American Medical Association*, Volume 282, Number 16, 1999, pages 1530–1538), a 61% increase in the prevalence of obesity between 1991 and 2000 (CDC, "Prevalence of Obesity Among U.S. Adults, by Characteristics," www.cdc.gov/nccdphp/dnpa/obesity/trend/prev_char.htm), a 9% increase in population between 1991 and 2000 (U.S. Census Bureau, page 8), and 38.8 million obese Americans in 2000 (CDC, "Overweight and Obesity: Frequently Asked Questions," www.cdc.gov/nccdphp/dnpa/obesity/faq.htm). These figures may also be off—different sources give different estimates for each of these quantities.

7. Inciardi, pages 167 and 172.

8. James Q. Wilson, "Against the Legalization of Drugs," *Commentary* 89, 1990, page 26.

9. As Jacob Sullum has shown (*Saying Yes: In Defense of Drug Use*, New York: Tarcher/Putnam, 2003), many drug users have normal and successful lives, and it is widely known that most users are not addicts.

10. ONDCP, *National Drug Control Strategy 2002*, Washington, D.C.: Government Printing Office, www.whitehousedrugpolicy.gov/publications/policy/ 03ndcs/, pages 1–2.

11. Husak, page 2.

12. Based on 73,389 drug inmates in federal prison in 2000 (U.S. Department of Justice (U.S. DOJ), "Prisoners in 2001," Washington, D.C.: Government Printing Office, 2002, www.ojp.usdoj.gov/bjs/pub/pdf/p01.pdf, page 14), 251,000 drug inmates in state prisons in 2000 (U.S. DOJ, "Prisoners in 2001," page 13), and 137,000 drug inmates in local jails. The last statistic is based on the 2000 jail population of 621,149 (U.S. DOJ, "Prisoners in 2001," page 2) and the 1996 rate of 22% drug offenders in local jails (U.S. DOJ, "Profile of Jail Inmates 1996," Washington, D.C.: Government Printing Office, 1998, www.ojp.usdoj.gov/bjs/pub/pdf/pji96.pdf, page 1). The numbers have probably increased since then.

13. Husak, page 15; see his chapter two for an extended discussion of various proposed rationales for drug prohibition, including many issues that I lack space to discuss here.

14. Husak (*Drugs and Rights*, Cambridge University Press, 1992, pages 166–168), similarly, argues that no one has a right that I be a good neighbor,

proficient student, and so on, and that only "harms" that violate rights can justify criminal sanctions.

15. See Inciardi for an instance of ignoring and Lungren (page 180) for an instance of dismissal without argument. (Daniel Lungren, "Legalization Would Be a Mistake," in Timothy Lynch, ed., *After Prohibition* (Washington, D.C.: Cato Institute, 2000).) Wilson (page 24) addresses the issue, if at all, by arguing that drug use makes users worse parents, spouses, employers, and co-workers. This fails to refute the contention that individuals have a right to use drugs.

16. ONDCP, *National Drug Control Strategy 2002*, page 3.

17. Inciardi, page 205.

18. Bill Clinton, Al Gore, Newt Gingrich and Clarence Thomas (reported by David Phinney, "Dodging the Drug Question," ABC News, August 19, 1999, http://abcnews.go.com/sections/politics/DailyNews/prez _questions990819.html). George W. Bush has refused to state whether he has ever used illegal drugs.

19. U.S. Census Bureau, page 122.

CHAPTER 27

The Experience Machine

Robert Nozick

Robert Nozick (1938–2002) was Joseph Pellegrino University Professor of Philosophy at Harvard University. The following selection is from his book *Anarchy, State, and Utopia*, which is widely regarded as one of the most brilliant and entertaining works in the history of political philosophy. In this excerpt, Nozick uses a thought-experiment to explore questions about what matters to us *other than what our experiences are like.* How we answer these questions will cast light on the ethics of drug use, television watching, and perhaps even sleeping late.

. . . Suppose there were an experience machine that would give you any experience you desired. Superduper neuropsychologists could stimulate your brain so that you would think and feel you were writing a great novel, or making a friend, or reading an interesting book. All the time you would be floating in a tank, with electrodes attached to your brain. Should you plug into this machine for life, preprogramming your life's experiences? If you are worried about missing out on desirable experiences, we can suppose that business enterprises have researched thoroughly the lives of many others. You can pick and choose from their large library or smorgasbord of such experiences, selecting your life's experiences for, say, the next two years. After two years have passed, you will have ten minutes or ten hours out of the tank, to select the experiences of your *next* two years. Of course, while in the tank you won't know that you're there; you'll think it's all actually happening. Others can also plug in to have the experiences they want, so there's no need to stay unplugged to serve them. (Ignore problems

From *Anarchy, State and Utopia* by Robert Nozick. Copyright © 1974 by Basic Books, Inc. Reprinted by permission of Basic Books, a member of Perseus Books, L.L.C.

such as who will service the machines if everyone plugs in.) Would you plug in? *What else can matter to us, other than how our lives feel from the inside?* Nor should you refrain because of the few moments of distress between the moment you've decided and the moment you're plugged. What's a few moments of distress compared to a lifetime of bliss (if that's what you choose), and why feel any distress at all if your decision *is* the best one?

What does matter to us in addition to our experiences? First, we want to *do* certain things, and not just have the experience of doing them. In the case of certain experiences, it is only because first we want to do the actions that we want the experiences of doing them or thinking we've done them. (But *why* do we want to do the activities rather than merely to experience them?) A second reason for not plugging in is that we want to *be* a certain way, to be a certain sort of person. Someone floating in a tank is an indeterminate blob. There is no answer to the question of what a person is like who has long been in the tank. Is he courageous, kind, intelligent, witty, loving? It's not merely that it's difficult to tell; there's no way he is. Plugging into the machine is a kind of suicide. It will seem to some, trapped by a picture, that nothing about what we are like can matter except as it gets reflected in our experiences. But should it be surprising that what *we are* is important to us? Why should we be concerned only with how our time is filled, but not with what we are?

Thirdly, plugging into an experience machine limits us to a man-made reality, to a world no deeper or more important than that which people can construct. There is no *actual* contact with any deeper reality, though the experience of it can be simulated. Many persons desire to leave themselves open to such contact and to a plumbing of deeper significance. This clarifies the intensity of the conflict over psychoactive drugs, which some view as mere local experience machines, and others view as avenues to a deeper reality; what some view as equivalent to surrender to the experience machine, others view as following one of the reasons *not* to surrender!

We learn that something matters to us in addition to experience by imagining an experience machine and then realizing that we would not use it. We can continue to imagine a sequence of machines each designed to fill lacks suggested for the earlier machines. For example, since the experience machine doesn't meet our desire to *be* a certain way, imagine a transformation machine which transforms us into whatever sort of person we'd like to be (compatible with our staying us). Surely one would not use the transformation machine to become as one would wish, and thereupon plug into the experience machine! So something matters in addition to one's experiences *and* what one is like. Nor is the reason merely that one's experiences are unconnected with what one is like. For the experience machine might be limited to provide only experiences possible to the sort of person plugged in. Is it that we want to make a difference in the world? Consider then the result machine, which produces in the world any result you would produce and injects your vector input into any joint activity. We shall not pursue here the fascinating details of these or other machines. What is most disturbing about them is their living of our lives for us. Is it misguided to search for *particular* additional functions beyond the competence of machines to do for us? Perhaps what we desire is to live (an active verb) ourselves, in contact with reality. (And this, machines cannot do *for* us.) Without elaborating on the implications of this, which I believe connect surprisingly with issues about free will and causal accounts of knowledge, we need merely note the intricacy of the question of what matters *for people* other than their experiences. . . .

CHAPTER **28**

*T*he Feminist Revelation

Christina Hoff Sommers

There are more females in the United States than males. Yet women make up only 14% of U.S. senators and 16% of U.S. representatives—and these are the highest figures in the history of those institutions. No woman has ever been president, nor has any woman ever been the presidential nominee of a major political party. In politics, men have the power.

In other areas of life, too, women fare worse. In the business world, the "glass ceiling" still exists: Fewer than 10 Fortune 500 companies are run by women. In 2004, women who worked full-time made only 77% of what men made, an average of $31,223 as compared to $40,798.

Meanwhile, men commit more crimes than women. Over 90% of the inmates in state and federal prisons are male. On death row, the percentage of men is 98.7%. And many of the crimes men commit are crimes against women. According to the National Crime Victimization Survey, there were almost 200,000 cases of sexual assault in 2003.

In light of such facts, many philosophers think that our society is deeply sexist. In the following selection, however, Christina Hoff Sommers argues that "gender feminists" have gone too far in their suggested remedies. Sommers is a resident scholar at the American Enterprise Institute in Washington, DC. Her most recent book, with Sally Satel, is *One Nation under Therapy: How the Helping Culture Is Eroding Self-Reliance.*

In the *Proceedings of the American Philosophical Association* . . . , we find the view that "the power of philosophy lies in its radicalness."[1] The author, Tom Foster Digby, tells us that in our own day "the radical potency of philosophy is particularly well-illustrated by contemporary feminist philosophy" in ways that "could eventually reorder human

Christina Hoff Sommers, "The Feminist Revelation," *Social Philosophy & Policy,* Vol. 8, Issue 1. Reprinted with the permission of Cambridge University Press.

life."[2] The claim that philosophy is essentially radical has deep historical roots.

Aristotle and Plato each created a distinctive style of social philosophy. . . . I shall call Aristotle's way of doing social philosophy "whiggish," having in mind that the Oxford English Dictionary characterizes "whig" as "a word that says in one syllable what 'conservative liberal' says in seven." Later whigs shared with Aristotle the conviction that traditional arrangements have great moral weight, and that common opinion is a primary source of moral truth. The paradigm example of a whig moral philosopher is Henry Sidgwick, with his constant appeal to Common Sense and to "established morality."[3] On the more liberal side, we have philosophers like David Hume who cautions us to "adjust [political] innovations as much as possible to the ancient fabric," and William James who insists that the liberal philosopher must reject radicalism.[4]

In modern times, many social philosophers have followed the more radical example of Plato, who was convinced that common opinion was benighted and in need of much consciousness-raising. Looking on society as a Cave that distorted real values, Plato showed a great readiness to discount traditional arrangements. He was perhaps the first philosopher to construct an ideal of a society that reflected principles of justice, inspiring generations of utopian social philosophers.

Tom Foster Digby thus belongs to a long and distinguished Platonist tradition that views philosophy as an organon for radical social reform. The opposing Aristotelian/whiggish tradition is today far weaker and certainly less popular among social philosophers: most feminist philosophers repudiate it altogether. Dr. Digby has high praise for the feminist social critics who are exposing the contemporary Cave as sexist ("androcentric") and unjust; he predicts that "feminist philosophy will one day be seen as one of the pivotal developments in the history of philosophy."[5] Digby's assessment reflects the view of the feminists themselves, who are convinced that feminist philosophy is initiating an intellectual revolution of historical dimensions. My own view that this judgment is intemperate and altogether unwarranted will be made evident throughout the ensuing discussion.

I. Feminism as a Radical Paradigm

For the benefit of those who have not been edified by much reading in feminist philosophy, I shall cite some characteristic positions of some leading feminist philosophers. It is practically impossible to do justice to all the newest turns of feminist theory. Feminist literature is in constant ferment; there is a kind of feminism of the week, but keeping track of it would engage all one's time. I shall therefore outline Alison Jaggar's useful and influential typology of contemporary feminist theory.[6] Jaggar identifies four dominant feminist "frameworks": liberal, Marxist, radical, and socialist.

   1. Liberal feminism, according to Jaggar, has its origins in the social contract theories of the sixteenth and seventeenth centuries. Liberal feminists demand that principles of liberty and equality be applied to women, and they actively work to remove laws and to reform institutions that restrict women's autonomy or range of opportunity. Historically, liberals have worked to accomplish the following for women: suffrage, the right to own property, the right to obtain a divorce, access to credit and educational opportunities, and other rights enjoyed by men. Liberals do not, however, challenge the basic assumptions of democratic capitalism. . . . Jaggar also discusses a more radical and contemporary version of liberalism (which I shall call egalitarianism). Jaggar gives no examples, but the views of Susan Okin and Richard Wasserstrom come to mind.[7] Both deploy liberal principles in order to make the case for complete equality between men and women. Okin argues for a feminist reading of John Rawls. She believes that if the participants in the original position were ignorant of their sex, they would probably opt for a genderless society in which the family as we know it is abolished in favor of an egalitarian alternative.

> The family is the linchpin of gender, reproducing it from one generation to the next . . . [F]amily life as typically practiced in our society is not just, either to women or to children. Moreover, it is not conductive to the rearing of citizens with a strong sense of justice. . . . A just future would be one without gender.[8]

Okin doesn't specify the changes entailed by a sexually neutral social contract. Richard Wasserstrom, on the other hand, gives a detailed account of an ideal "sexually assimilated" society in which the gender system has been overthrown.

> [T]here would be no expectation that the family was composed of one adult male and one adult female, rather than, say, just two adults—if two adults seemed the appropriate number . . . [P]ersons would not be socialized so as to see or understand themselves or others as essentially or significantly who they were . . . because they were either male or female. . . . Bisexuality, not heterosexuality or homosexuality, would be the typical intimate sexual relationship in the ideal society that was assimilationist in respect to sex.[9]

2. Marxist feminists constitute the next major group in Jaggar's typology. Following Friedrich Engels, Marxist feminists hold that women's oppression will be abolished in the classless society; the discriminatory aspect of the gender difference will be overcome when the class struggle is won. There do not seem to be many current feminist theorists writing under this banner, but Jaggar and others discriminate the Marxist perspective since it has been a critical influence on radical feminism and socialist feminism—the other two major categories in Jaggar's typology.

3. Radical feminism emerged from the liberation movements of the 1960s. It sees women as the most oppressed group in history, and denies that this oppression can be removed merely by changing the economic system or even overthrowing the class system. Women are oppressed by men; the recognition of this fact is the starting point of radical feminist philosophy, and it gives it a confrontational and highly controversial character.

Two of the contemporary theorists mentioned by Jaggar, Mary Daly and Andrea Dworkin, have worked out an imaginative and elaborate view of the "patriarchy" in which men are variously characterized as death-affirming rapists and warmongers. Daly calls them "Necrophiliacs."[10] According to Andrea Dworkin:

> Men love death. In everything they make they hollow out a central place for death . . . in male culture slow murder is the heart of eros, fast murder is the heart of action, and systemized murder is the heart of history.[11]

Women, by contrast, are life-affirming, caring, and nurturing. Radical feminists seek to give expression to women's experience in a new feminine epistemology while exposing the masculinist aspects of classical epistemology as denigrating and hostile to women's ways of knowing. The political character of the male point of view affects the most abstract disciplines. Here is how Catherine MacKinnon articulates this claim:

> [Feminism's] project is to uncover and claim as valid the experience of women. . . . This defines the task of feminism not only because male dominance is perhaps the most pervasive and tenacious system of power in history, but because it is metaphysically nearly perfect. . . . Its force is exercised as consent, its authority as participation . . .[12]

Virginia Held looks forward to the day when the "patriarchy is overthrown" and women do the "organizing."

Instead of organizing human life in terms of expected male tendencies toward aggression, competition and efforts to over-power . . . one might try to organize human life to nurture cre-ativity, cooperation and imagination, with the point of view of those who give birth and nurture taken as primary.[13]

Some radical feminists follow de Beauvoir in abjuring moth-erhood itself as oppressive to women. In her "Motherhood: The Annihilation of Women," Jeffner Allen tells us what being a mother really means:

A mother is she whose body is used as a resource to reproduce men and the world of men. . . . Motherhood is dangerous to women because it continues the structure within which females must be women and mothers, and, conversely, because it denies to females the creation of a subjectivity and world that is open and free.[14]

4. Socialist feminism is a synthesis of Marxism and radical femi-nism: its goal is to abolish both class and gender. "Socialist feminism," says Jaggar, "seeks a society in which 'masculinity' and 'femininity' no longer exist."[15] After noting that the ideal society is not immediately realizable, Jaggar points to some things that socialist feminists believe can be done right away:

One institution to which some socialist feminists are seeking immediate alternatives is the stereotypical 20th century nuclear family . . . [They] see this structure as a corner-stone of women's oppression: it enforces women's dependence on men, it enforces heterosexuality, and it imposes the prevailing masculine and feminine character structures on the next generation. In addi-tion, the traditional nuclear family is a bulwark of the capitalist system . . .[16]

Jaggar, who finds this version of feminism most plausible, notes that uninitiated women in the capitalist, patriarchal cave are subject to common illusions that serve to reinforce male dominance. "The ideology of romantic love has now become so pervasive that most women in contemporary capitalism probably believe they marry for love rather than for economic support."[17] The socialist feminist utopia includes technological as well as social transformations:

[W]e must remember that the ultimate transformation of human nature at which socialist feminists aim goes beyond the liberal conception of psychological androgyny, to a possible transforma-tion of "physical" human capacities, some of which, until now, have been seen as biologically limited to one sex.[18]

Socialist and radical feminists are divided on how the revolution will come to pass. Jaggar continues:

> Socialist feminists, by contrast [to radical feminists], are suffi-
> ciently Marxist to be skeptical that the white male ruling class
> would give up its power without a violent revolution; however
> they are confident that such a struggle could be won by the over-
> whelming majority of the population whom they view as their
> potential allies.[19]

Jaggar mentions several other contemporary feminist sub-
groups: lesbian separatists, anarcha-feminists, Freudian feminists, eco-
feminists, radical women of color, and French "post-structuralist"
feminists. They share a common goal of articulating the experiences
of women that, for some, serve as the basis of a distinctively "feminist
epistemology." All take characteristic pride in their revolutionary perspective on society and the family.

II. Liberal Feminism and Gender Feminism

Feminist thinkers of a liberal (that is, Millian) persuasion are not at
the core of contemporary feminist philosophy, and they are not
among those Digby praises. Jaggar harks back to the nineteenth century for examples of influential liberal feminists. Liberal feminism is a
significant force outside the academy.[20] But it is not the favored standpoint among academic feminists; in particular, liberal feminism does
not inspire contemporary feminist philosophers.

Liberal feminists are content to achieve equality of opportunity
and full legal equality; they are not, in principle, at war with the "gendered family" or with other aspects of society that place value on
masculine and feminine differences. As Jaggar correctly, if somewhat
disparagingly, says:

> For the liberal feminist . . . the roots of women's oppression lie in
> women's lack of equal civil rights and equal educational oppor-
> tunities. There is little attempt at historical speculation as to why
> such a lack should exist. Because the roots are so easily visible,
> women's oppression can be tackled immediately by a direct attack
> on sexist discrimination. When this discrimination has been elim-
> inated, women will have been liberated.[21]

Liberal feminists are not out to second-guess women on what
they really prefer. On the whole, they follow John Stuart Mill in being
attentive to the preferences, aspirations, and ideals of women—even

when these include such "gendered" choices as conventional marriage and motherhood. In short, the liberal feminists are more liberal
than feminist—or, rather, they are feminists in wanting for women
what any liberal wants for anyone suffering from bias: namely, fair
treatment.

The feminist schools Jaggar mentions—egalitarian, Marxist, radical, and socialist—all tend to see popular women's culture as something that needs to be "critiqued" and, perhaps, eliminated. These
gender feminists, as I shall call them, view social reality in terms of the
"sex-gender system." In Sandra Harding's words, this system is a

> system of male-dominance made possible by men's control of
> women's productive and reproductive labor, where "reproduc-
> tion" is broadly construed to include sexuality, family life, and
> kinship formations, as well as the birthing which biologically
> reproduces the species . . . [The sex/gender system] appears to
> be a fundamental variable organizing social life throughout most
> recorded history and in every culture today.[22]

Leading contemporary feminist philosophers have adopted this
perspective on history, society, and culture. In addition to demanding
a radical restructuring of society, the gender feminist calls for an epistemological revolution that will expose masculinist bias and ultimately
remove its mark from our cultural and social heritage. As a liberal feminist, I am saddened to see that the radical perspective has proved so
beguiling to the majority of feminist academics. In what follows, I shall
examine some of the attitudes and assumptions of gender feminism
and some of the consequences for philosophical feminism of adopting the gender perspective.

III. Transforming Human Nature

The gender feminist is radical in her Platonist confidence that a genderless ideal could be promoted by raising the consciousness of the
dwellers in the patriarchal cave. Two assumptions, one negative and
the other positive, are at the ground of her optimism. First, there is the
negative thesis that there are no inherited human traits determining a
sex/gender difference that would form a significant barrier to the real-
ization of the egalitarian, assimilationist ideal. Here, perhaps, the feminists follow Simone de Beauvoir, who denied there was such a thing
as a distinctive human nature. But American feminists are also convinced of Richard Rorty's dictum that "socialization goes all the way

down," determining almost all the functions and practices that are specific to human beings.[23] This leaves room for the second assumption, which I call the thesis of corrigibility: the positive thesis that what we think of as human nature is plastic and corrigible, offering real possibilities for radical social change brought about by conscious manipulation of the beliefs and institutions that now largely define our social relations and mores.

On this view, human nature as we have hitherto understood it is, in large part, a myth invented by men to oppress women. For example, unlike the desire for food—which is biologically given, but not specifically human—the widespread desire for heterosexual relationships is thought to be sociologically determined. It is, in that sense, a gendered and not a sexual phenomenon. That is, it is determined by society, not by biology. More generally, a genderless society would in no way run up against any genetic or biological constraints.[24]

If acculturation is not the elaboration of any specifically human biological traits—if it is historical, social, accidental, or political—then it is essentially mutable. This doctrine, that human nature has no fixed essence, if added to the more positive doctrine that sociology goes all the way down, is then assumed to entail the thesis of corrigibility.

The feminists here make a common mistake: they conflate mutability with corrigibility. It is one thing to maintain (rightly or wrongly) that human nature is diverse and mutable, and that in each society it is the product of particular historical and social forces; it is quite another to claim that because human nature is changeable, it is politically corrigible. For it does not follow that we have either the knowledge or the ability to effect the kinds of changes adumbrated by the gender feminists. To assume that we can effectively and responsibly intervene to change the mores that in fundamental ways define or determine us to be as we are—heterosexual, family-centered, genderized, and non-assimilationist—is to assume that we can take *full* charge of our social history. But nothing in history suggests that corrigibility goes all the way down.

My point is that the whig as well as the radical can embrace the idea that human nature is socially defined. But the whig is sensitive to the possibility that, in its own way, a particular social history may be as great a barrier to effective radical change as the "biological nature" that the feminists inveigh against. On the other hand, such evidence as we have argues for extreme modesty in assessing our

abilities to bring about radical change without courting unforesee-
able disasters.

Let me say that I do not wish to take any particular stand on the
nature/nurture question. I plead ignorance and even some confusion
as to how to set about talking about it. I am saying that the feminist
theorists do not appear to have a better grasp of the problem than anyone else, and that their confidence in the proposition that, say, a genderless society is achievable and a clearly worthwhile goal of moral
education is quite unwarranted.

We are now aware that large-scale human intervention into
natural systems can be disastrous. We know that natural history has
its reasons and its wisdom, and that we are largely ignorant of both.
For the present, at any rate, ecology is a modest science whose practical advice seems to be confined to telling us to *desist* from any
large-scale intervention because of our appalling ignorance. I believe
that much of this whiggish moral applies to the proponents of radical social reform. The sociological lessons are what the whig intuitively understands, but what the radical in her optimistic zeal is so
willing to ignore.

It is ironically true that so many who are sensitive and consider-
ate when it comes to issues of ecology are so intemperate when it
comes to embracing an activist and radical social philosophy whose
goal is to eliminate such things as the "gendered family." Perhaps we
need a group of moral ecologists who would protect our fragile but
vital social institutions (some of which have taken millennia to evolve)
in the way ecologists help us to protect systems in nature.

Now I do not mean to say that we cannot look at utopian ideals
for guidance in making needed changes; I simply mean that we cannot deploy any ideal in the wholesale utopian manner that the gender feminists do—as blueprints for the radical reform of preferences,
values, aspirations, and prejudices. For those who do not like the
word "conservative" I offer the more accurate and, perhaps, less ten-
dentious term "conservationist." The careful and socially responsible
philosopher—the Aristotelian whig—is a liberal and a conservationist; she wants reform, but she treads carefully in her dealings with
such fundamental institutions as the family or the rearing of children.
By contrast, the feminist who believes in the pervasiveness of the
sex/gender system of male oppression is led to look upon the women
she wants to liberate as a duped constituency whose actual preferences need not be taken seriously.

IV. The Benighted Constituency

Feminists recognize that to make palatable such novelties as a genderless society, communal parenting, or bisexuality would require radical measures in "reeducating" both men and women. Many would
restructure education to counter and ultimately to remove the widespread preference for heterosexual relationships. This is precisely
reminiscent of Plato's call for a *new* consciousness that dispels the illusions of the Cave and a *new* mode of "socialization" that will inculcate
the attitudes appropriate to the well-functioning just and genderless
society. That any such socialization is implementable and workable is
highly dubious. But whatever one may say of its feasibility, this feature
of the feminist perspective on social criticism—its readiness to reedu-
cate the benighted majority by "raising" its consciousness—is morally
and politically unattractive. Here, the gender feminist—like other radical social philosophers—shows her illiberal colors. Where the liberal
attends to the actual professed aspirations of those she wants to help,
the radical is impatient with them. The goal of restructuring human
beings and human society by changing what the average person pro-
fessedly wants in favor of what he or she "ought to want" is an essential
feature of gender feminism. In this fundamental respect, gender feminism is crudely illiberal and undemocratic.

It is indeed the case that most American women are not in sympathy with some of the fundamental assumptions of gender feminism.
But that has not inhibited feminist theorists from claiming to be posi-
tioned at the "standpoint of women," whence they report on the
insights afforded them by "the woman's perspective." Some interesting answers to the question "Why aren't all women feminists?" are
cited by Jaggar:

> Within radical feminism, two main lines of reasoning are offered
> to explain women's submission to domination. One line stresses
> the lack of objective options for women, portraying them as
> almost totally trapped by the patriarchy . . . submitting to men in
> order to survive. The other line . . . sees women as deluded,
> tricked or bewildered by the patriarchal culture, patriarchal sci-
> ence, and even the language of the patriarchy.[25]

Jaggar herself speaks of "perhaps . . . developing a feminist version of false consciousness," and cites psychoanalytic and Marxist
explanations of why so many contemporary women have the wrong
kinds of preferences and the inability to grasp their own true interests. Catherine MacKinnon's theory about why so many women

failed to support the Equal Rights Amendment is characteristically condescending:

> I think that these women . . . feared the meaning of sex equality in their lives, because sex inequality gave them what little they had, so little that they felt they couldn't afford to lose it. They hung on to their crumbs, as if that was all they were ever going to get.[26]

It is not hard to see that such accounts of why so many women are not feminists leave the feminist theorists quite free to discount all grass-roots opposition to feminism. Non-feminist sentiment is conveniently seen as the product of a socialization that has educated women to their subordinate roles. It therefore need not be taken seriously except as an obstacle in the path of realizing the genderless ideal. . . .

V. Feminist Misogyny

Women have been socialized to want the role of mother, to marry good providers, to like clothes that render them "sex objects." The feminist is depressed by all such symptoms of a craven femininity. What is to be done with the duped majority of women who choose conventional motherhood? Simone de Beauvoir's candor, as far as it goes, is refreshing:

> No woman should be authorized to stay at home and raise her children . . . one should not have the choice precisely because if there is such a choice, too many women will make that one.[27]

However, de Beauvoir does not tell us anything about the kind of society in which Big Sister has the authority and power to prevent women from living the lives they may prefer. . . .

It is important to be aware of how the radical approach, which is so dismissive of established morality, has led the feminist to an undemocratic elitism that is so condescending to its claimed constituency. But it is equally important to understand that the roots of condescension are to be located in philosophical radicalism itself, which perverts the true task of moral philosophy and social criticism by its confident and principled disregard of traditional morality and common values. Radical philosophers characteristically believe themselves to have a clear perception of the "objective interests" of the people they want to help. Where liberal reformers are dependent on finding out about the ideals and preferences of those they help, radicals come to the task of social reform already equipped with a principled knowledge of what their constituents "really" want and need. Deploying their under-standing of the "objective interests" of women, gender feminists tend to disregard the values of men and women who may like many aspects of *la différence*. The values of the uninitiated are "subjective" and must be discounted when they conflict with the genderless ideal. . . .

It seems clear (to me, at any rate) that the primary job of social philosophy is to make good theoretical sense of the moral world in which we live. Even as we grant that ideals of justice and equality are needed to guide us in repairing the moral imperfections of our insti-tutions and social arrangements, we must be on guard against any deployment of these ideals that is illiberally insensitive to moral com-mon sense. When the feminists advocate abolishing the family, or when political radicals advocate the undermining of a democratic gov-ernment, they violate our preanalytic commitments to common-sense morality. Plato believed that the morality of the Cave was largely illu-sory "appearance." But a reasonable moral theory aims generally at saving appearances and making sense of them, and not at a wholesale dismissal of established morality as an illusion. And good social criti-cism should be based on a reasonable moral theory. . . .

Notes

1. Tom Foster Digby, "Philosophy as Radicalism," *Proceedings and Addresses of the American Philosophical Association*, vol. 61, no. 5 (June 1988), p. 860.

2. Ibid., pp. 860–61.

3. See Ernest Barker's introduction to Aristotle's *Politics*, where he argues that Aristotle was "a Whig of the type of Locke or Burke." *Politics of Aristotle*, ed. and trans. Ernest Barker (Oxford: Oxford University Press, 1973).

4. Both David Hume and William James warn against the hazards of social and political radicalism. Here is Hume on the subject of political experimentation: "To . . . try experiments merely upon the credit of sup-posed argument and philosophy can never be the part of a wise magistrate, who will bear a reverence to what carries the mark of age; and though he may attempt some improvements for the public good, yet will he adjust his innovations as much as possible to the ancient fabric . . ." (*Essays on Moral and Political Subjects*, pt. II, essay XVI). William James saw the rejection of radicalism as central to the pragmatic method. "[Experience] has proved that the laws and usages of the land are what yield the maximum of satisfaction. . . . The presumption in cases of conflict must always be in favor of the

conventionally recognized good. The philosopher must be a conservative . . ." ("The Moral Philosopher and the Moral Life," *Essays in Pragmatism* (New York: Hafner, 1948, p. 80)).

5. Digby, p. 860.

6. Alison Jaggar, *Feminist Politics and Human Nature* (Totowa: Rowman and Allanheld, 1983). A similar typology is described by Rosemary Tong in "Feminism Philosophy: Standpoints and Differences," *American Philosophical Association Newsletter on Feminism and Philosophy* (April 1988), pp. 8–11.

7. See Richard Wasserstrom, "Racism and Sexism," *Philosophy and Social Issues* (Notre Dame: University of Notre Dame Press, 1980), p. 26; Susan Moller Okin, *Justice, Gender and the Family* (New York: Basic Books, 1989).

8. Okin, pp. 170–71.

9. Wasserstrom, p. 26.

10. Mary Daly, *Gyn/Ecology: The Metaethics of Radical Feminism* (Boston: Beacon Press, 1978), p. 59.

11. Andrea Dworkin, "Why So-Called Radical Men Love and Need Pornography," ed. Laura Lederer, *Take Back the Night: Women on Pornography* (New York: William Morris, 1980), p. 139.

12. Catherine MacKinnon, *Toward a Feminist Theory of the State* (Cambridge: Harvard University Press, 1989), pp. 116–17.

13. Virginia Held, "Birth and Death," *Ethics*, vol. 99, no. 2 (January 1989), p. 388.

14. Jeffner Allen, "Motherhood: The Annihilation of Woman," ed. Joyce Trebilcot, *Mothering, Essays in Feminist Theory* (Totowa: Rowman and Allanheld, 1984), p. 315.

15. Alison Jaggar, p. 340.

16. Ibid., p. 336.

17. Ibid., p. 219.

18. Ibid., p. 132.

19. Ibid., p. 340 (part of this passage was misprinted in the first edition; see the 1988 edition for correct text).

20. Sylvia Hewlett is a good example of a working liberal feminist. She left the academy when her academic sisters did not give her adequate support in her attempts to manage a family and an academic career. See her *A Lesser Life: The Myth of Women's Liberation in America* (New York: William Morrow, 1985).

21. Alison Jaggar, eds. Alison Jaggar and Paula Rothenberg, *Feminist Frameworks* (New York: McGraw-Hill, 1984), p. 85.

22. Sandra Harding, "Why Has the Sex/Gender System become Visible Only Now?", eds. Sandra Harding and Merrill Hintikka, *Discovering Reality: Feminist Perspectives on Science* (Dordrecht: D. Reidel, 1983), p. 312.

23. Richard Rorty, *Contingency, Irony, and Solidarity* (Cambridge: Cambridge University Press, 1989), p. 185.

24. Many feminist philosophers are convinced that babies are born bisexual and are then transformed into "males" and "females" by their parents. See, for example, Ann Ferguson, "Androgyny as an Ideal for Human Development," eds. M. Vetterling-Braggin, F. Elliston, and J. English, *Feminism and Philosophy* (Totowa, NJ: Rowman and Littlefield, 1977), p. 61; Gayle Rubin, "The Traffic in Women: Notes on the 'Political Economy of Sex'," ed. Rayna R. Reita, *Toward an Anthropology of Women* (New York: Monthly Review Press, 1975), pp. 157–210; and Harding, p. 127.

25. Jaggar, p. 149.

26. Catherine MacKinnon, *Feminism Unmodified* (Cambridge: Harvard University Press, 1989), p. 226.

27. From "Sex, Society, and the Female Dilemma: A Dialogue between Simone de Beauvoir and Betty Friedan," *Saturday Review* (June 14, 1975); quoted in Nicholas Davidson, *The Failure of Feminism* (Buffalo: Prometheus Books, 1988), p. 17.

CHAPTER 29

Is Racial Discrimination Arbitrary?

Peter Singer

When the Major League Baseball season ended in 1973, Atlanta Braves slugger Hank Aaron was just one swing away from the greatest prize in baseball: Babe Ruth's record of 714 career home runs. History was in the making; the Bambino was about to get hammered. Aaron's first at-bat of the '74 season saw number 714. Number 715 came on April 8, 1974, before a sellout crowd in Atlanta. Today, outside the Braves' stadium, there is a statue of Hank Aaron, and though the stadium has moved, a sign in the outfield still commemorates the spot where home run 715 cleared the fence.

There is, however, an unpleasant side to this story. Aaron now recalls those "glory" days as being the worst days of his life. Why? Because Aaron is African-American, and for daring to break Babe Ruth's record, he had to endure a torrent of hatred. In 1973, he received 930,000 pieces of mail, most of it filled with racial slurs. As he got near Ruth's record, Aaron holed up in his apartment, afraid to go outside. The FBI uncovered a plot to kill his daughter, who lived in Nashville. And when he actually hit number 715, Aaron's mother Estella jumped out of the stands and rushed onto the field, not out of joy, but because she believed that her son was about to be murdered.

Racial discrimination violates one of our most deeply held moral beliefs: that people should not be treated badly for arbitrary reasons like the color of their skin. The hatred Hank Aaron had to endure was clearly vile. However, other cases of differential treatment are less clear. Peter Singer discusses three such cases in this selection.

For information on Peter Singer, see Chapters 15 and 19.

Peter Singer, "Is Racial Discrimination Arbitrary?" *Philosophia*, Vol. 8, No. 1, October 1978. Used by permission.

1. Introduction

There is nowadays wide agreement that racism is wrong. To describe a policy, law, movement, or nation as "racist" is to condemn it. It may be thought that since we all agree that racism is wrong, it is unnecessary to speculate on exactly what it is and why it is wrong. This indifference to moral fundamentals could, however, prove dangerous. For one thing, the fact that most people agree today that racism is wrong does not mean that this attitude will always be so widely shared. Even if we had no fears for the future, though, we need to have some understanding of what it is about racism that is wrong if we are to handle satisfactorily all the problems we face today. For instance, there is the contentious issue of "reverse discrimination" or discrimination in favor of members of oppressed minority groups. It must be granted that a university which admits members of minority groups who do not achieve the minimum standard that others must reach in order to be admitted is discriminating on racial lines. Is such discrimination therefore wrong?

Or, to take another issue, the efforts of Arab nations to have the United Nations declare Zionism a form of racism provoked an extremely hostile reaction in nations friendly to Israel, particularly the United States, but it led to virtually no discussion of whether Zionism is a form of racism. Yet the charge is not altogether without plausibility, for if Jews are a race, then Zionism promotes the idea of a state dominated by one race, and this has practical consequences in, for instance, Israel's immigration laws. Again, to consider whether this makes Zionism a form of racism we need to understand what it is that makes a policy racist and wrong. . . .

If we ask those who regard racial discrimination as wrong to say why it is wrong, it is commonly said that it is wrong to pick on race as a reason for treating one person differently from others, because race is irrelevant to whether a person should be given a job, the vote, higher education, or any benefits or burdens of this sort. The irrelevance of race, it is said, makes it quite arbitrary to give these things to people of one race while withholding them from those of another race. I shall refer to this account of what is wrong with racial discrimination as the "standard objection" to racial discrimination.

A sophisticated theory of justice can be invoked in support of this standard objection to racial discrimination. Justice requires, as Aristotle so plausibly said, that equals be treated equally and unequals be treated unequally. To this we must add the obvious proviso that the equalities or inequalities should be relevant to the treatment in question. Now when we consider things like employment, it becomes clear that the relevant inequalities between candidates for a vacant position are inequalities in their ability to carry out the duties of the position and, perhaps, inequalities in the extent to which they will benefit through being offered the position. Race does not seem to be relevant at all. Similarly with the vote, capacity for rational choice between candidates or policies might be held a relevant characteristic, but race should not be; and so on for other goods. It is hard to think of anything for which race in itself is a relevant characteristic, and hence to use race as a basis for discrimination is arbitrarily to single out an irrelevant factor, no doubt because of a bias or prejudice against those of a different race.

As we shall see, this account of why racial discrimination is wrong is inadequate because there are many situations in which, from at least one point of view, the racial factor is by no means irrelevant, and therefore it can be denied that racial discrimination in these situations is arbitrary.

One type of situation in which race must be admitted to be relevant to the purposes of the person discriminating need not delay us at this stage; this is the situation in which those purposes themselves favor a particular race. Thus if the purpose of Hitler and the other Nazi leaders was, among other things, to produce a world in which there were no Jews, it was certainly not irrelevant to their purposes that those rounded up and murdered by the SS were Jews rather than so-called "Aryans." But the fundamental wrongness of the aims of the Nazis makes the "relevance" of race to those aims totally inefficacious so far as justifying Nazi racial discrimination is concerned. While their type of racial discrimination may not have been arbitrary discrimination in the usual sense, it was no less wrong for that. *Why* it was wrong is something that I hope will become clearer later in this article. Meanwhile I shall look at some less cataclysmic forms of racial discrimination, for too much contemporary discussion of racial discrimination has focused on the most blatant instances: Nazi Germany, [the former situation in] South Africa, and the American "Deep South" during the period of legally enforced racial segregation. These forms of racism are not the type that face us now in our own societies . . . and to discuss racial discrimination in terms of these examples today is to present an oversimplified picture of the problem of racial discrimination. By looking at some of the reasons for racial discrimination that might actually be offered today in countries all over the world I hope to show that the real situation is usually much more complex than consideration of the more blatant instances of racial discrimination would lead us to believe.

2. Examples

I shall start by describing an example of racial discrimination which may at first glance seem to be an allowable exception to a general rule that racial discrimination is arbitrary and therefore wrong; and I shall then suggest that this case has parallels with other cases we may not be so willing to allow as exceptions.

Case 1. A film director is making a film about the lives of blacks living in New York's Harlem. He advertises for black actors. A white actor turns up, but the director refuses to allow him to audition, saying that the film is about blacks and there are no roles for whites. The actor replies that, with the appropriate wig and make-up, he can look just like a black; moreover he can imitate the mannerisms, gestures, and speech of Harlem blacks. Nevertheless the director refuses to consider him for the role, because it is essential to the director's conception of the film that the black experience be authentically portrayed, and however good a white actor might be, the director would not be satisfied with the authenticity of the portrayal.

The film director is discriminating along racial lines, yet he cannot be said to be discriminating arbitrarily. His discrimination is apt for his purpose. Moreover his purpose is a legitimate one. So the standard objection to racial discrimination cannot be made in this instance.

Racial discrimination may be acceptable in an area like casting for films or the theater, when the race of a character in the film or play is important, because this is one of the seemingly few areas in which a person's race is directly relevant to his capacity to perform a given task. As such, it may be thought, these areas can easily be distinguished from other areas of employment, as well as from areas like housing, education, the right to vote, and so on, where race has no relevance at all. Unfortunately there are many other situations in which race is not as totally irrelevant as this view assumes.

Case 2. The owner of a cake shop with a largely white and racially prejudiced clientele wishes to hire an assistant. The owner has no prejudice against blacks himself, but is reluctant to employ one, for fear that his customers will go elsewhere. If his fears are well-founded (and this is not impossible) then the race of a candidate for the position is, again, relevant to the purpose of the employer, which in this case is to maintain the profitability of his business.

What can we say about this case? We cannot deny the connection between race and the owner's purposes, and so we must recognize that the owner's discrimination is not arbitrary, and does not necessarily indicate a bias or prejudice on his part. Nor can we say that the owner's purpose is an illegitimate one, for making a profit from the sale of cakes is not generally regarded as wrong, at least if the amount of profit made is modest.

We can, of course, look at other aspects of the matter. We can object to the racial discrimination shown by customers who will search out shops staffed by whites only—such people do discriminate arbitrarily, for race is irrelevant to the quality of the goods and the proficiency of service in a shop—but is this not simply a fact that the shop-owner must live with, however much he may wish he could change it? We might argue that by pandering to the prejudices of his customers, the owner is allowing those prejudices to continue unchallenged; whereas if he and other shopkeepers took no notice of them, people would eventually become used to mixing with those of another race, and prejudices would be eroded. Yet it is surely too much to ask an individual shop-owner to risk his livelihood in a lone and probably vain effort to break down prejudice. Few of the most dedicated opponents of racism do as much. If there were national legislation which distributed the burden more evenly, by a general prohibition of discrimination on racial grounds (with some recognized exceptions for cases like casting for a film or play) the situation would be different. Then we could reasonably ask every shop-owner to play his part. Whether there should be such legislation is a different question from whether the shop-owner may be blamed for discriminating in the absence of legislation. I shall discuss the issue of legislation shortly, after we consider a different kind of racial discrimination that, again, is not arbitrary.

Case 3. A landlord discriminates against blacks in letting the accommodation he owns. Let us say that he is not so rigid as never to let an apartment to a black, but if a black person and a white person appear to be equally suitable as tenants, with equally good references and so on, the landlord invariably prefers the white. He defends his policy along the following lines:

> If more than a very small proportion of my tenants get behind in their rent and then disappear without paying the arrears, I will be out of business. Over the years, I have found that more blacks do

this than whites. I admit that there are many honest blacks (some of my best tenants have been black) and many dishonest whites, but, for some reason I do not claim to understand, the odds on a white tenant defaulting are longer than on a black doing so, even when their references and other credentials appear equally good. In this business you can't run a full-scale probe of every prospective tenant—and if I tried I would be abused for invading privacy—so you have to go by the average rather than the individual. That is why blacks have to have better indications of reliability than whites before I will let to them.

Now the landlord's impression of a higher rate of default among blacks than among comparable whites may itself be the result of prejudice on his part. Perhaps in most cases when landlords say this kind of thing, there is no real factual basis to their allegations. People have grown up with racial stereotypes, and these stereotypes are reinforced by a tendency to notice occurrences which conform to the stereotype and to disregard those which conflict with it. So if unreliability is part of the stereotype of blacks held by many whites, they may take more notice of blacks who abscond without paying the rent than of blacks who are reliable tenants; and conversely they will take less notice of absconding whites and more of those whites who conform to their ideas of normal white behaviour.

If it is prejudice that is responsible for the landlord's views about black and white tenants, and there is no factual basis for his claims, then the problem becomes one of eliminating this prejudice and getting the landlord to see his mistake. This is by no means an easy task, but it is not a task for philosophers, and it does not concern us here, for we are interested in attempts to justify racial discrimination, and an attempted justification based on an inaccurate description of a situation can be rejected without raising the deeper issue of justification.

On the other hand, the landlord's impression of a higher rate of default among black tenants *could* be entirely accurate. (It might be explicable in terms of the different cultural and economic circumstances in which blacks are brought up.) Whether or not we think this likely, we need to ask what its implications would be for the justifiability of the racial discrimination exercised by the landlord. To refuse even to consider this question would be to rest all one's objections to the landlord's practice on the falsity of his claims, and thereby to fail to examine the possibility that the landlord's practice could be open to objection even if his impressions on tenant reliability are accurate.

If the landlord's impressions were accurate, we would have to concede, once again, that racial discrimination in this situation is not arbitrary; that it is, instead, relevant to the purposes of the landlord. We must also admit that these purposes—making a living from letting property that one owns—are not themselves objectionable, provided the rents are reasonable, and so on. Nor can we, this time, locate the origin of the problem in the prejudices of others, except insofar as the problem has its origin in the prejudices of those responsible for the conditions of deprivation in which many of the present generation of blacks grew up—but it is too late to do anything to alter those prejudices anyway, since they belong to previous generations.

We have now looked at three examples of racial discrimination, and can begin to examine the parallels and differences between them. Many people, as I have already said, would make no objection to the discriminatory hiring practice of the film director in the first of these cases. But we can now see that if we try to justify the actions of the film director in this case on the grounds that his purpose is a legitimate one and the discrimination he uses is relevant for his purpose, we will have to accept the actions of the cake-shop owner and the landlord as well. I suspect that many of those ready to accept the discriminatory practice in the first case will be much more reluctant about the other two cases. But what morally significant difference is there between them?

It might be suggested that the difference between them lies in the nature of what blacks are being deprived of, and their title to it. The argument would run like this: No one has a right to be selected to act in a film; the director must have absolute discretion to hire whomsoever he wishes to hire. After all, no one can force the director to make the film at all, and if he didn't make it, no one would be hired to play in it; if he does decide to make it, therefore, he must be allowed to make it on his own terms. Moreover, since so few people ever get the chance to appear in a film, it would be absurd to hold that the director violates someone's rights by not giving him something which most people will never have anyway. On the other hand, people do have a right to employment, and to housing. To discriminate against blacks in an ordinary employment situation, or in the letting of accommodation, threatens their basic rights and therefore should not be tolerated.

Plausible as it appears, this way of distinguishing the first case from the other two will not do. Consider the first and second cases: almost everything that we have said about the film director applies to the cake-shop owner as well. No one can force the cake-shop owner to keep his shop open, and if he didn't, no one would be hired to work in it. If in the film director's case this was a reason for allowing him to make the film on his own terms, it must be a reason for allowing the shop-owner to run his shop on his own terms. In fact, such reasoning, which would allow unlimited discrimination in restaurants, hotels, and shops, is invalid. There are plenty of examples where we would not agree that the fact that someone did not have to make an offer or provide an opportunity at all means that if he does do it he must be allowed to make the offer or provide the opportunity on his own terms. The United States Civil Rights Act of 1965 certainly does not recognize this line of argument, for it prohibits those offering food and lodgings to the public from excluding customers on racial grounds. We may, as a society, decide that we shall not allow people to make certain offers, if the way in which the offers are made will cause hardship or offense to others. In so doing we are balancing people's freedom to do as they please against the harm this may do to others, and coming down on the side of preventing harm rather than enlarging freedom. This is a perfectly defensible position, if the harm is sufficiently serious and the restriction of freedom not grave.

Nor does it seem possible to distinguish the first and second cases by the claim that since so few people ever get the chance to appear in a film, no one's rights are violated if they are not given something that most people will never have anyway. For if the number of jobs in cake-shops was small, and the demand for such jobs high, it would also be true that few people would ever have the chance to work in a cake-shop. It would be odd if such an increase in competition for the job justified an otherwise unjustifiable policy of hiring whites only. Moreover, this argument would allow a film director to discriminate on racial lines even if race was irrelevant to the roles he was casting; and that is quite a different situation from the one we have been discussing.

The best way to distinguish the situations of the film director and the shop-owner is by reference to the nature of the employment offered, and to the reasons why racial discrimination in these cases is not arbitrary. In casting for a film about blacks, the race of the actor auditioning is intrinsically significant, independently of the attitudes of those connected with the film. In the case of hiring a shop assistant, race is relevant only because of the attitudes of those connected (as customers) with the shop; it has nothing to do with the selling of cakes in itself, but only with the selling of cakes to racially prejudiced customers.

This means that in the case of the shop assistant we could eliminate the relevance of race if we could eliminate the prejudices of the customers; by contrast there is no way in which we could eliminate the relevance of the race of an actor auditioning for a role in a film about blacks, without altering the nature of the film. Moreover, in the case of the shop-owner racial discrimination probably serves to perpetuate the very prejudices that make such discrimination relevant and (from the point of view of the owner seeking to maintain his profits) necessary. Thus people who can buy all their cakes and other necessities in shops staffed only by whites will never come into the kind of contact with comparable blacks which might break down their aversion to being served by blacks; whereas if shop-owners were to hire more blacks, their customers would no doubt become used to it and in time might wonder why they ever opposed the idea. (Compare the change of attitudes toward racial integration in the American South since the 1956 United States Supreme Court decision against segregated schools and subsequent measures against segregation were put into effect.)

Hence if we are opposed to arbitrary discrimination we have reason to take steps against racial discrimination in situations like Case 2, because such discrimination, while not itself arbitrary, both feeds on and gives support to discrimination by others which is arbitrary. In prohibiting it we would, admittedly, be preventing the employer from discriminating in a way that is relevant to his purposes; but if the causal hypothesis suggested in the previous paragraph is correct, this situation would only be temporary, and after some time the circumstances inducing the employer to discriminate racially would have been eliminated.

The case of the landlord presents a more difficult problem. If the facts he alleges are true his nonarbitrary reasons for discrimination against blacks are real enough. They do not depend on present arbitrary discrimination by others, and they may persist beyond an interval in which there is no discrimination. Whatever the roots of hypothetical racial differences in reliability as tenants might be, they would probably go too deep to be eradicated solely by a short period in which there was no racial discrimination.

We should recognize, then, that if the facts are as alleged, to legislate against the landlord's racially discriminatory practice is to impose a long-term disadvantage upon him. At the very least, he will have to take greater care in ascertaining the suitability of prospective tenants. Perhaps he will turn to data-collecting agencies for assistance, thus contributing to the growth of institutions that are threats, potential or actual, to our privacy. Perhaps, if these methods are unavailable or unavailing, the landlord will have to take greater losses than he otherwise would have, and perhaps this will lead to increased rents or even to a reduction in the amount of rentable housing available.

None of this forces us to conclude that we should not legislate against the landlord's racial discrimination. There are good reasons why we should seek to eliminate racial discrimination even when such discrimination is neither arbitrary in itself nor relevant only because of the arbitrary prejudices of others. These reasons may be so important as to make the disadvantage imposed on the landlord comparatively insignificant.

An obvious point that can be made against the landlord is that he is judging people, at least in part, as members of a race rather than as individuals. The landlord does not deny that some black prospective tenants he turns away would make better tenants than some white prospective tenants he accepts. Some highly eligible black prospective tenants are refused accommodation simply because they are black. If the landlord assessed every prospective tenant as an individual this would not happen. . . .

There are plenty of reasons why in situations like admitting people to higher education or providing them with employment or other benefits we should regard people as individuals and not as members of some larger group. For one thing we will be able to make a selection better suited for our own purposes, for selecting or discarding whole groups of people will generally result in, at best, a crude approximation to the results we hope to achieve. This is certainly true in an area like education. On the other hand it must be admitted that in some situations a crude approximation is all that can be achieved anyway. The landlord claims that his situation is one of these, and that as he cannot reliably tell which individuals will make suitable tenants, he is justified in resorting to so crude a means of selection as race. Here we need to turn our attention from the landlord to the prospective black tenant.

To be judged merely as a member of a group when it is one's individual qualities on which the verdict should be given is to be treated as less than the unique individual that we see ourselves as. Even where our individual qualities would merit less than we receive as a member of a group—if we are promoted over better-qualified people because we went to the "right" private school—the benefit is usually less welcome than it would be if it had been merited by our own attributes. Of course in this case qualms are easily stilled by the fact that a benefit has been received, never mind how. In the contrary case, however, when something of value has been lost, the sense of loss will be compounded by the feeling that one was not assessed on one's own merits, but merely as a member of a group.

To this general preference for individual as against group assessment must be added a consideration arising from the nature of the group. To be denied a benefit because one was, say, a member of the Communist Party, would be unjust and a violation of basic principles of political liberty, but if one has chosen to join the Communist Party, then one is, after all, being assessed for what one has done, and one can choose between living with the consequences of continued party membership or leaving the party. Race, of course, is not something that one chooses to adopt or that one can ever choose to give up. The person who is denied advantages because of his race is totally unable to alter this particular circumstance of his existence and so may feel with added sharpness that his life is clouded, not merely because he is not being judged as an individual, but because of something over which he has no control at all. This makes racial discrimination peculiarly invidious.

So we have the viewpoint of the victim of racial discrimination to offset against the landlord's argument in favor, and it seems that the victim has more at stake and hence should be given preference, even if the landlord's reason for discriminating is nonarbitrary and hence in a sense legitimate. The case against racial discrimination becomes stronger still when we consider the long-term social effects of discrimination.

When members of a racial minority are overwhelmingly among the poorest members of a society, living in a deprived area, holding jobs low in pay and status, or no jobs at all, and less well educated than the average member of the community, racial discrimination serves to perpetuate a divided society in which race becomes a badge of a much broader inferiority. It is the association of race with economic status and educational disadvantages which in turn gives rise to the situation in which there could be a coloring of truth to the claim that race is a relevant ground for discriminating between prospective tenants, applicants for employment, and so on. Thus there is, in the end, a parallel between the situation of the landlord and the cake-shop owner, for both, by their discrimination, contribute to the maintenance of the grounds for claiming that this discrimination is nonarbitrary. Hence prohibition of such discrimination can be justified as breaking this circle of deprivation and discrimination. The difference between the situations, as I have already said, is that in the case of the cake-shop owner it is only a prejudice against contact with blacks that needs to be broken down, and experience has shown that such prejudices do evaporate in a relatively short period of time. In the case of the landlord, however, it is the whole social and economic position of blacks that needs to be changed, and while overcoming discrimination would be an essential part of this process it may not be sufficient. That is why, if the facts are as the landlord alleges them to be, prohibition of racial discrimination is likely to impose more of a long-term disadvantage on the landlord than on the shop-owner—a disadvantage which is, however, outweighed by the costs of continuing the circle of racial discrimination and deprivation for those discriminated against; and the costs of greater social inequality and racial divisiveness for the community as a whole. . . .

CHAPTER 30

*L*etter from the Birmingham City Jail

Martin Luther King, Jr.

Born in 1929, Martin Luther King, Jr., followed in his father's footsteps and became a Baptist minister. In 1956, while he was pastor of the Dexter Avenue Baptist Church in Montgomery, Alabama, he led a boycott of that city's segregated public buses, and then went on to become the leading spokesman for the American civil rights movement. He was awarded the Nobel Peace Prize in 1964. Dr. King was assassinated in 1968.

In 1963, while incarcerated in an Alabama jail, he read a statement that had been issued by some of his fellow clergymen. The statement sympathized with the goals of his movement but questioned the wisdom of his tactics. King advocated—and practiced—nonviolent civil disobedience, whereas these critics argued that the law should be obeyed even by those who want to change it. Using a pen smuggled in to him by his lawyers and some tattered scraps of paper that were lying about, King wrote an "open letter" replying to them. This "Letter from the Birmingham City Jail" was printed in many liberal magazines and newspapers until almost a million copies were in circulation. It became the single most famous document of the movement.

MY DEAR FELLOW CLERGYMEN,

While confined here in the Birmingham city jail, I came across your recent statement calling our present activities "unwise and untimely." Seldom, if ever, do I pause to answer criticism of my work

Reprinted by arrangement with the Estate of Martin Luther King, Jr., c/o Writers House, Inc., as agent for the proprietor. Copyright 1963 by Martin Luther King, Jr., copyright renewed 1991 by Coretta Scott King.

and ideas. If I sought to answer all of the criticisms that cross my desk, my secretaries would be engaged in little else in the course of the day, and I would have no time for constructive work. But since I feel that you are men of genuine good will and your criticisms are sincerely set forth, I would like to answer your statement in what I hope will be patient and reasonable terms.

You may well ask, "Why direct action? Why sit-ins, marches, etc.? Isn't negotiation a better path?" You are exactly right in your call for negotiation. Indeed, this is the purpose of direct action. Nonviolent direct action seeks to create such a crisis and establish such creative tension that a community that has constantly refused to negotiate is forced to confront the issue. It seeks so to dramatize the issue that it can no longer be ignored. I just referred to the creation of tension as a part of the work of the nonviolent resister. This may sound rather shocking. But I must confess that I am not afraid of the word *tension*. I have earnestly worked and preached against violent tension, but there is a type of constructive nonviolent tension that is necessary for growth. Just as Socrates felt that it was necessary to create a tension in the mind so that individuals could rise from the bondage of myths and half-truths to the unfettered realm of creative analysis and objective appraisal, we must see the need of having nonviolent gadflies to create the kind of tension in society that will help men to rise from the dark depths of prejudice and racism to the majestic heights of understanding and brotherhood. So the purpose of the direct action is to create a situation so crisis-packed that it will inevitably open the door to negotiation. We, therefore, concur with you in your call for negotiation. Too long has our beloved Southland been bogged down in the tragic attempt to live in monologue rather than dialogue.

One of the basic points in your statement is that our acts are untimely. Some have asked, "Why didn't you give the new administration time to act?" The only answer that I can give to this inquiry is that the new administration must be prodded about as much as the outgoing one before it acts. We will be sadly mistaken if we feel that the election of Mr. Boutwell will bring the millennium to Birmingham. While Mr. Boutwell is much more articulate and gentle than Mr. Connor, they are both segregationists, dedicated to the task of maintaining the status quo. The hope I see in Mr. Boutwell is that he will be reasonable enough to see the futility of massive resistance to desegregation. But he will not see this without pressure from the devotees of civil rights. My friends, I must say to you that we have not made a single gain in civil rights without determined legal and nonviolent pressure. History is the long and tragic story of the fact that privileged groups seldom give up their privileges voluntarily. Individuals may see the moral light and voluntarily give up their unjust posture; but as Reinhold Niebuhr has reminded us, groups are more immoral than individuals.

We know through painful experience that freedom is never voluntarily given by the oppressor; it must be demanded by the oppressed. Frankly, I have never yet engaged in a direct action movement that was "well-timed," according to the timetable of those who have not suffered unduly from the disease of segregation. For years now I have heard the word "Wait!" It rings in the ear of every Negro with a piercing familiarity. This "Wait" has almost always meant "Never." It has been a tranquilizing thalidomide, relieving the emotional stress for a moment, only to give birth to an ill-formed infant of frustration. We must come to see with the distinguished jurist of yesterday that "justice too long delayed is justice denied." We have waited for more than 340 years for our constitutional and God-given rights. The nations of Asia and Africa are moving with jetlike speed toward the goal of political independence, and we still creep at horse and buggy pace toward the gaining of a cup of coffee at a lunch counter. I guess it is easy for those who have never felt the stinging darts of segregation to say, "Wait." But when you have seen vicious mobs lynch your mothers and fathers at will and drown your sisters and brothers at whim; when you have seen hate-filled policemen curse, kick, brutalize and even kill your black brothers and sisters with impunity; when you see the vast majority of your twenty million Negro brothers smothering in an airtight cage of poverty in the midst of an affluent society; when you suddenly find your tongue twisted and your speech stammering as you seek to explain to your six-year-old daughter why she can't go to the public amusement park that has just been advertised on television, and see tears welling up in her little eyes when she is told that Funtown is closed to colored children, and see the depressing clouds of inferiority begin to form in her little mental sky, and see her begin to distort her little personality by unconsciously developing a bitterness toward white people; when you have to concoct an answer for a five-year-old son asking in agonizing pathos: "Daddy, why do white people treat colored people so mean?"; when you take a cross-country drive and find it necessary to sleep night after night in the uncomfortable corners of your automobile because no motel will accept you; when you are humiliated day in and day out by nagging signs reading "white" and "colored"; when your first name becomes "nigger" and your middle name becomes "boy" (however old you are) and your last name becomes "John," and when your wife and mother are never given the respected title "Mrs."; when you are harried by day and haunted by night by the fact that you are a Negro, living constantly at tiptoe stance never quite knowing what to expect next, and plagued with inner fears and outer resentments; when you are forever fighting a degenerating sense of "nobodiness"; then you will understand why we find it difficult to wait. There comes a time when the cup of endurance runs over, and men are no longer willing to be plunged into an abyss of injustice where they experience the blackness of corroding despair. I hope, sirs, you can understand our legitimate and unavoidable impatience.

You express a great deal of anxiety over our willingness to break laws. This is certainly a legitimate concern. Since we so diligently urge people to obey the Supreme Court's decision of 1954 outlawing segregation in the public schools, it is rather strange and paradoxical to find us consciously breaking laws. One may well ask, "How can you advocate breaking some laws and obeying others?" The answer is found in the fact that there are two types of laws: there are *just* and there are *unjust* laws. I would agree with Saint Augustine that "An unjust law is no law at all."

Now what is the difference between the two? How does one determine when a law is just or unjust? A just law is a man-made code that squares with the moral law or the law of God. An unjust law is a code that is out of harmony with the moral law. To put it in the terms of Saint Thomas Aquinas, an unjust law is a human law that is not rooted in eternal and natural law. Any law that uplifts human personality is just. Any law that degrades human personality is unjust. All segregation statutes are unjust because segregation distorts the soul and damages the personality. It gives the segregator a false sense of superiority, and the segregated a false sense of inferiority. To use the words of Martin Buber, the great Jewish philosopher, segregation substitutes an "I-it" relationship for the "I-thou" relationship, and ends up relegating persons to the status of things. So segregation is not only politically, economically and sociologically unsound, but it is morally wrong and sinful. Paul Tillich has said that sin is separation. Isn't segregation an existential expression of man's tragic separation, an expression of his awful estrangement, his terrible sinfulness? So I can urge men to disobey segregation ordinances because they are morally wrong.

Let us turn to a more concrete example of just and unjust laws. An unjust law is a code that a majority inflicts on a minority that is not binding on itself. This is difference made legal. On the other hand a just law is a code that a majority compels a minority to follow that it is willing to follow itself. This is sameness made legal.

Let me give another explanation. An unjust law is a code inflicted upon a minority which that minority had no part in enacting or creating because they did not have the unhampered right to vote. Who can say that the legislature of Alabama which set up the segregation laws was democratically elected? Throughout the state of Alabama all types of conniving methods are used to prevent Negroes from becoming registered voters and there are some counties without a single Negro registered to vote despite the fact that the Negro constitutes a majority of the population. Can any law set up in such a state be considered democratically structured?

These are just a few examples of unjust and just laws. There are some instances when a law is just on its face and unjust in its application. For instance, I was arrested Friday on a charge of parading without a permit. Now there is nothing wrong with an ordinance which requires a permit for a parade, but when the ordinance is used to preserve segregation and to deny citizens the First Amendment privilege of peaceful assembly and peaceful protest, then it becomes unjust.

I hope you can see the distinction I am trying to point out. In no sense do I advocate evading or defying the law as the rabid segregationist would do. This would lead to anarchy. One who breaks an unjust law must do it *openly, lovingly* (not hatefully as the white mothers did in New Orleans when they were seen on television screaming, "nigger, nigger, nigger"), and with a willingness to accept the penalty. I submit that an individual who breaks a law that conscience tells him is unjust, and willingly accepts the penalty by staying in jail to arouse the conscience of the community over its injustice, is in reality expressing the very highest respect for law.

Of course, there is nothing new about this kind of civil disobedience. It was seen sublimely in the refusal of Shadrach, Meshach and Abednego to obey the laws of Nebuchadnezzar because a higher moral law was involved. It was practiced superbly by the early Christians who were willing to face hungry lions and the excruciating pain of chopping blocks, before submitting to certain unjust laws of the Roman Empire. To a degree academic freedom is a reality today because Socrates practiced civil disobedience.

We can never forget that everything Hitler did in Germany was "legal" and everything the Hungarian freedom fighters did in Hungary was "illegal." It was "illegal" to aid and comfort a Jew in Hitler's Germany. But I am sure that if I had lived in Germany during that time I would have aided and comforted my Jewish brothers even though it was illegal. If I lived in a Communist country today where certain principles dear to the Christian faith are suppressed, I believe I would openly advocate disobeying these anti-religious laws. I must make two honest confessions to you, my Christian and Jewish brothers. First, I must confess that over the last few years I have been gravely disappointed with the white moderate. I have almost reached the regrettable conclusion that the Negro's great stumbling block in the stride toward freedom is not the White Citizens Counciler or the Ku Klux Klanner, but the white moderate who is more devoted to "order" than to justice; who prefers a negative peace which is the absence of tension to a positive peace which is the presence of justice; who constantly says, "I agree with you in the goal you seek, but I can't agree with your methods of direct action"; who paternalistically feels that he can set the timetable for another man's freedom; who lives by the myth of time and who constantly advised the Negro to wait until a "more convenient season." Shallow understanding from people of good will is more frustrating than absolute misunderstanding from people of ill will. Lukewarm acceptance is much more bewildering than outright rejection.

I had hoped that the white moderate would understand that law and order exist for the purpose of establishing justice, and that when they fail to do this they become dangerously structured dams that block the flow of social progress. I had hoped that the white moderate would understand that the present tension of the South is merely a necessary phase of the transition from an obnoxious negative peace, where the Negro passively accepted his unjust plight, to a substance-filled positive peace, where all men will respect the dignity and worth of human personality. Actually, we who engage in nonviolent direct action are not the creators of tension. We merely bring to the surface the hidden tension that is already alive. We bring it out in the open where it can be seen and dealt with. Like a boil that can never be cured as long as it is covered up but must be opened with all its pus-flowing ugliness to the natural medicines of air and light, injustice must likewise be exposed, with all of the tension its exposing creates, to the light of human conscience and the air of national opinion before it can be cured.

In your statement you asserted that our actions, even though peaceful, must be condemned because they precipitate violence. But can this assertion be logically made? Isn't this like condemning the robbed man because his possession of money precipitated the evil act of robbery? Isn't this like condemning Socrates because his unswerving commitment to truth and his philosophical delvings precipitated the misguided popular mind to make him drink the hemlock? Isn't this like condemning Jesus because His unique God-consciousness and never-ceasing devotion to His will precipitated the evil act of crucifixion? We must come to see, as federal courts have consistently affirmed, that it is immoral to urge an individual to withdraw his efforts to gain his basic constitutional rights because the quest precipitates violence. Society must protect the robbed and punish the robber. . . .

I must close now. But before closing I am impelled to mention one other point in your statement that troubled me profoundly. You warmly commended the Birmingham police force for keeping "order" and "preventing violence." I don't believe you would have so warmly commended the police force if you had seen its angry violent dogs literally biting six unarmed, nonviolent Negroes. I don't believe you would so quickly commend the policemen if you would observe their ugly and inhuman treatment of Negroes here in the city jail; if you would watch them push and curse old Negro women and young Negro girls; if you would see them slap and kick old Negro men and young boys; if you will observe them, as they did on two occasions, refuse to give us food because we wanted to sing our grace together. I'm sorry that I can't join you in your praise for the police department.

It is true that they have been rather disciplined in their public handling of the demonstrators. In this sense they have been rather publicly "nonviolent." But for what purpose? To preserve the evil system of segregation. Over the last few years I have consistently preached that nonviolence demands that the means we use must be as pure as the ends we seek. So I have tried to make it clear that it is wrong to use immoral means to attain moral ends. But now I must affirm that it is just as wrong, or even more so, to use moral means to preserve immoral ends. Maybe Mr. Connor and his policemen have been rather publicly nonviolent, as Chief Pritchett was in Albany, Georgia, but they have used the moral means of nonviolence to maintain the immoral end of flagrant racial injustice. T. S. Eliot has said that there is no greater treason than to do the right deed for the wrong reason.

I wish you had commended the Negro sit-inners and demonstrators of Birmingham for their sublime courage, their willingness to suffer and their amazing discipline in the midst of the most inhuman provocation. One day the South will recognize its real heroes. They will be the James Merediths, courageously and with a majestic sense of purpose facing jeering and hostile mobs and the agonizing loneliness that characterizes the life of the pioneer. They will be old, oppressed, battered Negro women, symbolized in a seventy-two-year-old woman of Montgomery, Alabama, who rose up with a sense of dignity and with her people decided not to ride the segregated buses, and responded to one who inquired about her tiredness with ungrammatical profundity: "My feet is tired, but my soul is rested." They will be the young high school and college students, young ministers of the gospel and a host of their elders courageously and nonviolently sitting-in at lunch counters and willingly going to jail for conscience's sake. One day the South will know that when these disinherited children of God sat down at lunch counters they were in reality standing up for the best in the American dream and the most sacred values in our Judeo-Christian heritage, and thusly, carrying our whole nation back to those great wells of democracy which were dug deep by the Founding Fathers in the formulation of the Constitution and the Declaration of Independence. . . .

I hope this letter finds you strong in the faith. I also hope that circumstances will soon make it possible for me to meet each of you, not as an integrationist or a civil rights leader, but as a fellow clergyman and a Christian brother. Let us all hope that the dark clouds of racial prejudice will soon pass away and the deep fog of misunderstanding will be lifted from our fear-drenched communities and in some not too distant tomorrow the radiant stars of love and brotherhood will shine over our great nation with all of their scintillating beauty.

Yours for the cause of Peace and Brotherhood,

MARTIN LUTHER KING, JR.

CHAPTER 31

In Defense of Quotas

James Rachels

Affirmative action programs began in the 1960s as a way of redressing past and present discrimination against African-Americans. Later, these programs were expanded to include other groups, such as women, Hispanics, and people with disabilities.

There are two kinds of affirmative action: quotas and racially sensitive policies. *Quotas* set numerical requirements for admissions, hirings, or promotions. For example, a quota would be imposed on a country club if it were told to admit at least five members of a specific minority within a year's time. *Racially sensitive policies* merely consider race as one factor in making a decision; no quota is imposed. For instance, some universities now have policies to promote "diversity," where one kind of diversity is racial diversity. In *California v. Bakke* (1978) the U.S. Supreme Court ruled that quotas are unconstitutional but that racially sensitive policies are constitutionally permitted.

The only African-American now sitting on the Supreme Court, Clarence Thomas, strongly opposes affirmative action. "In my mind," he writes, "government-sponsored racial discrimination based on benign prejudice is just as noxious as discrimination inspired by malicious prejudice. In each instance, it is racial discrimination, plain and simple." James Rachels disagrees. In the following selection, Rachels specifies some conditions under which quotas seem justified.

For information on James Rachels, see Chapter 17.

"Good sense," said Descartes, "is of all things in the world the most equally distributed, for everybody thinks himself so abundantly provided with it, that even those most difficult to please in all other matters

---

James Rachels, *Can Ethics Provide Answers?* from *Ethical Issues in Contemporary Society,* edited by John Howie and George Schedler. © 1995 by the Board of Trustees, Southern Illinois University, reprinted by permission.

do not commonly desire more of it than they already possess."[1] Much the same might be said about prejudice: everyone believes himself or herself to be objective and free of bias. We recognize that other people may be prejudiced, but we imagine that we ourselves see things as they really are.

But of course this is a mistake. We feel that we are unprejudiced only because we are unaware of our biases and how they work. This is true not only of bigots but of relatively open-minded people as well. It is a mistake for any of us to think that we are free of bias. Even when we are striving hardest to be objective, prejudices of all sorts can creep into our thinking without our noticing it.

To illustrate this, we may consider a type of example that does not often occur to us. We are familiar enough with prejudice based on race or gender. But those are not the only ways in which we discriminate. There is an impressive body of evidence that we are also prejudiced against people because of their height. I do not mean abnormally short or tall people—dwarfs or giants. That sort of prejudice is familiar enough. The less widely-recognized form of prejudice is against shorter people whose height falls within the normal range. Let me briefly mention some of the investigations that show this.[2]

In one study, 140 job-placement officers were asked to choose between two applicants with exactly the same qualifications, but one was described, parenthetically, as being 6'1" while the other candidate was listed as 5'5". One hundred two of the recruiters judged the taller candidate to be better qualified, while only one preferred the shorter candidate. The rest of them—a mere 27 percent—recognized that the two were equally qualified.

Other studies have shown that a person's earning potential is affected more by height than by, say, educational performance. One study compared the starting salaries of male librarians between 6'1" and 6'3" with the starting salaries of male librarians less than 6'. The same comparison was then made between those who had been in the top half of their classes academically and those in the bottom half. The average difference in starting salary between the taller and shorter graduates was found to be more than three times greater than the difference between the salaries of the more and less academically gifted. Another study using a sample of over five thousand men found that after twenty-five years of pursuing their varied careers, those who were 5'6" or 5'7" were earning on average $2,500 per year less than those who were 6'0" or 6'1".

The moral seems to be: if you could choose between being tall and being smart, from a crass economic standpoint, it's better to be tall.

The same sort of prejudice influences the way we vote. Of all U.S. presidents, only two—James Madison and Benjamin Harrison— were shorter than the average height for American males at the time of their election. And since 1904, the taller candidate has emerged victorious in 80 percent of presidential elections. Another moral might be drawn: if you are trying to predict the outcome of such an election, forget the other factors and put your money on the taller man.

Prejudice against short people seems importantly different from racist or sexist prejudice, because the latter sorts of prejudice seem to be motivated, at least in part, by the fact that members of the dominant group derive advantages from the discriminatory practices. These advantages are often economic. However, this seems much less plausible where height is concerned. It seems more likely that prejudice regarding height has some other, deeper psychological source. John S. Gillis, a psychologist who has written at length about this, has speculated that the source of our association of height with ability is to be found in childhood experiences:

> All of us experience a real association between height and power throughout our childhood. Adults tower over us physically as children, and they are the ones who control every single important thing in our lives. This may be the fountainhead of heightism. Each of us begins life with a dozen years or so of learning that the bigger person is more powerful and intelligent. This learning takes place not so much on an intellectual level but, more importantly, on the emotional level. Our attitudes and feelings are shaped in ways of which we are unaware.[3]

Whatever the source of these feelings, it is clear that they have deep and long-lasting effects.

The facts about "heightism" are quite remarkable. They suggest a number of points that should be of interest to anyone who is thinking about the philosophical problem of equality, especially as it relates to the formulation and assessment of social policies. First, the studies I have cited show that prejudice can have its influence quite unconsciously. No one—or so nearly no one as makes no difference—realizes that he thinks less well of shorter people. Yet the available evidence shows that this prejudice exists, and that it is widespread. The people who are affected by it are simply unaware of it.

Second, this evidence also suggests that people are very good at rationalizing their prejudiced judgments. The men and women whose actions were studied in these investigations—those who hired, promoted, and gave pay raises to the taller candidates—were, no doubt, reasonable people who could "explain" each decision by reference to the lucky employee's objective qualifications. No one believed that he was simply rewarding height. Yet the evidence shows that this is what was happening much of the time. The behavior induced by prejudice includes, importantly, the verbal behavior that "justifies" the prejudiced judgments.

These points, taken together, have a discouraging implication. They suggest that it is difficult even for people of good will to prevent such prejudice from influencing their deliberations. If I am prejudiced in ways that I do not fully realize and I am skilled at coming up with reasons to "justify" the decisions that prejudice leads me to make, then my good intention to "think objectively"—no matter how sincerely I want to do this—may be depressingly ineffective.

The Justification of Quotas

People ought to be treated fairly. Yet we know that our assessments of people are often corrupted by prejudice. Does this make any difference in the sorts of policies that should be adopted?

Choosing Widgets. Suppose you are the president of a manufacturing company and each year in the course of your business you need a supply of widgets. Widgets vary greatly in quality, and from among the hundreds available you need to get the ten best you can find. You are not able to devote much of your own time to this task, but luckily you have an assistant who is one of the most astute widget evaluators in the land. "Examine all the available widgets," you tell her, "and bring me the ten best."

In the fullness of time your assistant brings you ten good widgets, and all seems well. But then you notice that all ten were made at the Buffalo Widget Works. This is odd, because you know that the Albany Widget Works makes an equally good product; and moreover, you know that the pool from which your assistant made her selection contained equal numbers of Albany widgets and Buffalo widgets. So why should the ten best all come from Buffalo? One would expect that, on average, five would come from Buffalo and five from Albany. But perhaps this was just a statistical fluke, and it will all average out over time.

The next year, however, much the same thing happens. You need ten widgets; you assign your assistant to identify the best; and she brings you nine made in Buffalo and only one made in Albany. "Why?" you ask, and in response she assures you that, even though the Albany company does make excellent widgets, most of the best ones available this year happened to be from Buffalo. To prove the point she gives you quite an intelligent and persuasive analysis of the merits of the widgets in this year's pool. You are so impressed that you name her Vice President for Widget Procurement (VPWP).

In subsequent years the story is repeated again and again, with only slight variations. Each year you are told that almost all the best available widgets are from Buffalo. You begin to feel sure that something peculiar is going on. Briefly, you wonder whether your VPWP is accepting bribes from the Buffalo company, but you reject that hypothesis. She is an honest woman, and you cannot help but believe that she is using her best judgment. Then you consider whether, in fact, the Buffalo widgets are simply better than the Albany widgets. But you reject this possibility also; other experts testify that they are equally good.

Finally, you make a discovery that explains everything. It turns out that your vice president was raised in Buffalo, where there is a strong sense of civic pride, and an even stronger sense of rivalry with Albany. Children in Buffalo, it seems, have it drilled into them that everything about Buffalo is better than anything about Albany. Moreover, before coming to work for you, your VPWP worked for the Buffalo Chamber of Commerce and was in charge of promoting Buffalo products. Obviously, then, she is prejudiced, and that explains why she almost always judges Buffalo widgets to be superior.

What are you to do? You could forget about it; after all, the widgets you are getting from Buffalo are pretty good. But you don't want to do that; it is important to you to have the very best widgets you can get. So you talk to your VPWP, you confront her with your suspicion that she is prejudiced, and you stress the importance of getting the best widgets regardless of whether they are from Buffalo or Albany. She is a bit offended by this because she is a good woman and she believes herself to be impartial. Again, she assures you that she is selecting the best widgets available, and if they happen to be from Buffalo, she can't help it. And as time passes, nothing changes; she continues to select mostly Buffalo widgets.

Now what? You are certain she is prejudiced, but because the prejudice is entirely unconscious, your VPWP seems unable to overcome it or even to recognize it. You could get a new VPWP. But you don't want to do that, because this woman is an excellent judge of widgets, except for this one problem. Then an obvious solution occurs to you. You could simply change your instructions. Instead of saying, each year, "Bring me the ten best widgets," you could say, "Bring me the five best Buffalo widgets and the five best Albany widgets." She might not like that—she might take it as an insult to her ability to judge widgets impartially—but, if it is true that Albany widgets are equally as good as Buffalo widgets, this would result in your getting a better overall quality of widget, on average, year in and year out. . . .

The VPWP might, however, offer an interesting objection. She might point out that, in carrying out your new instructions, she would sometimes have to include in the total of ten an Albany widget that is inferior to a Buffalo widget that was also available. You will have to admit that this is so. But your problem is a practical one. You can trust the VPWP to judge which are the best Albany widgets, and you can trust her to judge which are the best Buffalo widgets. But you cannot trust her to compare objectively the relative merits of a widget from one city with a widget from the other city. In these circumstances, your new instructions give you a better chance of ending up with the best overall supply. Or to put it another way: you want the best-qualified widgets to get the jobs, and the quota system you have established will see to that more effectively than the alternative method of simply allowing your VPWP to exercise her judgment.

Hiring People. In the workplace, people ought to be treated equally, but often they are not. Among the important reasons is prejudice; after all, somebody has to decide who is to be hired, or promoted, or given a pay raise, and those who get to make such decisions are only human and might be prejudiced. Social policies ought to be devised with this in mind. Such policies should contain provisions to ensure that people are given equal treatment, insofar as this is possible, despite the fact that those policies must be administered by imperfect human beings.

Of all the kinds of policies that have been devised to combat discrimination, quotas are the most despised. Almost no one has a good word to say about them. Yet the widget example suggests that, under certain circumstances, quotas can be defensible. Can a similar argument be constructed, not for choosing widgets, but for hiring people?

Suppose you are the dean of a college, and you are concerned that only the best-qualified scholars are hired for your faculty. You notice, however, that your philosophy department never hires any women. (They did hire one woman, years ago, so they have a token female. But that's as far as it has gone.) So you investigate. You discover that there are, indeed, lots of women philosophers looking for jobs each year. And you have no reason to think that these women are, on average, any less capable than their male colleagues. So you talk to the (male) chairperson of the department and you urge him to be careful to give full and fair consideration to the female applicants. Being a good liberal fellow, he finds this agreeable enough—although he may be a little offended by the suggestion that he is not already giving the women due consideration. But the talk has little apparent effect. Whenever candidates are being considered, he continues to report, with evident sincerity, that in the particular group under review a male has emerged as the best qualified. And so, he says each year, if we want to hire the best-qualified applicant we have to hire the male, at least this time.

This is repeated annually, with minor variations. One variation is that the best female philosopher in the pool may be listed as the department's top choice. But when, predictably enough, she turns out to be unavailable (having been snapped up by a more prestigious university), no women in the second tier are considered to be good alternatives. Here you notice a disturbing asymmetry: although the very best males are also going to other universities, the males in the second tier are considered good alternatives. Momentarily, then, you consider whether the problem could be that philosophical talent is distributed in a funny way: while the very best women are equal to the very best men, at the next level down, the men suddenly dominate. But that seems unlikely.

After further efforts have been made along these lines, without result, you might eventually conclude that there is an unconscious prejudice at work. Your department, despite its good intentions and its one female member, is biased. It isn't hard to understand why this could be so. In addition to the usual sources of prejudice against women—the stereotypes, the picture of women as less rational than men, and so forth—an all-male or mostly male group enjoys a kind of camaraderie that might seem impossible if females were significantly included. In choosing a new colleague, the matter of how someone would "fit in" with the existing group will always have some influence. This will work against females, no matter their talents as teachers and scholars.

Finally, then, you may conclude that the existing prejudice cannot be countered by any measure short of issuing a new instruction, and you tell the philosophy department that it must hire some additional women, in numbers at least in proportion to the number of women in the applicant pool. The reply, of course, will be that this policy could result in hiring a less qualified woman over a better qualified man. But the answer is the same as in the example about the widgets. You are not trying to give women a special break, any more than you were trying to give Albany widgets a special break. Nor are you trying to redress the injustices that women have suffered in the past; nor are you trying to provide "role models" for female students. You may be pleased if your policy has these effects, but the purpose of your policy is not to achieve them. Your only purpose is to get the best-qualified scholars for your faculty, regardless of their gender. The fact of unconscious prejudice makes the usual system of simply allowing your experts—the philosophy department—to exercise their judgment an imperfect system for accomplishing that purpose. Allowing them to exercise their judgment within the limits of a quota system, on the other hand, may be more effective, because it reduces the influence of unconscious prejudice.

It is sure to be objected that people are not widgets, and so the two cases are not analogous. But they do seem to be analogous in the relevant respects. The features of the widget example that justified imposing a quota were: (1) There was a selection process that involved human judgment. (2) The result of the process was that individuals from a certain group were regularly rated higher than members of another group. (3) There was no reason to think that the members of the former group were in fact better than the members of the latter group. (4) There was reason to think that the human beings who were judging these individuals might have been prejudiced against members of the latter group. The case of hiring women faculty also has these four features. That is what permits the construction of a similar argument.

This argument takes into account a feature of the selection process that is often ignored when quotas (or "affirmative action," or "reverse discrimination") are discussed. Often, the question is put like this: assuming that X is better qualified than Y, is it justifiable to adopt a policy that would permit hiring or promoting Y rather than X? Then various reasons are produced that might justify this, such as that a preferential policy redresses wrongs, or that it helps to combat racism or sexism. The debate then focuses on whether such reasons are sufficient. But when the issue is approached in this way, a critical point is overlooked. People do not come prelabeled as better or worse qualified. Before we can say that X is better qualified than Y, someone has to have made that judgment. And this is where prejudice is most likely to enter the picture. A male philosopher, judging other philosophers, might very well rate women lower, without even realizing he is doing so. The argument we are considering is intended to address this problem, which arises before the terms of the conventional discussion are even set.

Of course, this argument does not purport to show that any system of quotas, applied in any circumstances, is fair. The argument is only a defense of quotas used in a certain way in certain circumstances. But the circumstances I have described are not uncommon. Actual quota systems, of the sort that have been established and tested in the courts during the past three decades, often have just this character: they are instituted to counter the prejudice, conscious or otherwise, that corrupts judgments of merit. Here is a real case that illustrates this.

In 1972 there were no blacks in the Alabama State Police. In the 37-year history of the force, there had never been any. Then the NAACP brought suit to end this vestige of segregation. They won their case in the trial court when federal district Judge Frank Johnson condemned what he termed a "blatant and continuous pattern and practice of discrimination." Judge Johnson did not, however, simply order the Alabama authorities to stop discriminating and start making their decisions impartially. He knew that such an order would be treated with amused contempt; the authorities would have been only too happy to continue as before, "impartially" finding that no blacks were qualified. So in order to prevent this and to ensure that the Alabamians could not avoid hiring qualified blacks, Johnson ordered that the state hire and promote one qualified black for every white trooper hired or promoted, until 25 percent of the force was black.

Judge Johnson's order was appealed to the Eleventh Circuit Court, where it was upheld. Time went by while the state was supposed to be carrying out his instructions. In 1984, twelve years later, the district court reviewed the situation to see what progress had been made. Forced by the court to do so, the department had hired some blacks. But virtually none had been promoted. The court found that, among the six majors on the force, none was black. Of the 25 captains, none was black. Of the 35 lieutenants, none was black. Of the 65 sergeants, none was black. Of the 66 corporals, however, there were four blacks. The court declared: "This is intolerable and must not continue."

The state of Alabama's last hope was the U.S. Supreme Court, which heard the case and rendered its decision in 1987. By a five-to-four vote, the Supreme Court upheld Judge Johnson's orders, and the *Birmingham News* ran a front-page story describing the "bitter feelings" of the white troopers, who viewed the ruling as a "setback." A spokesman for the Alabama Department of Public Safety assured the newspaper, "The department will comply with this ruling." It was clear enough from the official statements, however, that "complying with the ruling" would force the department to take steps—actually promoting blacks—that it would never take voluntarily.[4]

The Circumstances in Which Quotas Are Justified. The imposition of a quota may be justified as a way of countering the effects of prejudice. As I have said, this argument does not justify just any old quota. Our argument envisions the imposition of a quota as a corrective to a "normal" decision-making process that has gone wrong. For present purposes we may define a normal process as follows: (1) The goal of the process is to identify the best-qualified individuals for the purpose at hand. (2) The nature of the qualifications is specified. (3) A pool of candidates is assembled. (4) The qualifications of the individuals in the pool are assessed, using the specified criteria, and the individuals are ranked from best to worst. (5) The jobs, promotions, or whatever are awarded to the best-qualified individuals.

This process may go wrong in any number of ways, of course, some of them not involving prejudice. We are not concerned here with all the ways in which things can go wrong. We are concerned only with the following set of circumstances: First, we notice that, as the selection process is carried out, individuals from a certain group are regularly rated higher than members of another group. Second, we can find no reason to think that the members of the former group are in fact better than the members of the latter group; on the contrary, there is reason to think the members of the two groups are, on average, equally well qualified. And third, there is reason to think that the people performing the assessments are prejudiced against members of the latter group. These are the circumstances in which our argument says the imposition of a quota may be justified.

Even in these circumstances, however, the use of a quota does not eliminate human judgment, and so it does not guarantee that prejudice will disappear from the equation. Prejudice is eliminated from one part of the process, but it may reappear at a different point.

Consider again the male philosophy professors who always recommended the hiring of other males. In our example, the dean concluded that the male philosophers were prejudiced. In order to reach this conclusion, however, the dean had to make the judgment that female philosophers are equally as talented as males. (Otherwise, there would have been no grounds for thinking that the philosophy department's preference for hiring males was the result of bias.) An analogous judgment had to be made by Judge Johnson. He had to assume that black people were as qualified as whites for employment and promotion in the Alabama State Police. But prejudice can infect these general assessments just as it can influence the specific judgments that were being made by the philosophy professors and the highway patrol officials.

Therefore, our argument seems to require the assumption that some people—the hypothetical dean and, more to the point, actual federal court judges—are less prejudiced than others.

This assumption, however, seems correct. Some people are in fact less prejudiced than others; that is why prejudiced decisions can sometimes be successfully appealed. In general, people who are a step removed from a decision-making process are in a better position to be unbiased, or at least to recognize their biases and act to correct them, than those who are close to the "front lines." Part of the reason is that they have less at stake personally. The dean does not have to live in the philosophy department, and the judge does not have to work in the highway patrol. Another part of the reason is that in many instances the officials who impose the quotas are better educated and are more practiced in dealing with prejudice than those on whom the quotas are imposed. Judge Johnson was one of the most distinguished southern jurists with long experience in handling civil rights cases. The argument that I have presented does indeed assume that he was more capable of thinking objectively about what was going on, as well as about the likely qualifications of blacks, than the officials of the Alabama highway patrol. If that assumption is false, then our argument in defense of his action collapses. But I do not think that assumption is false.

Our argument has one other limitation that should be mentioned. It does not apply in the case of decisions made solely on the basis of "objective" criteria—test scores and the like—assuming, of course, that the tests really are objective and do not contain hidden bias. We can imagine procedures that, by using only such objective criteria, leave no room for the operation of prejudice. So in such cases the "normal" procedure will work well enough. The best-qualified will win out, and quotas will be unnecessary.

But such cases will be rare. Consider the range of cases that must be dealt with in the real world. Is there any decision procedure that a rational person would adopt for hiring teachers that would not disclose that an applicant for a teaching job was female? Should we be willing to hire teachers without an interview? Is there any imaginable multiple-choice test that one would be willing to use as the sole criterion for promotion in a police department? Would we want to eliminate the use of the assessments of those who have observed the officer's performance?

Moreover, it should also be remembered that so-called objective criteria often involve the use of tainted evidence. Suppose, in order to be perfectly impartial, I resolve to make a hiring decision using only objective criteria such as college grades. In this way I prevent any prejudices that I might have from coming into play. So far, so good. But the grades themselves were handed out by teachers whose prejudices could have come into play during the grading process.

Objections and Replies. The quota policy mandated by Judge Johnson continues to cause controversy. Newspaper columnist James J. Kilpatrick summed up the case against the judge's order succinctly. In the process of complying with the judge's ruling, he wrote, "white troopers with higher test scores and objectively better qualifications lost out. They themselves had engaged in no discrimination. They were the innocent victims of a remedial process addressed to blacks as a group. Were those whites denied equal protection of the law?"[5] These familiar objections are often taken to vitiate the whole idea of quotas as such. Do they undercut the argument presented here? In the time-honored way, we may consider these objections one by one.

Objection: People ought to be hired or promoted on the basis of their qualifications, and not on the basis of their race or sex. To give preference to a black merely because he is black, or to a woman merely because she is a woman, is no more defensible than to prefer a white man because he is white or male.

Reply: The whole point of the argument is that quotas may be justified as part of a plan to make sure that people are hired or promoted on the basis of their qualifications. The sort of policy that I have discussed does not involve hiring or promoting on the basis of race or gender, but only on the basis of qualifications. Quota policies are being defended, in some circumstances, because they are the most effective policies for achieving that goal.

Objection: The white male who is passed over is not responsible for the injustices that were done to blacks in the past; therefore it is unfair to make him pay the price for it. As Kilpatrick pointed out, the Alabama state troopers who were not promoted were not responsible for the injustices that were done to blacks, so why should they now be penalized?

Reply: Again, this misses the point. The argument does not envision the use of quotas as a response to past discrimination, but as a way of preventing, or at least minimizing, *present* discrimination. Sometimes people who defend the use of quotas or other such policies defend them as only temporary measures to be used reluctantly until racism and sexism have been eliminated. It may be agreed that if racist and sexist prejudice were eliminated, there would be no need for race- or gender-based quotas. But unfortunately, despite the progress that has been made, there is little reason to expect this to happen anytime soon.

Objection: To repeat the most obvious objection: Wouldn't there be some instances of injustice (that is, instances in which a less well qualified individual is preferred to a better-qualified individual) under a policy of quotas that otherwise wouldn't occur? And isn't this inherently unfair?

Reply: Of course this will inevitably happen. But the question is whether there would be fewer injustices under this policy than under the alternative of "hiring strictly according to qualifications," which means, in practice, hiring according to assessments of qualifications made by biased judges. Some philosophers have also urged that it is not acceptable to treat someone unjustly for the purpose of preventing other injustices, but that point, even if it is correct, doesn't apply here. The choice here is between two policies neither of which is perfect and each of which would inevitably involve some injustices. The relevant question is, which policy would involve more?

Objection: Finally, there is an objection that will surely have occurred to many readers. If our argument were accepted, wouldn't it lead to all sorts of quotas—not only to quotas favoring blacks and women, but also to quotas favoring short people, for example? After all, as has been pointed out here, short people are also the victims of bias.

Reply: If it were possible to devise practical policies that would ensure fair treatment for short people, I can see no reason to object. However, I do not know whether there are particular circumstances in which quotas would be practicable and effective, so I do not know whether such a policy would be defensible. The problem is that prejudice against short people has never been perceived as a serious social issue; consequently it has received little study, and it is less well understood and its effects are less well documented than, say, racist or sexist prejudice. But I know of no reason to rule out in advance the adoption of policies that would counter this sort of bias.

This admission might be taken to be a reductio ad absurdum of our argument. The very idea of quotas in favor of short people may seem so silly that if the argument leads to this, then the argument may be thought absurd. But why? One might well fear the intrusion of the heavy hand of government in still another area. Yet, if in fact short people are being treated unfairly—if they are singled out for unfavorable treatment because of an irrelevant characteristic—this seems, on its face, just as objectionable as any other form of discrimination and just as good a cause for corrective action. "Heightism" is not now a social issue. But it could become one.

In the meantime, those who have studied the subject have made some modest suggestions. John S. Gillis, the psychologist I quoted above, has made this form of prejudice his special concern. Here are a few of the things he proposes we do:[6] Employers should become aware of height bias and try to ensure that it does not influence personnel decisions. (The effects of such individual efforts might be small and imperfect, but they are better than nothing.) To help break the psychological connection between height and worth, we should avoid using the word "stature" to refer to status, caliber, and prestige. Teachers should stop the common practice of lining up schoolchildren according to height, which suggests to the children that this correlates with something important. Gillis also urges that metric measurements be used to indicate height. This, he says, would help to break "the mystique of the six-footer"—being 6 feet tall is perceived as a grand thing for a man, but being 183 centimeters tall doesn't have the same ring. These are all modest and reasonable proposals. The imposition of quotas in hiring and the like would be a much more drastic measure, which probably would not be wise until such time as heightism is established as a more pressing social concern.

Notes

1. Elizabeth S. Haldane and G. R. T. Ross, *The Philosophical Works of Descartes* (New York: Dover Books, 1955), 1:81.

2. The following information is drawn from John S. Gillis, *Too Tall, Too Small* (Champaign, Ill: Institute for Personality and Ability Testing, 1982).

3. Gillis, *Too Tall,* 125.

4. *Birmingham News,* 26 February 1987, sec. A, p. 1.

5. James J. Kilpatrick, "Reverse Discrimination Is Still Discrimination," *Birmingham News,* 5 November 1986, sec. A, p. 9.

6. Gillis, *Too Tall,* chap. 7.